The Practice of Family Therapy

Key Elements Across Models

The Practice of Family Therapy
Key Elements Across Models

Suzanne Midori Hanna
Joseph H. Brown
University of Louisville

Brooks/Cole Publishing Company

I(T)P™ An International Thomson Publishing Company

Pacific Grove • Albany • Bonn • Boston • Cincinnati • Detroit • London • Madrid • Melbourne
Mexico City • New York • Paris • San Francisco • Singapore • Tokyo • Toronto • Washington

A CLAIREMONT BOOK

Sponsoring Editor: *Claire Verduin*
Marketing Representative: *Jay Honeck*
Marketing Team: *Connie Jirovsky,*
    Jean Vevers Thompson
Editorial Associate: *Gay C. Bond*
Production Editor: *Marjorie Z. Sanders*
Manuscript Editor: *Bernard Gilbert*

Interior Design: *Roy R. Neuhaus*
Cover Design: *Cloyce J. Wall*
Art Coordinator and Interior Illustration: *Lisa Torri*
Typesetting: *Joan Mueller Cochrane*
Cover Printing: *Lehigh Press Lithographers/Autoscreen*
Printing and Binding: *Arcata Graphics/Fairfield*

For more information, contact:

BROOKS/COLE PUBLISHING COMPANY
511 Forest Lodge Road
Pacific Grove, CA 93950
USA

International Thomson Publishing Europe
Berkshire House 168–173
High Holborn
London WC1V 7AA
England

Thomas Nelson Australia
102 Dodds Street
South Melbourne, 3205
Victoria, Australia

Nelson Canada
1120 Birchmont Road
Scarborough, Ontario
Canada M1K 5G4

International Thomson Editores
Campos Eliseos 385, Piso 7
Col. Polanco
11560 México D. F. México

International Thomson Publishing GmbH
Königswinterer Strasse 418
53227 Bonn
Germany

International Thomson Publishing Asia
221 Henderson Road
#05–10 Henderson Building
Singapore 0315

International Thomson Publishing Japan
Hirakawacho Kyowa Building, 3F
2-2-1 Hirakawacho
Chiyoda-ku, Tokyo 102
Japan

Printed in the United States of America

10 9 8 7 6 5 4 3 2 1

Library of Congress Cataloging-in-Publication Data

Hanna, Suzanne Midori, [date]
    The practice of family therapy : key elements across models /
Suzanne Midori Hanna, Joseph H. Brown.
        p. cm.
    Includes bibliographical references and index.
    ISBN 0-534-25098-X
    1. Family psychotherapy. I. Brown, Joseph H. II. Title.
RC488.5.H337 1994
616.89'156—dc20   94-16803
                                                    CIP

Contents

Preface

This book has been designed to help entry-level family therapists learn the concepts and skills necessary for clinical work with individuals, couples, and families. The curriculum reflects the many changes that have occurred in the field of family therapy since the early years of our practice. By incorporating constructivist and competency-based thinking, we encourage family therapy educators to integrate these changes into their teaching. In addition, we feel it is important to integrate issues of gender and race into a book on entry-level skills.

The practice of family therapy grew out of diverse influences within mental health, social sciences, and our evolving culture. The early years of the field were dominated by innovative, creative therapists who wanted to break away from the prevailing perspectives of their time. They viewed traditional mental health as placing too much emphasis on the individual as the site of the problem, too much emphasis on history to explain causality, too much emphasis on pathology to construct treatment strategies, and too much emphasis on objectivity; many of them considered psychotherapy to be a very subjective process. These pioneers found that seeing the problem differently produced different avenues of intervention.

Specifically, they argued that problems were relational and evolved out of inadequate or dysfunctional relationships. Problems were characterized not as existing within an individual but as *systemic*—as existing between individuals with different life experiences and patterns of behavior.

Once freed to consider problems from multiple perspectives, therapists developed diverse techniques designed to meet specific situations. Their personal solutions to clinical situations seemed exciting to other therapists with a desire to be more effective. The thinking of family therapy began to expand rapidly as therapists eager to see problems differently sought out the early innovators for training and supervision. Those innovators quickly evolved into heads of major schools of therapy and were able to promulgate their view of how to work with problems systemically. For many years, attention focused on the differences among the various schools, but many contemporary family therapists have begun to recognize the importance of creating an environment in which the useful distinctions of each model could be successfully integrated into an individual's practice.

Concurrent with this movement toward integration has been a tendency to focus more upon the individual in assessment and treatment. This has come about for both conceptual and practical reasons. As it became obvious that systems were made up of subsystems, it followed that the individual was also a legitimate type of system.

On the practical side, the mental health field as a whole has moved more slowly toward a family systems approach than first hoped. Many agencies still do not have supervisory staff capable of training less experienced staff in marital and family therapy, and many universities are still teaching graduates the differences between major schools rather than preparing them with entry-level family therapy skills. Therefore, clinical staff often find that, although they know the problems are family-related, they lack the skills to actually implement family systems concepts into treatment.

This book is based on our belief that beginning practitioners need to know how to work from a systemic and interactional perspective, whether they are serving an individual, a couple, or a family. When they are able to develop multiple views of a problem and integrate common skills from each theoretical model, therapists will be more likely to adapt their systemic practice to a specific treatment setting. Thus, we have attempted to present the material in a form that practitioners can generalize to various presenting problems, family configurations, and work settings. Organized into three main sections, the content follows the logical order of the therapeutic process.

Part One: From Theory to Practice

Chapter One begins with a brief review of the diversity within the field, on the basis of a specific case example. Differences in content and process between models are emphasized, in order to provide the beginning student with a conceptual background form which to appreciate the challenge of integration.

In contrast, Chapter Two reviews the common elements that can be found across models, in terms of the therapist's role, interventions, and assumptions about change. This chapter begins the process of integration by identifying areas of overlap among the various schools that can serve as a starting point.

Chapter Three overviews stages in the process of family therapy. These stages are discussed as part of a general progression through the therapeutic process that all models contain either implicitly or explicitly. We recommend that the therapist discuss these stages explicitly with clients, as a way of encouraging collaboration in the therapeutic process.

Part Two: Basic Family Therapy Assessment Skills

Chapters Four and Five provide detailed instructions on how to conduct intake and initial interviews. This information constitutes a way of organizing the beginning stage of treatment; administrative and relational processes that promote clarity in the early stages of the therapeutic process are itemized. The major points in these chapters are summarized in a series of boxes, which serve as a guide to help entry-level clinicians stay on task. A final section of Chapter Five addresses common questions and dilemmas that entry-level clinicians may confront, such as how to address alcohol abuse, violence, and family secrets.

Chapter Six examines major models in the field as representing areas of content that the practitioner may explore during an assessment stage of therapy. Each section provides a list of questions that the family therapist can use to maintain a sense of direction while conducting an assessment. Suggestions are made regarding the circumstances in which each model might be most useful. Proceeding from macro factors such as gender and race to micro factors such as individual phenomenology, the chapter also helps the student of family therapy to see the value of exploring content on a multidimensional continuum.

To conclude the section on assessment skills, Chapter Seven reviews assessment techniques that have broad-based utility. While some might associate genograms and circular questions with a specific family model, this chapter clarifies how these techniques can be used to accommodate multiple views of the problem. In the same manner, tracking interactional sequences is described in a way that generalizes across models, and tracking longitudinal sequences introduces a way of integrating historical information into treatment that is both systemic and interactional.

Part Three: Treatment Skills

Chapter Eight helps the practitioner to gain a sense of direction in therapy by focusing on how to develop concrete goals, how to enlist the involvement of family members, and how to structure collaboration with large systems involved with the family, such as school representatives. Lists of guidelines help the reader remember key principles.

Chapter Nine describes skills necessary to facilitate change in family process. This chapter breaks down complex skills into behaviors that can be easily learned. The chapter can also be used as a supervisory resource, by matching the therapist's therapeutic intent with several skills designed to accomplish that intent. Some skills relate to facilitating cognitive change and others to facilitating behavioral change. Taken together, these sections provide a foundation for integrating the most common forms of cognitive-behavioral therapy found in the literature.

Chapter Ten integrates assessment and treatment skills through the use of case examples. Partial transcripts, case summaries, and supervisory commentary provide a view of the case from "behind the mirror" as such case progresses from session to session. The case studies illustrate how the therapist utilizes skills and concepts explained in earlier chapters.

Chapter Eleven is aimed at helping family therapists understand how an evaluative process can be an integral part of treatment. We provide material on the evaluation of family therapy from multiple perspectives, in terms of both process and outcomes. A section on evaluations for termination or follow-up offers practical guidelines by which the clinician can help clients continue the process of change and mobilize their resources. In the final section, we discuss the possibility of integrating clinical practice with clinical research—by seeing the two as examples of systematic inquiry. Evaluation provides a context for learning from client feedback, which is essential if the beginning clinician is to advance to intermediate-level practice.

Acknowledgments

Of the many people who have contributed to this project, our thanks must first go to Dana Christensen, whose thinking was instrumental in launching its early stages. As we progressed, we did so with the valuable help of our program assistant, Donnetta Davis, who organized the office staff during all stages of production. We are grateful to Jennifer Brown for assisting us in the last stages of manuscript preparation. Wayne Oates and Carolyn Brown reviewed various parts of our manuscript and added valuable perspectives. Claire Verduin, Marjorie Sanders, and their colleagues provided the patience and encouragement we needed in order to address the valuable feedback from our reviewers. We extend our thanks to the reviewers for their helpful suggestions: Margaret Blake, University of Northern Colorado; Jeremiah Donigian, SUNY–Brockport; Lennis G. Echterling, James Madison University; Lawrence H. Ganong, University of Missouri–Columbia; Clarence Hibbs, Pepperdine University; Arthur M. Horne, University of Georgia; Marvin Knittel, University of Nebraska at Kearney; and Carol A. Werlinich, University of Maryland.

Perhaps our most important thanks go to those unsuspecting students and families who, by opening their lives to us as an arena for our own learning, have taught us the profound respect due to all those who continue to meet daily human challenges with sincerity, dignity, and persistence.

Suzanne Midori Hanna
Joseph H. Brown

Part One

FROM THEORY TO PRACTICE

Chapter One

Family Therapy: A Field of Diversity

T he history of marital and family therapy has always been one of professional diversity. The early interests of clergy, physicians, and child-welfare advocates led researchers across the United States to study communication and behavior within the families of schizophrenics. The collaboration between these groups led to an exchange of publications and joint presentations at major national conferences. As it evolved, the practice of these groups produced a paradigmatic shift in thinking: Rather than view problems within the individual, therapists began to see problems within the relationship.

From these developments, the field of family therapy emerged in the mid-twentieth century. With the organized efforts of those early pioneers came a variety of family therapy practices and backgrounds. From anthropology and communications to psychiatry and hypnosis, the ancestors of present-day family therapy extrapolated the knowledge of their original discipline and integrated it with other knowledge bases. Their synthesis occurred as these multidisciplinary networks dialogued and debated across the country. Gradually, experimentation gave way to models of intervention that developed around the practices of various charismatic innovators.

Today, the field of family therapy is characterized by numerous approaches, all claiming this common heritage. Nichols and Schwartz (1991) note that:

> Theoretical positions tend to be stated in doctrinaire terms that maximize their distinctions. While this makes interesting reading, it is somewhat misleading. The truth is that the different systems of family therapy are more alike in practice than their theories suggest. Moreover, each new approach tends to become more eclectic over time. Practitioners start out as relative purists, but eventually discover the validity of theoretical concepts from other approaches and the usefulness of other people's techniques. The result is that, with increasing experience, most family therapists gradually become more eclectic. (pp. 512–513)

The intent of this book is to find a common ground from which to begin practicing family therapy. While the remaining chapters address the overlap between models, this chapter is intended to introduce distinctions between the major categories of family therapy practice. It does not contain every model practiced at present, and discussion is limited to those concepts and interventions that are considered unique to a given approach. However, this brief survey illustrates the variety that exists and the many avenues of creativity open to contemporary family therapists. Table 1.1 summarizes the concepts and interventions generally associated with some of the leading figures in the field, and Chapter Five covers many of these concepts in greater depth.

By reviewing these general models and identifying their unique contributions, beginning family therapists will have an introduction to concepts and skills that they may ultimately integrate into their practice. To illustrate the primary differences between the various approaches, the same case material will be examined through different perspectives, illustrating how a family therapist from each approach might address the issues in practice.

Table 1.2

Model	Leading Figures	Concepts Emphasized	Goals	Unique Interventions
Structural	Minuchin	Hierarchy, boundary, subsystem, alignment, coalition	Strengthen parental subsystem / Realign coalitions	Joining / Enactments / Unbalancing
Strategic	Haley / M.R.I.	Symptoms as messages / Solutions as problems / Utopian thinking	Interrupt problematic sequences / Second-order change of unsuccessful "solutions"	Directives / Reframing / Paradox
Intergenerational	Bowen	Differentiation / Family projection process / Family losses	Decrease emotional reactivity / Address losses	Genogram
	Boszormenyi-Nagy	Relational ethics / Family ledger	Restore trust and fairness	Multidirected partiality
Experiential	Satir	Self-concept / Communication / Family rules	Relieve family pain	Sculpting / Acceptance / Communication skills
	Whitaker	Growth as an interpersonal process / Therapy as an encounter	Interpersonal competence	Use of self / Modeling / Confrontation / Cotherapy
Contemporary	Milan team	Hypothesizing / Circularity / Neutrality / Information that makes a difference	Relief of symptom	Circular questions / Positive connotation / Paradoxical directives / Externalization
	Michael White	Oppression / Liberation / Narratives / Unique outcomes	Rewrite problem-saturated story	Questions of influence / Questions as invitations

Sample Case: The Nelsons

Paul Nelson, 14, was admitted to a residential group home for adolescent males when his truancy and behavior problems became such that his parents could no longer keep him at home. A caseworker was assigned through juvenile court, and Paul was placed in a local facility where parents were involved in parent education and family therapy. The adolescents had a structured school experience and could earn weekend visits home through good behavior.

Paul's parents—Roy, 45, and Lilly, 42—were a white, working-class couple who had three children, Ed, Janet, and Paul. Ed, 18, had dropped out of high school two years before and was working at a local gas station. His girlfriend, Roxanne, 17, was pregnant. Ed was living at home, trying to save enough money to support this forthcoming child. At the time of treatment, Ed was uncertain whether he would marry Roxanne, although they were currently seeing each other on a regular basis. Janet, 17, was in her senior year of high school. She was an "A" student and enjoyed such school activities as cheerleading and chorus. She hoped to finish high school and go on to college. Paul had been held back in the seventh grade because of absences and was in the eighth grade at the time of his placement.

Structural Family Therapy

In this approach, family therapists focus on the interactions and activities of family members to determine the organization or structure of the family. Symptoms are regarded as a consequence of organizational difficulties. This theory is closely identified with Salvador Minuchin, M.D., who emphasized how, when, and to whom family members currently relate as a way of understanding the problem.

In the case of the Nelsons, family therapists using this model would be interested in determining who interacts with whom, for what purpose, and how often. For example, when Paul was truant from school, who would be first to find out? What would be their reaction? Who would be told next? What would be their reaction? What would Paul do in response to their reactions? How would other family members get involved? While gathering this information, structural family therapists would also observe whether the family relationships appeared close, distant, chaotic, or rigid. Who sits by whom during the initial session? Could their placement in the session be symbolic of how relationships are conducted at home? In this case, Paul's parents accompany him to the first session, and he sits next to his mother. During the session, the therapist notices that Lilly often leans toward Paul and away from her husband.

The therapist asks the Nelson family to describe their interactional process related to Paul's truancy and discovers that, when Mrs. Nelson is called by the school, she responds by leaving work and confronting Paul. When Paul refuses to interact with her and withdraws to his room, she complains to Mr. Nelson about the situation. Mr. Nelson usually responds by confronting Paul about his behavior and threatening him with punishment if his behavior does not improve. When Janet becomes aware of the problem, she usually spends time with Paul, encouraging him to behave better. She has also become Lilly's sounding board, providing a listening ear as her mother worries out loud. The therapist asks Paul about his relationship with each member of the family. Of his parents, he spends the most time with Lilly and is uncomfortable with Roy. Of his siblings, he is closest to Janet and feels some disgust that Ed has "gotten himself into trouble." Roy and Lilly are asked about the time they spend together. Because they work different shifts, they have very little time together until the weekend. Recently, Roy has been asked to work overtime at the meat-packing plant, as a result of layoffs and employee reductions.

The structural family therapist might hypothesize from this information that the marital subsystem has become distant as a result of the family's economic situation. In addition, Lilly seems to be overinvolved with Janet and Paul in contrasting ways. By confiding in Janet, she has elevated Janet from the status of child to that of peer. By engaging in repetitive interactions with Paul, she is equally enmeshed with him, but in a way that produces opposition rather than peer status. Because Paul has been persistent in his misbehavior, he has rendered the parental subsystem ineffective at this time, obtaining a level of power that is inappropriate.

Structural goals are based on hypotheses formulated from interactional sequences in the family (Aponte & Van Deusen, 1981). These goals are often specified in the form of altered transactional patterns or sequences of behavior related to the problem. Goals for the Nelson family include a strengthening of the marital subsystem in order to unite them around parental functions. For example, instead of a pattern in which each makes ineffective threats to Paul, their sequence might be changed so that their first interaction is with each other, allowing them to decide on a position or plan of action. Additional goals would be to help Roy become closer to his children and to help Lilly develop some distance in her responses. Since they have developed complementary roles with their children (that is, one close, one distant), another goal would be for them to develop more flexible personal boundaries, becoming more balanced in their roles and less rigid and extreme.

Therapeutic Process

In structural family therapy, the therapist's goal at the beginning of the session is to join with the family—to become a part of the family system. Joining requires the therapist to build rapport by being personable and responsive to family members. Colapinto (1991) suggests that the role of the structural family therapist is that of producer, stage director, protagonist, and narrator. Further, he suggests:

> The structural model requires from the therapist a respectful curiosity about diverse forms of family experience and strengths, a commitment to help families change, a preference for concrete behavioral changes

over talk about changed feelings, a disposition to construct hypotheses on the basis of scanty data and to have them corrected through a close encounter with clients, the ability to set clear goals and to express them frankly, a willingness to direct, a directedness of expression, a tolerance for intensity in human transactions, and the courage to raise intensity when necessary. (p. 436)

In the session with the Nelsons, the structural therapist joins the family by discussing Roy's work and Lilly's hobbies. Paul is asked about his hobbies and what musical groups he prefers. The therapist looks for strengths in the system as well as patterns of interaction. As patterns become evident and hypotheses are formulated, the therapist becomes directive, asking the family to participate in specifically designed enactments. For example, Paul and Roy are asked to sit together and discuss a family activity. The therapist nudges them to be direct and honest with each other. Lilly is asked to explore her own reaction to the suggestion that Roy become more involved in addressing Paul's behavior. When she tries to interrupt the discussion between Roy and Paul, the therapist interrupts her interruption and directs Roy and Paul to continue. Suggestions are made regarding ways that Roy and Lilly can alter their roles. The therapist shares personal stories that demonstrate an empathy with the family's struggle. As Roy's isolation becomes more evident, the therapist works to strengthen the therapeutic bond with him, pointing out his strengths and acknowledging his good intentions. As the session concludes, the family is asked to bring the other two siblings next time. Eventually, the therapist discovers that Roy's mother is also very involved with Paul and persuades the family to include her in sessions as well.

The structural therapist relies heavily on in-session interventions to produce initial behavioral changes. These changes are thought to stimulate cognitive and perceptual changes as well. By involving many family members, the structural therapist hopes to help the family reorganize itself so that the parental subsystem is strengthened with appropriate hierarchical boundaries.

Strategic Family Therapy

Strategic models of family therapy emphasize a particular approach or strategy for each presenting problem. Principal contributors to this type of practice are communication theorists at the Mental Research Institute (M.R.I.) in Palo Alto, California, including Don Jackson, Paul Watzlawick, Gregory Bateson, and Jay Haley. Jackson's early collaborations with Bateson led to many significant contributions such as the double-bind theory of schizophrenia (Bateson, Jackson, Haley, & Weakland, 1956). Their ideas about symptoms as a form of communication provided a theoretical model for strategic therapy. Concurrently, Milton Erickson was pioneering hypnotic and paradoxical techniques that emphasize the uniqueness of the symptom and the importance of behavioral directives. Haley incorporated these ideas into the model he called strategic family therapy.

Symptoms in the family are interpreted as metaphors that also describe some aspect of the family system. The idea of metaphor is used in the symbolic rather than the literary sense. Because metaphors often communicate meaning on more than one level, the symptom can contain an explicit message ("I have a stomach ache") as well as an implicit message ("I want more affection"). Since these therapists view all behavior as communication, a symptom is a communicative act between two or more members that symbolizes some problem within the interpersonal network (Watzlawick, Weakland, & Fisch, 1974).

Symptoms often occur when a family is stuck at a particular stage in the family life cycle; that is, while Paul Nelson's behavior may be a metaphor for conflictual interactions between his parents, his behavior may also be saying something about the family's adaptation to a new stage in the life cycle (the launching stage). In this way, the symptom is often an attempted solution for some other problem that goes unacknowledged or unnoticed by others in the system. Such metaphorical messages help the therapist to conceptualize the relationship between symptoms and interactional patterns within the family.

The strategic family therapist would assume that Paul Nelson's behavior is a metaphor or nonverbal message about something else going on in the family. It might be related to problems in the marriage, challenges in entering the launching stage of the family life-cycle, or some other aspect of the family's well-being that has not yet come to light. As strategic therapists explore opinions and interactions within the family, they will be searching for possible clues to clarify the message of the symptom.

In developing a treatment strategy, therapists at M.R.I. emphasized an analysis of the client's attempted solutions as a way of assessing which interactions were unsuccessful (Watzlawick et al., 1974). Their work ushered in a type of strategic family therapy known as brief family therapy. After getting a definition of the problem, brief family therapists explore what solutions have been tried to resolve the problem (Weakland, Fisch, Watzlawick, & Bodin, 1974). Often the family's attempt to solve the problem actually has worsened the original situation. In exploring the Nelsons' attempts at solving the problem of Paul's behavior, the therapist discovers that their primary solutions have been verbal (nagging, criticizing, and threatening), as have the responses (Paul's refusal to answer); furthermore, none of these attempted solutions has been successful. These would be considered first-order attempts at change, rather than second-order solutions that do change the nature of the interaction. A second-order solution would require Lilly and Roy to identify options they could implement in order to be more action-oriented and less verbal and negative. To withhold privileges or other pleasures generally would be considered a more action-oriented option, provided the parents can accomplish that with a minimum of argument or discussion. In addition, since Paul may be aligned with Lilly, a second-order plan might also incorporate a shift in the relationship, by having Lilly administer the consequences while Roy rewards Paul's good behavior.

Therapeutic Process

The strategic family therapist serves as a stage director who provides directives to the family. The therapist hypothesizes about each problem and provides a directive to the family in an attempt to solve it. In the process of discussing the problem, the Nelson family is asked what changes they would like to see in the family. The therapist asks, "What do we need to work on?" or, "What would need to happen for you to be successful here?" Lilly begins to explain something about Paul's recent behavior, focusing primarily on her own frustration and helplessness. As family members describe the problem, the therapist is careful not to confirm the family's perception that (1) the identified patient is the problem and (2) the identified patient or symptom is unchangeable (Stanton, 1981). By accepting the family's definition of the problem, the therapist would be participating in its perpetuation (Madanes, 1981). Instead, it is critical to redefine the presenting problem from an individual condition (for example, Paul's stubbornness) to a behavioral or interactional difficulty that can be alleviated (for example, not going to school or obeying parents).

The therapist begins to look for sequential patterns of behavior. When one family member speaks, does another family member interrupt or reject what is being said? When this happens, what happens next? The therapist is thinking about the sequence of interactions surrounding the presenting problem. Lilly is the first to speak. Roy remains silent. Both Roy and Paul wait to be spoken to by the therapist. When the therapist asks Roy to describe what happens when "Paul gets stubborn," Roy outlines the usual sequence of interactions: his arrival from work, Lilly's complaints about Paul's truancy, Roy's questions to Paul about why he is behaving this way, and Paul's silence. At that point, in exasperation, Roy tells Paul that, if he keeps up with his behavior, he will "never amount to much of anything." With this, finally, Paul retreats to his room and begins to listen to his collection of heavy metal music.

The therapist now directs Roy and Lilly to discuss the problem, to see if they can talk about it in the presence of Paul. When Paul interferes, the therapist identifies a problem area and directs Lilly to ignore his comment and return to her discussion with Roy. The therapist is careful not to be central to this interaction. As Roy and Lilly interact, family structure and hierarchy begin to emerge. As noted in the structural example, Lilly is overinvolved with Paul, whereas Roy is underinvolved. When the therapist asks Roy and Paul to talk without interference from Lilly, the directive has both diagnostic and therapeutic value. The therapist works on the premise that small initial changes will lead to greater changes in the Nelsons as time goes on (Weakland et al., 1974).

As the therapist helps the family to interact differently in the session, it is important to attribute "positive motives to clients" (Stanton, 1981, p. 376). Problem behaviors are relabeled to have more positive meaning. For example, a positive label for Lilly's interference is "caring," and Paul's anger is relabeled as "desired attention." The new labels aim to provide family members with a new way of thinking about the problem, so that it can be resolved. Further interaction with the therapist might generate a list of attempted solutions other than "caring" that Roy and Lilly have employed, so that they can begin to see what has worked to their benefit and what has not.

As the session concludes, the strategic therapist must decide what type of task to assign for the week. Sometimes, strategic therapists use straightforward tasks, on the assumption that clients will comply with the suggestions. At other times, strategic therapists use paradoxical directives, on the assumption that clients are ambivalent about change, even though they are in distress from the problem. Families with a schizophrenic member or an addict and those in which one or more members are characterized by "personality disorder" generally have difficulty completing straightforward tasks (Stanton, 1981). These families are very effective in getting the therapist to work hard for improvement while they resist his or her efforts (Haley, 1976b).

Since the therapist is new to the Nelson family, a straightforward task is assigned. This serves the purpose of assessing the family's ability to comply with direct suggestion and providing direction for changes in their interactional sequences. Since Paul is currently in residential treatment, some of the family's typical interactions are already disrupted. Therefore, the therapist assigns Roy to be in charge of the weekly telephone call to Paul and suggests that he ask Paul about his future ambitions. What would he like to be when he grows up? Whom does he consider to be his heroes? If he had a million dollars, how would he spend it? The therapist suggests that Roy keep his opinions and advice to himself, so that he can focus entirely on understanding and recording what Paul says. Once Roy returns and reports on his efforts with the task, the therapist can decide whether more straightforward tasks are in order, or whether to shift focus toward more indirect and paradoxical tasks.

Strategic models assume that change takes place through client response to in-session directives and out-of-session tasks. The interruption of current behavior patterns is thought to be the most important starting point of change. This entry point allows family members to experience the new and strange with the help of the therapist. With that experience comes the increased likelihood that the family will view new possibilities for themselves and extend their experimental behaviors outside of the session. Positive labels and an analysis of solutions strengthen this momentum by stimulating changes in thinking.

Intergenerational Family Therapy

Intergenerational family therapy includes the work of several pioneers who share an attention to family dynamics across several generations and a history in psychodynamic theory. These practitioners conceptualize families and their problems in terms of psychological dynamics passed from generation to generation. They see the past as operating in the present and have evolved theories that help them chart a therapeutic course across time.

The practitioners who will be sampled for this category are Murray Bowen, M.D., who pioneered family treatment and research of schizophrenia in the 1960s, and Ivan Boszormenyi-Nagy, M.D. (the last syllable is pronounced "Nahzsh"), who developed contextual family therapy, which is based on the concepts of loyalty and trust in family relationships. While they each developed various ideas that are unique to their separate approaches, together they represent the primary roots of most intergenerational therapy practiced today.

Intergenerational therapists would assume that the parenting and marital patterns of the Nelsons have been influenced by experie‍   parent's family of origin. Unlike structural and strategic the‍   itioners of this model consider information about past rela‍   aningful springboard from which to design interventions in‍ the present. Bowenians would assert that both Roy and Lilly respond out of emotion rather than rationality when addressing Paul's behavior. This imbalance of emotionality over rationality is referred to as a lack of differentiation. The fact that they engage in repetitive interactions that bring about the same unsatisfactory results is an indication of the intense anxiety that motivates their behavior. This model suggests that, if the Nelsons can begin to discern the difference between the anxiety of their current behavior and the logic of alternative solutions, they can develop more healthy relationships in the future.

Additionally, Bowenians assume that patterns of differentiation are transmitted from parents to children. They would reason that Paul and his siblings are mirrors of a transmitted family process (family projection process) rooted in the historical evolution of previous generations. As parents pass on their level of differentiation to children, relationships are often fused (too close and too emotionally reactive). This model of family therapy would assume that each member of the family acts impulsively out of emotion or tradition and is unaware of how the power of reason could generate improved relational patterns. Thus, Paul's behavior would be thought of as coming from some gut-level instinct that manifests the same level of differentiation as his parents'.

In exploring the historical development of the Nelsons, a family map called a genogram is constructed. This diagram identifies each member of their three-generational extended family, noting dates of births, deaths, marriages, and divorces. The intergenerational family therapist discovers that Roy's mother lives in their neighborhood and has been widowed for five years. As family members begin discussing the loss of Grandpa, Paul becomes animated and talkative for the first time. He relates his memories of Grandpa, giving particular emphasis to the sadness that he can still vividly remember feeling on the day of the funeral. Other family members also describe the family vacations that Grandpa organized and the great void his death left in the family. Since his death, there have been no family vacations. The year after his death, Lilly went to work outside the home for the first time. Paul was 10 at the time.

Intergenerational family therapists often inquire about deaths and losses experienced in the family. The occurrence of such events is often linked with the subsequent development of symptoms in the family (Petker, 1982). When viewing the problem as part of a sequence of family events, some families will be seen as going through "emotional shock waves," from which they may not have recovered fully (Bowen, 1978). The Nelsons can be seen as having not recovered fully from Grandpa's death. The void in the family was not filled by anyone else taking on the planning of family vacations. For Paul, the void may have widened when Lilly went to work and Janet graduated from elementary school, leaving him to attend his school alone for the first time. The historical development of the Nelsons illustrates how a lack of differentiation can be passed down through the generations and also how it can be exacerbated through traumatic life events.

Other intergenerational therapists might utilize contextual family therapy in helping the Nelsons. Boszormenyi-Nagy (1987) might assume that each person in the family is motivated, in part, by a subjective sense of fairness that can only be understood from their unique development (relational ethics). Paul's motivation for skipping school could come from an unspoken sense of entitlement based on some contribution that he perceives himself to be making to the family. For example, having seen his brother drop out of school at age 16 (a perceived privilege), Paul may think he is entitled to the same privilege in return for the loyalty he manifests to his mother against his father. Understandably, Roy and Lilly may also be motivated by a sense of justice that comes from their experience in their own families ("We were expected to obey our parents unconditionally, and we are entitled to the same obedience from our children"). This "ledger system" provides a framework by which the family therapist discovers each person's subjective justification for his or her current behavior (Boszormenyi-Nagy & Krasner, 1986).

From an intergenerational perspective, the goals for this family could include teaching Roy and Lilly how to differentiate, helping the entire family to recover more fully from Grandpa's death, and rebalancing the family ledger system to improve their sense of trust and fairness.

Therapeutic Process

In an intergenerational session, the therapist remains central to the process. Bowen usually worked with individuals or couples, gathering family information and coaching them into new behaviors. Boszormenyi-Nagy usually works with the entire family, learning about their sense of loyalty and fairness within the family. The first session with the Nelsons includes all members of the household. For this model of practice, no purpose is served by asking family members to interact with each other. Instead, family therapists ask questions about the history of the symptom, paying specific attention to significant life events in the chronology of the family. This is how the therapist discovers the nodal event of Grandpa's death. However, the therapist begins by asking about the parents' courtship and marriage, and then traces significant life-cycle transitions from that time to the present. It emerges that Paul's behavior did not become problematic until the sixth grade, approximately one year after Grandpa's death. This was also the year that Lilly went to work. During the early parts of the interview, Roy and Lilly describe the first years of their marriage as very happy. Lilly's parents died when she was young, and she was happy to be "adopted" into Roy's family, since he was an only child and she liked his parents very much.

When the family becomes emotional during the discussion about Grandpa, the therapist asks each person for their reflections and memories; the therapist models differentiated (calm) behavior that is empathic but not emotionally reactive to their level of emotion. When they express anger toward each other over current conflicts, the therapist does not take sides but seeks understanding of each point of view, allowing each member to confirm or correct the therapist's understanding (multidirected partiality). As each side of the conflict is clarified, the therapist begins to ask questions intended to diffuse emotional reactivity and to help each member listen to the other. Throughout the session, the therapist engages in continuous self-monitoring, in order to manage personal anxiety that might allow triangulation to occur. When Paul begins to accuse his parents of being unfair, the therapist is most interested in having Paul express his thoughts and feelings, not in discovering all areas of the parents' perceived unfairness. Since Paul is actually talking to the therapist, he is able to develop some emotional distance about the problem instead of engaging in the same repetitive interactions with his parents. Roy and Lilly are given the opportunity to listen to Paul with some distance instead of having to respond to him in direct interaction. In this manner, the process provides opportunities for the therapist to help family members differentiate, and the actual content of their discussions is of lesser importance.

As this session comes to a close, the therapist has received an overview of the Nelson family history, of their emotional evolution with each other, and of the significant events that may have influenced their current lack of differentiation. In Bowenian therapy, this overview might actually be accomplished in several sessions. Eventually, family members will be given assignments such as gathering more family history, writing letters (to the living or the dead) that will be reviewed with the therapist, visiting relatives, or visiting the cemetery. With the Nelsons, the therapist decides to ask them to plan a hypothetical family vacation, since they have not had one in five years. Now that Paul is in a residential facility, the weekly telephone call to his family can be used in vacation planning, so that his views will also be represented. Paul is also asked to write a letter to his Grandpa. In subsequent sessions, reviews of the assignments provide useful information to help detriangle relationships and help the family discuss their unresolved issues; the therapist coaches family members with their assignments so that emotional reactivity decreases as each issue is addressed.

Experiential Family Therapy

Experiential family therapists focus on the subjective needs of the individual in the family and work to facilitate a family process that will address the individuality of each member. They are similar to intergenerational therapists in their focus on the subjective; however, they place more value on emotional expression as part of the growth process. They also resemble structural and strategic therapists in their emphasis on present interactions. Carl Whitaker and Virginia Satir, though very different in personal style, best represent the distinguishing characteristics of an experiential approach. These clinicians believe that all individuals have the right to be themselves; however, family and social needs may often suppress the individuality and self-expression by which a person becomes fully understood and known in the family. As parents are the "architects of the family" (Satir, 1972), it is incumbent on them to provide sufficient structure and nurturance so that the individuality of each child can be fostered.

In the Nelson family, communication is rigid and focuses mainly on superficial topics that do not reveal their vulnerabilities, hurts, hopes, fears, and dreams. Lilly can be affectionate with her children but spends most of her time nagging Paul about his problems and preaching to Ed about his predicament. Roy is often silent. When he begins to talk about himself, he launches into long monologues about the men he works with on the assembly line at the meat-packing plant; he describes the pranks they pull on each other to break the monotony of the work. In experiential family therapy, this family would be thought of as lacking enough creativity and flexibility to adapt to the transitions that challenge them. The restricted range of emotional expression in the family prevents family members from feeling loved and accepted for who they are.

In exploring the climate for personal growth in the Nelsons, the experiential therapist discovers that Ed dropped out of school with his parents' permission. He felt discouraged about his school performance and did not want the continued humiliation of failure. He was never a behavior problem at school or at home. However, as the family discussed ways in which they tried to help Ed with his studies, it emerged that both Lilly and Roy had no understanding of the math techniques being taught at the high school and they felt intimidated and helpless in the process. They would usually become angry and embarrassed when he received his report card, telling him he should ask his teachers for more help. When Ed announced that he wanted permission to drop out of school, Roy had few words to say and Lilly was relieved.

Currently, the Nelsons exhibit the same sense of alienation from each other. When discussing Ed's present attempts to earn enough money to support his forthcoming child, the conversation moves quickly away from the hurt that the parents are feeling; Roy shrugs his shoulders in confusion and Lilly sermonizes. Experiential family therapists would view the Nelsons as needing more nurturance. With empathy and support from the therapist, the parents come to accept their own emotional experience, thereby becoming more intimate and caring. As self-awareness increases, the quality of communication improves, fostering self-esteem and growth in family members.

Lilly and Roy manifest their low self-esteem through the embarrassment and helplessness they feel regarding their children's struggles. By fostering self-acceptance, the experiential family therapist helps parents to become who they want to be. Roy and Lilly can learn to forgive themselves for not being perfect parents. As they do this, they can also risk more intimate self-expression with each other. As they learn to tolerate intimacy (and the accompanying risk of conflict), their acceptance of themselves and each other generalizes to their children. Interactions become opportunities for family members to be heard and understood, rather than contests to control or judge.

Therapeutic Process

An experiential session with the Nelsons includes the entire family. The therapist employs self-disclosure, revealing feelings and experience relevant to therapeutic goals. By modeling good communication, the therapist begins to teach the Nelsons how to tolerate honest emotional expression. Meeting each family member, the therapist makes a gesture or expression that personalizes the therapeutic experience and helps each family member to feel accepted. At the same time, the therapist demonstrates self-acceptance through having the courage to admit mistakes and fallibility. As introductions proceed, the therapist looks for opportunities to demonstrate frankness and candor, commenting on some aspect of each individual that normally might be ignored in typical communication. In addition to modeling and teaching, the therapist facilitates the family's process during the session so that effective communication can occur. Ed is asked, "How do you know when your Dad is feeling good toward you? What does he do to show his love?" Roy is asked, "Do you love Ed? What are the ways you prefer to show your love?" As the family squirms at such uncharacteristic openness, the therapist models respect for their fears and discomfort. Through encouragement, the therapist develops rapport with the family through empathy, questions, and directives. The therapist also models genuineness by disclosing fears, embarrassments, fantasies, and foibles. In so doing, experiential family therapists trust the universality of human experience to help family members identify with them.

Compared to other practitioners, experiential family therapists are less systematic in their use of specified interventions, because of their emphasis on spontaneity and creativity. Consistent patterns of intervention usually stem from the therapist's style. For example, if Carl Whitaker were meeting with the Nelsons, he would focus first on Roy, in order to address the alienation that keeps him from being a more nurturing father. He might also become argumentative with Paul, to encourage the honest expression of the anger that conceals his pain (Napier & Whitaker, 1978). If Virginia Satir were meeting with the Nelsons, she might start by asking Paul to help her construct a live sculpture of his family, by placing family members in physical locations that represent the degree of emotional distance present within the family. As the sculpture is constructed, she would use the resulting scene as a catalyst for honest communication about relationships in the family. Satir would emphasize nurturance, whereas Whitaker makes liberal use of confrontation and modeling with frankness.

As treatment continues in experiential family therapy, the Nelsons find each session to contain some opportunity for emotional experience and interaction with each other, through the therapist's directives and various techniques borrowed from Gestalt psychotherapy. Experiential practitioners believe that change occurs through increased intimacy and through interactions that help family members to resolve their hurt and anger toward each other with warmth and respect. Central to this process is the therapist's ability to model the confrontation of difficult issues with courage and humanity.

Contemporary Models of Family Therapy

In addition to the first-generation models of family therapy discussed thus far, other models of practice have been developed by those who made innovations in earlier approaches on the basis of their own experience—in particular, the Milan team from Italy and Michael White from Australia. These practitioners are social constructionists or constructivists, who assume that a given situation can be interpreted in many different ways. For example, they would argue that traditional approaches to family therapy represent many different ways of viewing the same case. The question of which view is most "correct" becomes irrelevant. Instead, they would ask which view is the most helpful to the family. They would also suggest that the family's view of the problem may be the most important to consider, since it may be restraining them from more effective solutions. They emphasize Bateson's idea that, if brought forth, information that provides a contrast to the family's dominant (or negative) mode of thinking is information that begins the change process.

The Milan Team

In 1967, Mara Selvini Palazzoli organized the Milan Center for Family Studies. Selvini Palazzoli was joined by Luigi Boscolo, Giuliana Prata, and Gianfranco Cecchin. This group developed a systemic approach for treating the families of anoretic, encopretic, and emotionally disturbed children. Their book *Paradox and Counterparadox* (Selvini Palazzoli, Boscolo, Cecchin, & Prata, 1978) provides the most comprehensive description of their early therapy, although the team eventually split into two interest groups, each emphasizing different aspects of their earlier work. Before this split, however, the entire team developed systematic practices such as circular questioning, hypothesizing, and neutrality (Selvini Palazzoli, Boscolo, Cecchin, & Prata, 1980a).

In their early strategic work, the team pursued research and practice in the area of cross-generational coalitions. They developed the invariant prescription, which is a standard directive given to every family. The directive instructs the parents to continue coming to therapy secretly without their children. Their early research suggested that when parents did this successfully, symptoms in the children remitted. However, if the secret was broken, symptoms would recur (Selvini Palazzoli, Cirillo, Selvini, & Sorrentino, 1989).

Following some of Bateson's earlier work in communication and knowledge systems, the Milan team has also pursued a less direct model that emphasizes changes in thinking. They use circular questions to assess family interactions, the historical evolution of the problem, and emotional issues still influencing the family. Then they look for opportunities to provide a positive connotation for problematic behaviors. Each family member is often provided with a positive connotation not only for the behavior of the identified patient but for any behavior that is thought to be maintaining the problem. Going beyond the strategic idea of positive labeling, these clinicians use positive connotation to elucidate how and why family members may be covertly cooperating with the problem (Boscolo, Cecchin, Hoffman, & Penn, 1987).

Therapeutic process   The Milan team would initially assume that Paul is in a secret coalition with one parent. Upon detecting Lilly as the most likely part of the alignment, they might move to sessions with Roy and Lilly alone.

Their main goal would be to help Lilly maintain different boundaries with the children and to help Roy become a more involved partner with Lilly.

In a session with the Nelsons, Milan therapists might spend most of the session asking circular questions that compare different points of view. Who first noticed the problem? What was happening in the family at that time? Who agrees and disagrees about what the problem is and what the solution should be? What is the next most important problem in the family after these concerns about Paul? Who is in the most pain in the family? The least pain?

After learning about the correlation of the problem with significant events in the family history, the therapists might tell the Nelsons that it is important for Paul to continue his behavior, because the alternative of having him grow up before the family fully recovers from Grandpa's death might result in a greater void in the family. Thus, it is wise to slow the process down. In addition, Roy is being a dutiful husband by keeping his distance so that Lilly can have closeness with her children as a way of filling the void that Grandpa left for all of them. In addition to this in-session intervention that targets changes in thinking, the Milan team might also create a ritual for the family (see Chapter Nine for a description) or prescribe other interactions that might help the family reorganize their behavior so as to accommodate developmental transitions.

By drawing on the family's generational and structural history and incorporating strategic interventions, the Milan team integrates key elements of other models. A focus on a developmental history of how the problem has evolved over time progresses toward a focus on present behaviors and future goals within the family. Behavioral and cognitive changes are addressed simultaneously by eliciting systemic information in session about multiple points of view within the family and assigning rituals or tasks out of session to help change interaction patterns.

As part of the social-construction movement in family therapy, the Milan team remains open to multiple interpretations of any problem. They consider indirect interventions to be the most appropriate for difficult cases because they are more respectful of the client's reality and minimize resistance to change by making paradoxical arguments for no change. These arguments indirectly legitimize client ambivalence toward change and provide an atmosphere that is accepting and respectful of these client dilemmas. By providing the Nelsons with the paradoxical suggestion that it might not be the right time for Paul to grow up, the therapists acknowledge hardship and adversity in the family; they hypothesize that the symptoms have developed accidentally from coping patterns that have evolved over time. In this way, family members are provided with a face-saving way to begin the change process, since no one is blamed for the problem and everyone's positive intentions are acknowledged.

Michael White

Michael White has continued the trend toward social construction in family therapy with his recent innovations. Just as constructionism asserts the validity of alternative points of view when addressing social problems, the playful interventions of Michael White also spring from a variety of theoretical tracks. In working with the Nelsons, White would assume that the dominant view held by much of the mental health system has led to their depersonalization and oppression. He would also assume that the family is feeling oppressed by the influence of their problems. By using social theory regarding oppression and liberation, White would help the Nelsons to notice their own expert knowledge— that is, to notice those times when the problem did not interfere with their lives. In helping the Nelsons to develop their own expert knowledge, he would use a concept developed by Bateson (1972) and look for small exceptions to their negative experiences—so-called unique outcomes. He would use this increased awareness of successes to help the family develop a new life story of victory, competence, and leadership.

White emphasizes the importance of characterizing the problem as some force or entity that is outside the identified patient and outside the family. In the case of the Nelsons, a "truant life-style" might become the label for the problem. This process of externalization is one of White's distinctive contributions to family therapy, based on his integration of sociological theories about oppression. He applies these concepts in redefining the role of the therapist.

Therapeutic process   A session with Michael White might consist of a progression through various sets of questions. The family might first be asked about the problem and how it influences or defeats the family. Then the therapist might ask Lilly and Roy to describe the times when things go well with Paul, even though they are few and far between. As they describe these times, White would spend much time elaborating upon these few experiences as examples of the family's expert knowledge of how they have influenced and controlled the problem.

When Paul fails to recognize anything positive about the exceptions, White would use his own observations of Paul to begin creating a picture of competence and cooperation. One of the ways he accomplishes this is to use strategic questions that provide a benevolent confrontation with present destructive cycles while pointing toward a hopeful future. He might ask Paul, "Which description would you prefer—Paul as a fellow who is being held hostage by a truant life-style, or Paul as a fellow who has battled the influences of a truant life-style and won?" He might ask Lilly and Roy if they would like to feel victorious over the oppressive influence of this life-style, and then he would illustrate how the exceptions they have described are the first steps toward freedom.

The Nelsons would find that White adapts easily to their own subculture. He would carefully note their words and their language, incorporating them into his analysis and into their story of liberation. As therapy proceeds, they would be invited to think about their lives and problems as an old story that they are rewriting together. He is the audience, director, and editor of the emerging work of art. The Nelsons are the authors and principal characters in the production. His playfulness demedicalizes and depathologizes family problems by placing the problem in an alternative knowledge base (literature and sociology). He prefers thinking of solutions in those terms rather than adopting the dominant language of traditional mental health practice. The goal is to liberate the Nelsons from their own oppression and from that of larger systems that stereotype, label, and objectify them.

As work progresses with the Nelsons, White would use sessions as a time for the family to report on their successes. When difficulties occur, they would be compared to situations that were even worse, in order to help the family maintain their sense of momentum. For example, Roy and Lilly might report discouragement arising from an episode in which they began to lecture Paul, falling back into old patterns. White might quickly ask them how they managed to lecture him for only 10 minutes instead of the usual 45 minutes, "like in the old days." He would focus his questions on how they were able to stop the old pattern so quickly and what they thought made the difference. If they remained discouraged, failing to see any progress, he might comment on their awareness and how quickly they became aware of the old trap. Further questions might be, "What difference do you think it will make in your future if you are able to continue this type of awareness? What would it say about you as parents if you are able to continue exercising this type of awareness?"

White has been successful in integrating the search for competencies with an analysis of interactional cycles and playful interventions. Probably his most famous example of playfulness is cited in the protocols he developed for working with encopretic children, externalizing the problem as "sneaky poo" and enlisting family members in a game to outsmart "sneaky poo" (Epston & White, 1992). Although his therapeutic process is quite different from that of the Milan team, he is also successful at helping families find a face-saving way out of their present difficulties. However, he is quick to discourage stereotyping of his interventions. In describing their type of work, Epston and White (1992) make this observation:

> We have been steadfast in our refusal to name our work in any consistent manner. We do not identify with any particular "school" of family therapy, and are strongly opposed to the idea of our own contribution being named as a school. We believe that such a naming would only subtract from our freedom to further explore various ideas and practices, and that it would make it difficult for others to recognize their own unique contributions to developments in this work, which we regard to be an "open book" . . . However, we are drawing attention to the fact that one of the aspects associated with this work that is of central importance to us is the spirit of adventure. We aim to preserve this spirit, and know that if we accomplish this our work will continue to evolve in ways that are enriching to our lives, and to the lives of those persons who seek our help. (pp. 8–9)

Summary

As the field of family therapy has developed over the past several decades, the movement toward distinct schools of thought has given way to integration of these major modes of thinking. While early pioneers spoke of their particular approach as a certain type of truth, the trend toward constructivist thinking has led toward greater acceptance of the family's unique reality (truth) and a flexible inclusion of contrasting points of view. Representative of such integration is Minuchin's (1987) reflection on the factors influencing his own practice:

> Recently, I was working with a family with three adult children whose mother committed suicide 20 years ago . . . I surprised myself by asking them to watch family movies and to mourn the mother's death. I thought Norman Paul might be proud of me. Another day I was seeing a family with an anoretic child . . . I found myself remembering some of the writings of Hilde Bruch. I didn't know she was one of my voices, but so it seems. Naturally pulling many voices together usefully demands an organizing frame. Briefly, the business of family therapy is change. . . . Within this framework the possibilities are many and varied, as are the voices that speak to me. . . . Within the possibilities open to us, the best in us always learns from the best of others. I am pleased to acknowledge that when I say to a man, "When did you divorce your wife and marry your office?", it is Carl [Whitaker]'s voice speaking. He might not recognize it in my accent, but it is there, as are all the others. (pp. 13–14)

The models presented in this chapter have discussed the Nelson family using many voices. While each model provides somewhat different concepts and language, the therapist's ability to integrate the family's reality with a given theoretical reality may really be at the heart of successful family therapy. The remaining chapters examine the elements shared by a number of family therapy approaches, in order to help the beginning practitioner develop the basic skills necessary for successful clinical work, regardless of the approach ultimately chosen.

Chapter Two

Toward Integrated Practice: Common Elements

The Role of the Therapist
    Therapist Behaviors
    Therapist Attitudes

Theories of Change
    Naturalistic Change
    Therapeutic Change
    Perceptual and Behavioral Change

T he field of family therapy has many conceptual models that guide the
practitioner, but this diversity can often be overwhelming for the beginning
practitioner. The structural therapist might assess the boundaries, coalitions, and hierarchy of a family (Minuchin & Fishman, 1981). The intergenerational therapist might focus on family beliefs, conflicts, and losses transferred
from one generation to another (Framo, 1981; Paul & Paul, 1975). M.R.I.
therapists might search for different points of view that might be at the root of a
symptomatic impasse in family interactions (Selvini Palazzoli et al., 1978). While
theoretical models offer practitioners a way to organize their thinking, trainees
must often incorporate concepts and techniques from various schools. This can
be confusing since different theoretical models use different terms to describe
similar concepts. For example, Bowen's concept of differentiation is similar to
Minuchin's concept of boundary. Likewise, the same specific techniques have
proven useful in a number of schools of family therapy: For example, several
approaches (structural, strategic, experiential, and contemporary) clarify communication, direct enactments, and describe the symptom (Nichols & Schwartz,
1991).

These overlapping concepts can be confusing, but the pursuit of conceptual purity has pitfalls of its own. The adoption of a rigid theoretical framework
may limit a family therapist's effectiveness; there is a tendency to distort
observations so as to conform to theoretical precepts. For example, if practitioners
are interested in assessing structural boundaries, they may only attend to specific
interactions (for example, when family members talk for each other). While
practitioners who utilize this approach can easily organize their observations,
they may also miss some important information that doesn't fit within that
framework (such as an important issue raised even though members are talking
for each other). To use an old cliche, a person with a hammer thinks everything
is a nail.

While some practitioners adhere to a particular theoretical orientation,
a recent major development in the field of family therapy has been the increased
emphasis on integrative practice (Lebow, 1987), rather than on theoretical
concepts or schools. The majority of practicing family therapists do not draw from
a single theory or school of techniques (Quinn & Davidson, 1984). Even those
therapists who have been trained in a single theory incorporate other theories
and techniques later on. Therapists integrate their own blend of methodologies
based on training, personality, and the population of families being served.

For the purpose of this book, integrative practice is that which moves
away from separate family therapy theories toward a systematic combination of
models. Broderick and Schrader (1991) write:

> Although there are still strong networks of therapists loyal to one or
> another pioneer, particularly in the areas of family therapy and sex
> therapy, the enormous majority of marriage and family and sex thera-
> pists today are trained in secular settings. That is, in programs that
> impartially have them read a wide range of current textbooks rather
> than those representing only one view. Perhaps, the university or
> agency will invite Haley or Bowen or Satir or Stuart or Masters for a

special workshop, and for a period of weeks everyone is a convert to that philosophy. These men and women are charismatic and articulate, but after a series of such appearances, learning from such specialized workshops tends to become integrated into the therapist's own views. (p. 34)

For many contemporary practitioners, integration begins at an early stage of training. The integrative approach attempts to focus on similarities between approaches and to identify common elements of the change process that can guide the practitioner. For example, some literature on family therapy training divides therapist skills into three categories: conceptual, perceptual, and executive (Tomm & Wright, 1979). In essence, these refer to how the family therapist thinks, observes, and behaves as a facilitator of change. The intent of such authors was to identify general guidelines that are not theory-specific. Other theoreticians consider change from a more universal perspective (a metaperspective), discussing how problems and solutions develop or whether humans can indeed change (Watzlawick et al., 1974). However, even without addressing specific theoretical biases, the family systems approach to facilitating change can still be complicated. Therefore, we have attempted to limit the array of options to those that seem most important for a beginning clinician.

With integration as our primary objective, the important questions are, What type of knowledge must every family therapist have in order to be therapeutic? What are the specific skills, attitudes, and ideas that are common to this area of practice? In answering these questions, we have found that some categories of learning are shared by all forms of family therapy practice. Those categories include knowledge as well as expertise, attitudes as well as specific concepts. Because these elements are central to most theories of family therapy, it is our belief that the practice of family therapy can be based on a synthesis of key principles across multiple models. The remainder of this chapter will review key elements of family therapy that are related to the behavioral and conceptual skills and knowledge of the practitioner. These elements can integrate several traditional and contemporary models of family therapy into a workable starting point for beginners. They are divided into two main categories: elements related to the role of the therapist and those related to specific theories of change. Each element will be illustrated by examples from various contributors in the national and international family therapy network, chosen for their impact on mainstream practice in the field of family therapy.

The Role of the Therapist

The therapeutic relationship is one of the most critical factors in the effectiveness of treatment (Pinsof & Catherall, 1986). The personal characteristics of the therapist determine how a particular intervention is delivered. Therapists must be able to utilize skills that fit with their own personality. Lebow (1987) explains:

> Training in integrative models should not merely teach technique and theory, but explicitly accent the generation of a therapeutic stance by the therapist. The ability to feel and be hopeful, empathic, assertive,

confrontative, and focused are all a part of being a therapist. To the extent possible, such skills should be directly taught, supplemented by personal therapy, to help overcome obstacles to attaining a therapeutic position. Each therapist ultimately needs to find a mode (or modes) of operating that is (are) comfortable and blends successfully with the theory, strategies, and techniques utilized. (p. 8)

The therapeutic position described here is multidimensional, encompassing the behaviors and attitudes of the therapist. These two dimensions find a number of similarities across the various models of family therapy.

Therapist Behaviors

Historically, family therapists focused on the etiology of the problem. Practitioners who emphasized the role of the family considered the goal to be the treatment of mental illnesses such as schizophrenia. For those therapists, the goal of therapy was healing, and the treatment of choice was the involvement of family members with the symptomatic person. This placed the therapist in a traditional doctor-patient relationship but with a more active, directive role than traditional psychoanalysis, which encouraged the therapist to remain aloof and detached. This change in therapist behavior toward more activity is illustrated by the following models.

Bowen (1978) became noted for his work with individual family members, coaching them toward a more rational perspective vis-à-vis their family of origin. Instead of remaining passive, he took an active, involved role in facilitating change. His intergenerational approach to family therapy was characterized by information gathering about the nuclear family, each spouse's family of origin, and the relationship of nodal events over time to the development of the symptom in question. Then, with this family story in place, he would coach the client into developing a strategy that could be executed over time, outside of sessions.

Minuchin, as he developed his model of structural family therapy, characterized his role as that of a director, actively moving in and out of involvement with the family during a treatment session. As a director, Minuchin would guide interaction between members in a session, develop rapport with hesitant members, or assign tasks for the family to perform in the session. While the directives given to the family are diverse, the clinician plays a specific role in this model: the role of a pragmatic stage manager who enacts old and new dramas that help the family reorganize their relational difficulties.

Communication theorists such as Watzlawick, Weakland, and Fisch (1974) introduced the gentle art of reframing into the repertoire of family therapists. In developing strategic family therapy, these authors defined reframing as a reconceptualization of some context that keeps the clients from exercising other options in solving their problem. These practitioners attempt to reconstruct their clients' view of the problem in a way that would produce new options. Therefore, they would generate multiple meanings for various problem behaviors. They found that, when they could help their clients assign a new meaning to an old problem, new attitudes brought forth new options for problem solving.

Experiential models such as those developed by Whitaker (1976) and Satir (1972) generally consider personal growth and self-responsibility as the goals of therapy for both the therapist and family members. These therapists believe that the use of self to foster family members' flexibility and range of choice will facilitate their growth and increased self-esteem. Although these clinicians have different personal styles, they are both noted for their dramatic and impactful interactions with clients. Both believe that, when the therapist is open and spontaneous, family members will learn to behave in the same way. Satir describes a therapist as a resource person and a model of congruent communication. The therapist helps family members to clarify and alter their values so that they can communicate openly with one another. The therapist teaches family members how to observe discrepancies between the intent and impact of their messages. The therapist becomes a standard by which family members can evaluate themselves and the effectiveness of the communication. Experiential family therapists refrain from emphasizing specific therapeutic techniques; however, their use of questions, empathic responses, clarification, and directives facilitates effective communication in the family. Family members learn to solve their own problems. The therapist trusts that the family will find a creative solution to their problem within the therapeutic relationship.

The Milan team developed a style of conducting family therapy based on "hypothesizing, circularity, and neutrality" (Selvini Palazzoli et al., 1980a). In this model, the therapist gathers information about the family through a continual series of questions. The intent of such questions can range from the exploratory ("Has it always been this way? When have things been different?") to the provocative ("When did you first realize that your father needed your support in dealing with your mother?"). When the intent is exploratory, the Milan team emphasizes the usefulness of questions that draw comparisons, whether between people, between points in time, or between definitions of the problem. When questions are provocative, they are used as an indirect way of making some implicit family dynamic explicit and verbalized.

Michael White focuses on "exceptions to the rule." Emphasizing the work of Gregory Bateson (1972), White looks for small positive exceptions to a negative pattern and amplifies this new reality. Convincing the family that change has already occurred, he promotes a strategy that will expand this newly discovered improvement. This information or insight about exceptions, discovered in session through persistent interpretations, becomes the basis for therapeutic directives and "experiments" (White, 1986) that lead to out-of-session changes for individuals and families.

Certainly, the above models illustrate the diversity within family therapy, but the therapist's active and involved role is seen in all the examples. That role can be operationalized into four main interventions found in all of the major schools of family therapy: the use of questions; the tracking of interactional sequences; reframing; and directives.

Questions Someone once said that wisdom is not in having the right answer, but in asking the right question. Although all models of family therapy use questions in some part of their practice, the Milan team, Michael White, and Murray Bowen rely heavily on the use of questions as interventions. In recent years, the literature has developed an increasing emphasis on the use of questions in family therapy (Fleuridas, Nelson, & Rosenthal, 1986; Penn, 1982; Tomm, 1984). When family therapists make systematic use of questions, it is for the purpose of eliciting information that will bring about change. Numerous accounts of the Milan team's questions began to surface in the literature in the 1980s (Tomm, 1984). These authors coined the phrase "circular questions" to refer to the line of questioning that they used in family interviews. The questions are of four types: problem definition, sequence of interaction, comparison/classification, and intervention. In addition, they reported an evolution from present-oriented questions to past-oriented questions to future-oriented questions in the course of the therapeutic process.

In the work of Michael White, questions are used for two primary purposes. First, the family therapist can ask questions as a way of looking for exceptions to the stated systematic behavior—for example, "When are the times that you are not fearful?" or, "When are the times that the two of you are getting along?" Second, the family therapist can use questions to gain the specifics of family interactions. Michael White refers to this as "relative influence questioning." Basically, these questions ask how the client is influenced by the problem and how the problem is influenced by the client. For example, if a couple comes to therapy complaining about their conflict, the therapist might ask, "How does conflict affect you? What do you do when you are being influenced by conflict?" The therapist actually personifies conflict and states the question as though there is an interaction between conflict and the person (externalization). Another set of questions would be, "What do you do that seems to overcome conflict? How do you have an influence on conflict?" In both instances, attention focuses on specific behaviors. What do the family members do? The family therapist must be able to visualize how people act and what people say when they are overcome by conflict and when they are overcoming conflict.

In addition, such questions yield a clear picture of the present while also providing a hopeful direction for the future. In keeping with a Batesonian perspective, these questions also introduce new information in the form of contrast. Very often, clients come in with perspectives that are distorted by their own pain; they fail to see the positive possibilities that lie in their own circumstances. Through the use of questions, family therapists help to uncover and emphasize small moments of progress that can become new patterns of relating. The choice of questions that call the clients' attention to new information keeps the family therapist active and directive; it is a fundamental skill in family therapy. In addition to circular questions and relative influence questions, the above models also focus on interactional patterns that unfold in family life over time. This focus, shared by virtually all models, is a basic skill for the beginning practitioner and merits detailed consideration.

Tracking interactional sequences Structural and strategic models are representative of those that define the therapeutic goal as structural or interactional change within the family system. Both models are chiefly interested in *how* family members interact with each other: Do family members speak for each other? When a child speaks, does Mom or Dad interrupt him or her? Do parents agree about how to solve the problem? Is the symptom a metaphor for something else in this family? How is the symptom maintained by the system and how does the system maintain the symptom? What system function could these symptoms serve? From these questions the therapist attempts to understand the sequence of interactions surrounding the presenting problem. By determining the sequence of interaction, the therapist gains information useful in developing an intervention to alleviate the problem.

While structural and strategic approaches emphasize the interactional sequence, each treats it somewhat differently. Strategic family therapists are more symptom-focused than structural therapists, and both are more symptom-oriented than the intergenerational therapists (Stanton, 1981). For instance, strategic therapists focus on dysfunctional sequences of interaction that contribute to the problem. Structuralists center their attention on how family members interact to carry out specific functions within each subsystem (marital, parental, and sibling). For both models, the emphasis on interactional change corresponds to a focus on behavioral change, even though each model may focus on different aspects of behavior. In these models, assessment and intervention is based on observations of interactional sequences.

Ericksonian and brief therapies also have a strong emphasis on tracking interactions with clients (Lankton, 1988; O'Hanlon, 1982). In these models, the therapist gathers very specific information about what a client *does* when depressed and what the client *does* when less depressed, or what a child *does* when a parent behaves in a certain way and what happens to the child's behavior if the parent behaves in an unexpected way. Interactional sequences that are nonproblematic are elicited by such questions as, "What is different about the times when you are less depressed?" or, "How do you get that to happen?" Specific interventions are designed to interrupt or change the behavioral patterns that appear to be the family's response to a presenting problem. Regardless of the school of thought, much of the activity of a family therapist is focused on gathering interactional and behavioral information about the family. Box 2.1 summarizes examples of how to track behavior and communication in interactional sequences. This information, in turn, becomes a foundation that enables families to make behavioral changes. In general, change will be behavioral, perceptual, or both. The next skill is aimed at perceptual change in families.

Reframing The term "reframe" or "reframing" is commonly used in contemporary psychotherapy, as well as in family therapy. It is possible that Watzlawick et al. (1974) were the first family therapy thinkers to use this term. Subsequently, Minuchin and Fishman (1981) promoted an intervention called "relabeling," and later the Milan team introduced the idea of "positive connotation." Stanton (1981) also has reported using an intervention called "ascribing noble intentions." Because these terms all have similar meanings and uses, we

---

Box 2.1

Questions to Track Interactional Sequences:
Who did *what* when?
What did she or he actually say or do?
What was happening right before this?
And when he or she said or did that, what happened next?
And then what happened?
Then what did they do?
And while this was going on, where was _____ , _____ , _____ (other family or household members)?
When she or he does that, then what happens?

Questions to Clarify Meanings and Messages:
What was actually said?
What were you thinking when he said that?
When you said _____ , what were you thinking?
When you thought _____ , how did you come to that conclusion?
        (Where did you get that idea?)

---

will limit our discussion to reframing and positive connotation, which adequately represent the important aspects of this general intervention.

Reframing is a reinterpretation of the problem or symptom. For example, if two adolescent brothers are engaging in rough and physically aggressive wrestling, their parents may conceptualize their behavior as "fighting." If these parents want their sons to quit this behavior, an attempted solution may include telling them to "stop fighting." However, when this solution doesn't work, it becomes tempting to try the same solution over and over again. If the family seeks the help of a therapist in trying to solve this problem, a possible intervention would be for the therapist to reframe the behavior known as fighting and refer to it as "the way in which they love each other." If their behavior is seen in this new light, it would encourage parents and others to point out how much these two young men love each other at a time when their wrestling is a problem to others. The rationale behind this reframe is that two adolescents trying to be "manly" would find the idea of open expressions of love to one another as "sissy"; consequently, the new label for their behavior might make them feel embarrassed, which, in turn, might encourage them to stop the behavior. The principle behind this strategy is that a new meaning attached to old behaviors will produce new behaviors that are associated with the new meaning.

After the concept of reframing was introduced to the family therapy profession, the term was generalized to refer to a relabeling or a new understanding of the problem. For example, if a wife becomes concerned that her husband's lack of communication connotes rejection, she may label his behavior as "distant" and label her own response as "feeling rejected." A family therapist may use reframing to help the wife consider other factors outside the relationship that might explain her husband in a different way: Perhaps he has recently lost his job; perhaps one of his parents has recently died; perhaps he has recently sustained a serious injury. Any of these circumstances might help this woman to define her husband's behavior as "pain or sorrow" rather than distance. Another possible explanation for this man's behavior might lie within the marital relationship. Perhaps they have recently had a child, and the wife is preoccupied with her new responsibilities as a mother. Thus, her husband may be feeling the effect of this change in their family system; the behavior that she interprets as rejection or distance may be explained by his feeling "left out" or "insecure." Very often, such feelings are difficult to communicate. In reframing, the therapist's ultimate goal is to help clients see the problem behaviors of their family members in a new light. In the last example, the wife's new perception of the situation might change her behavior, transforming her criticism into reassurance. In the first example, the effect of reframing might be that the adolescents become embarrassed when their behavior is noticed, rather than enjoying the attention.

In learning how to reframe a problem, the family therapist must be able to understand how the reframe will facilitate change. The therapist's own limited way of defining a certain problem may prove an obstacle to reframing: for example, if the family therapist has the same view of the problem behavior as the client, sincere use of reframing may be difficult. However, as the beginning practitioner comes to understand how many interpretations of human problems are possible, it will become progressively easier to develop more flexible and multiple views of every situation. In addition, the most effective reframes, though they may be expressed in dramatic language, usually involve a relabeling of the problem that has some truth to it, in the sense that it fits with the clients' point of view or experience. For example, in the case of the adolescent brothers, if their behavior was truly reinforced because of the attention they were receiving and not because of some deep-seated resentment for each other, this would suggest a fundamental bond between them that is ultimately positive—a coalition between them, rather than a chasm. Speaking of their behavior in terms of love, while dramatic, would be movement in the right direction. However, if their behavior stemmed from serious hostility or some other unrecognized issue, the reframe might have to address their attempts to communicate deep hurt.

Another way to begin experimenting with reframing is to consider several new terms for the problem behavior and decide which one might be most consistent with the clients' experience and goals, rather than with what the therapist thinks is the most accurate definition of the problem. If a certain reframe seems to strike an effective chord with the clients, even though the therapist doesn't actually believe it, the therapist could begin to be persuaded that what is most important is what fits for the clients, not what fits for the therapist. Beginning family therapists often struggle with the dilemma of sincerity when new definitions are awkward and untested. We encourage readers to conceptualize the training process as an experiment with different maps of the world and with learning how to identify the clients' map before their own. It may also be useful to note that it is possible to learn how to reframe the problem simply by using new language. A therapist's choice of words can be powerful, regardless of the personal conviction behind it. These new words, when effective, not only facilitate new options in clients but also transform a therapist's view of reality.

In some cases, negative problems can be relabeled to have more positive meaning. For example, "jealousy" could be relabeled as "caring," and "anger" could be relabeled as "desiring attention." Positive labels often provide family members with new ways to think about solving the problem (Stanton, 1981). For example, Madanes (1981) describes a woman whose "hysterical paralysis" was relabeled as "muscular cramp," and a man whose "depression" was relabeled as "irresponsibility." In each of these cases, the problem was relabeled in less severe terms so that it was within the client's control to change.

The Milan team coined the term "positive connotation" as they worked with families who had psychotic and anorectic young adults. They found their work to be more effective when they identified a positive aspect to some family member's problematic behavior. Examples of positive connotation include instances where a therapist may describe a benefit to a daughter's anorexia by suggesting that she is doing the family a service by giving them an opportunity to come together. In turn, the Milan team might reframe the family as being terrified of growing apart. By reframing one behavior and positively connoting another, they found that family members would respond between sessions with some meaningful change in their behavioral patterns. Another example involves an adolescent male who was deaf from birth. The young man was of great concern to many people because he persistently cross-dressed, wearing his sister's or other female clothing. When the consultant on the case discovered that the young man and his father were both first-born sons with younger female siblings, both were detached from their fathers, and the father was also detached from his mother and sisters, it was suggested that the boy's behavior could possibly be a message to his father about how to relate to women: "If you can't beat 'em, join 'em." Surprisingly, the parents found great comfort in such an interpretation. It provided them with a less shameful analysis of their son's problem. It was also more hopeful than labeling his behavior as a dysfunction.

Selvini Palazzoli (1986) suggests that rigidity in families can often be addressed through positive connotation. Because she believes that much rigidity is the expression of intense shame, positive connotation helps to bypass client shame in the service of developing new patterns for relating. In the above example, the positive connotation for cross-dressing provided an alternative view of the young man's struggle, by avoiding the shame of transvestism and the shame of having a deaf child who could not communicate in conventional ways.

While there are some similarities to the skills of positive connotation and reframing, the main difference is suggested by their names: Positive connotation is always intended to be positive from the client's perspective; conversely, reframing can be experienced by the client as either positive or negative and still be effective. The similarities between positive connotation and reframing are generally found when a therapist uses either skill to depathologize a presenting problem and relate it to normal occurrences such as the family's life-cycle stage, the identified patient's ordinal or sibling position, some significant event prior to the development of symptoms, ethnic factors, or some other circumstance in the client's background. In any case, reframing and positive connotation are used to bypass shame and blame, to create a hopeful acceptance of client characteristics, and to introduce multiple views of the presenting problem.

While the techniques already considered attempt to change family perceptions, the last skill to be discussed focuses on behavior change.

Directives   This category of interventions is usually associated theoretically with strategic family therapy. Madanes (1981) states that the directive is to strategic therapy "what interpretation is to psychoanalysis." However, considered more broadly, directives are found in all the major schools of family therapy—whether as an assigned task or ritual to be completed outside of the session or as one of the many maneuvers within the session that the therapist uses to direct interaction, clarify communication, or change behavior. In structural family therapy, the term "restructuring" refers to tasks aimed at changing some aspect of family organization, such as the balance of power or the nature of some coalition. For example, a mother who confides in her child regarding her marital difficulties might be directed to discuss some marital issue directly with her husband. A mother who favors one child over another might be asked to sit next to the less favored child. Through simple directives aimed at changing some behavioral pattern, the family therapist creates new possibilities by directing new interactions that the family does not initiate independently. Once begun, the in-session change is expected to have out-of-session influence.

Experiential family therapists often encourage increased self-disclosure or influence the direction of communication flow within the family. For example, Satir (1972) directs family members to follow three rules for effective communication: (1) Family members should speak in the first person and express what they think and feel (the therapist might ask, "I want to know how you feel about that"); (2) family members are asked to take responsibility for their feelings ("Tell me how you feel when he ignores you"); and (3) family members are required to level with each other ("Tell your son what you want him to do when he gets home"). Such directives shift the responsibility for communication as well as the content.

Other schools such as intergenerational family therapy generally use directives as assignments or projects that a client may incorporate into his or her long-term strategic plan for improving family relationships. For example, a young married woman told her therapist that her father had sexually abused her when she was an adolescent, after the sudden death of her mother. She was directed to explore all extended-family members for the person most likely to respond sympathetically to her disclosures on the matter. She was able to identify an aunt whose memory had remained positive despite years of distance and no contact. The family therapist encouraged her to reestablish contact with the aunt and to explore what possibilities might exist for an adult-to-adult relationship in the present. The aunt proved to be a source of comfort, and the woman soon planned a family vacation with her husband and children for a visit to this aunt, 1000 miles away. In this case, directives helped the client to entertain and explore possibilities for increased satisfaction within her natural environment.

Directives can be direct or indirect, depending on the skill level of the therapist. Indirect interventions include paradoxical prescriptions and the creation of rituals. Some guidelines for these strategic interventions will be reviewed in later chapters.

While this discussion of therapist behaviors does not claim to be all-inclusive, it is intended to help the beginning family therapist identify basic skills needed in clinical practice. In mastering these four interventions—questions, tracking interactional sequences, reframing, and directives—the clinician will realize that these form the basis for more advanced skills. In addition to these behavioral techniques, more advanced practice also requires certain therapist attitudes, which will now be discussed.

Therapist Attitudes

In a survey, Figley and Nelson (1989) asked family therapy supervisors to list the most basic skills that should be taught to beginning family therapists. Their results might be surprising to some:

> While the questionnaire asked the respondents to nominate generic skills, it is quite interesting that a large number of personal attributes were nominated. We had been thinking of behaviors in the context of therapy that could be taught to beginning therapists—behaviors that could be demonstrated, explained, and measured in some way . . . Our fellow educators/trainers seem to believe, based on these data, that the person of the therapist is as important, if not more so, than the skill of the therapist . . . It is probable that our respondents were aware that, for therapy training to be effective, a foundation of abilities, values, attitudes, and other traits is essential for effective family therapy. (p. 362)

In their survey, 5 of the top 16 ranked items were "possess integrity," "desire to learn," "intellectually curious," "flexible," and "take responsibility for mistakes." Although the authors saw these as personal attributes that could not be measured with behavioral methods, it is possible that even these qualities could be "demonstrated, explained, and measured in some way."

As the role of the family therapist has become more active and involved, there has been an accompanying shift in attitudes. Implicit in the more traditional doctor-patient relationship was the assumption that the therapist was the expert and authority who would pursue a cure for the client's distress. However, as interventions such as positive connotation have become popular, the therapist-client relationship has become more egalitarian. A focus away from deficits to strengths has also become more prevalent. The Milan team suggests that the therapist's stance should be "hopeful and curious" (Tomm, 1984). Experiential family therapists are described by Piercy and Sprenkle (1986) in the following way:

> Experiential family therapists participate actively and personally in therapy sessions; they do not attempt to hide behind a therapeutic mask. This means at times being vulnerable with family members and

> at other times being angry and upset. If the therapist expects the family
> to have the courage to be real, the therapist must also demonstrate that
> courage. (p. 53)

While there is debate in the field regarding which of these attributes is essential
to the process of facilitating change, there is generally a consensus that certain
personal qualities will likely enhance therapeutic effectiveness. Lankton, Lankton,
and Matthews (1991) write:

> We can make some generalization about two qualities of the therapist
> that are important variables in therapy. The first is that it is desirable
> that therapists have a great pragmatic understanding of people and of
> coping with life's exigencies. The second quality is an ability to step
> outside of oneself into the world of another person while at the same
> time retaining an awareness of that pragmatic understanding of coping
> with life. These two qualities are operational aspects of what is usually
> called empathy and sympathy. An excitement about learning is visible
> in the most successful therapist. And finally, the ability to articulate,
> especially the differences between one's own experience and that of
> the client, is highly valuable. (p. 274)

While this list of desired therapist qualities exemplifies the variety within the
field, it is possible to select certain contemporary trends from the myriad of
suggestions. These trends, while not exhaustive, are considered here as the best
starting point for the entry-level family therapist. They include an ability to
perceive client competencies and flexibility in shifting from one view to another.

Perception of client competency   In recent years, several family
therapists have begun emphasizing language that describes and labels competencies in clients. For example, Michael White (1986) will suggest that clients
can become experts on themselves. This highlights client strengths and down-
plays the authority of the therapist. Brief therapists such as O'Hanlon (1987)
have elaborated on the Ericksonian technique of referring to positive possibilities. For example, a brief therapist, after listening to a description of the
presenting problem, might ask the client to describe the times when things are
going well. This is representative of a trend toward competency-based treatment,
in which strengths and successes are systematically investigated and highlighted
as a central element in the treatment process.

More traditionally, this same element can be found in structural and
experiential family therapy. Minuchin and Fishman (1981) outlined their own
emphasis on client strengths as they integrated their values with other leaders in
the field:

> In every family there are positives. Positives are transmitted from the
> family of origin to the new family, and from there to the next genera-
> tion. Despite mistakes, unhappiness, and pain, there are also pleas-
> ures: spouses and children give to each other in ways that are
> growth-encouraging and supportive, contributing to each other's sense
> of competence and worth . . . The orientation of family therapists

toward "constructing a reality" that highlights deficits is therefore being challenged. Family therapists are finding that an exploration of strengths is essential to challenge family dysfunctions. The work of Virginia Satir, with its emphasis on growth, is oriented toward a search for normal alternatives. So is the work of Ivan Nagy [Boszormenyi-Nagy], with its emphasis on positive connotations and his exploration of the family value system. Carl Whitaker's technique of challenging the positions of family members and introducing role diffusion springs from his belief that out of this therapeutically induced chaos the family member can discover latent strength. Jay Haley and Chloe Madanes' view that the symptom is organized to protect the family and Mara Selvini Palazzoli's paradoxical interventions all point toward family strengths. (p. 268)

In a different way, Whitaker (1982) considers the goals of family therapy to be an increased sense of competency and self-worth. While each model may execute this objective in a different way, the trend toward a more positive, affirming mode of practice appears to be gaining considerable momentum. Partly on account of the rise of constructivist thinking in mental health circles, this competency-based approach is a key element found across multiple models. A second attribute essential to the family therapist's repertoire is flexibility.

Therapist flexibility   In defining therapist flexibility, it may be helpful to return to the research of Figley and Nelson (1989). Some of the attributes that family therapy supervisors regarded as important include "nonjudgmental," "respectful of differences," "understanding that one reality doesn't work for everyone," and "meet clients 'where they are.' " These are indicative of a family therapist who has learned to be flexible.

In discussing reframing, references were made to the need for flexible thinking in order to use that skill effectively. If the beginning family therapist can recognize his or her own limited view of the world, it will be easier to experiment with different perspectives. However, if beginning practitioners believe that there are few other ways to view a problem besides their own, it may be difficult to learn the art of reframing. In developing a greater sense of flexibility, constructivist views have encouraged practitioners to reconsider some assumptions that may limit flexibility and narrow the possibilities for creativity. Duncan and Parks (1988) elaborate:

Simply stated, reality, like beauty, rests entirely in the eye of the beholder; there is no objective reality or truth inherent in a given situation. Reality, therefore, is constructed by each individual in each circumstance. The process of construction is based in complex sociocultural interaction between the ever changing larger society, the family, and the biologically/psychologically developing individual. The constructivist position is central to a selective integration model. In the absence of a specific view of reality, the therapist is free to entertain the "reality" of any content that seems applicable in a given clinical situation. Rather than imposing the therapist's theoretical reality on the client, a theoretical language or specific content is chosen because it best matches the client's conceptualization and presentation of the problem. (p.156)

Similarly, Milton Erickson, who has been a primary influence on M.R.I., strategic, and Ericksonian models of therapy, stated that he invented a new theory for each individual (Lankton & Lankton, 1983).

In addition to such theoretical flexibility, it is also important for the family therapist to learn a type of "political" flexibility that requires the clinician to adopt a cooperative and hopeful stance, regardless of the family's own idiosyncrasies. For example, in research conducted on the treatment of adolescent substance abuse, the Purdue Brief Family Therapy Model (the P.B.F.T. model) listed the following curative factors related to successful change (Lewis, Piercy, Sprenkle, & Trepper, 1991):

1. The family feels the therapist is "with them" or "on their side."
2. The therapist engenders hope.
3. The therapist diminishes the family's fear of change.
4. The therapist avoids resistance.
5. The therapist respects the family's uniqueness.
6. The therapist mobilizes the family's resources. (p. 41)

These curative factors, shared by the models that the P.B.F.T. model integrates, begin to describe in greater detail therapist attitudes that are associated with successful outcomes in family therapy.

To summarize this view of selected therapist behaviors and attitudes, the role of the therapist may be described as active and involved in promoting competencies and flexible in accepting differences. In later chapters, we will continue to address important elements that can provide a sense of direction and order without sacrificing therapist flexibility. The next section examines key concepts related to the process of change.

Theories of Change

At the beginning of this chapter, we referred to the variety of theoretical orientations whose similarities and differences challenge the practitioner. We have already reviewed therapist behaviors and attitudes that can provide unity across these approaches; however, integration must also include guiding principles that will help to organize goals, observations, interactions, and, ultimately, the process of facilitating change. Accordingly, we have chosen to review the major models of therapy with respect to their specific theory of how change occurs. Such a review indicates that, when we address those concepts that have the most relevance to the actual practice of family therapy, once again, integration helps to simplify. The various theories used by family therapists can be grouped into two categories: Some address the occurrence of change outside of therapy, in the natural world; others address the necessary elements of change within the therapeutic context. In addition, some focus on behavioral change, while others emphasize perceptual change.

Naturalistic Change

In family therapy, life-cycle theory implies that change is an inevitable part of human and family development. In other words, the passing of time brings about a natural change in the family through the growth of its members. This perspective also suggests that family life is a continual sequence of periods of change, followed by periods of stability, followed by periods of change, and so on. For the family therapist who uses life-cycle theory, a problem brought to therapy would be placed in its developmental context in order to investigate the possible relationship between the onset of the problem and the developmental tasks that are normally associated with a given stage of life. If a client described the problem as chronic, ongoing depression, then the family therapist would explore what life stage the person was in during the onset of this depression and how the onset might be related to an unfinished task from an earlier developmental stage. Perhaps the onset of depression came at the death of a loved one and has been intermittent since that time. Perhaps the depression was noticed as children were leaving home or during the early stages of recovery in an alcoholic spouse. In this way, the family therapist tries to relate the onset of a problem to developmental transitions in family life.

Many times, just as problems are related to developmental changes, solutions may be related to other developmental changes. For example, many parents of high school seniors become frustrated with the tension and conflict sometimes present in their relationships with their children. Often, the tension disappears as the child prepares to leave home and become independent. A family therapist would use naturalistic theories of change by anticipating and expecting that changes can occur spontaneously within family life. This assumption could likely lead the therapist to look toward the future and help a family generate possible solutions to their problem as part of anticipated events in the future.

Another naturalistic theory of change within the field follows the notion of Bateson (1979) that change comes about from "information that makes a difference." He suggested that comparative information is information that makes a difference in the system. For example, a son's voice changing at the onset of puberty might signal his growth and influence his parents' behavior toward him. Or, if a husband says to his wife, "I'm not sure I married the right person," this would communicate information that makes a difference; it is comparative information about how he has changed in the marriage over time. If the wife was unaware of his changes, the new information would likely make a difference in her behavior, thoughts, and feelings. In this approach, then, comparative information is information about change, and information about change in a system will bring about other changes. To utilize this type of naturalistic theory in their practice, therapists ask questions that focus on comparisons within the family, in an attempt to find some aspect that the family has overlooked: Who is the most bothered by the problem? Who is the least bothered by the problem? Very often, such questions serve a dual purpose as both assessment and intervention: By eliciting information, they precipitate spontaneous change within the family.

Therapeutic Change

In contrast to these naturalistic theories about the nature of change, others focus solely on how change occurs in a family therapy session. Structural, strategic, and interactional theories generally suggest that behavioral change can be brought about without insight or cognition, by attending to interactional sequences and interrupting those that become associated with the identified problem. This is usually done within the session, focusing on present interactions. Intergenerational models, by contrast, focus on the emotional nature of out-of-session interactions and the clients' own reactions to them. The tools that the therapist uses are modeling and questions aimed toward fostering interactional and intrapsychic insight.

In the early literature of the field, explanations about how change was brought about through these models were either too vague or too complicated for beginning family therapists to emulate. For example, Haley (1967) wrote:

> Therapeutic change comes about through the interactional processes set off when a therapist intervenes actively and directively in particular ways in a family system. (p. 7)

On the mechanisms of change in structural therapy, Aponte and Van Deusen (1981) wrote:

> Change in structure produces change in functioning . . . the therapist will intervene in transactions that are manifestations of the problem-bearing structure in such a way that the system will internalize the structural changes and operate differently as a result . . . Structural change in treatment is induced by the maneuvers of therapists of all orientations . . . This approach serves as a framework for a broad range of therapeutic techniques, structural and otherwise. (p. 337)

In addition, Bodin (1981) described the principles of change used by the M.R.I. Brief Therapy Center in this way:

> These principles include an emphasis on observable behavior in the present rather than on historical genetic factors, since intrapsychic insight is not regarded as the royal road to change, although it may follow as an epiphenomenon or ex post facto rationalization as a result of change instigated through any of a number of techniques for reframing or behavioral prescription. (p. 303)

Similarly, Kerr (1981), who taught intergenerational family therapy, described the therapeutic process in this way:

> The early sessions were devoted to trying to help the spouses, through the therapist's questions, describe the nature of their emotional inter-action . . . A successful session is one in which one or both spouses have been able to think about the emotional process . . . instead of just continuing to react emotionally to each other . . . Objectivity and emotional detachment are reflected in the way the therapist sits, how often he talks, in the absence of preaching, in his tone of voice, and

sense of humor . . . The therapist's main task is to help people recognize and deal with their lack of objectivity when applying the concepts to their own situations . . . It is usually difficult for families really to see that one generation's problems are related to the previous generation's problems, but placing a three or four generation diagram on the blackboard and asking questions about it can be a step toward helping the family gain that kind of perspective. (pp. 255–259)

While all four of these descriptions provide the therapist with an emerging picture of what the therapist does to bring about change in the system, there is some variation in focus between behavioral and perceptual change. In addition, this early literature focused much attention on the distinguishing characteristics of the models, leaving the beginning clinician without a systematic model for integrating these differences. However, from this continuum of assumptions, helpful similarities can provide the beginning family therapist with a workable starting point.

Perceptual and Behavioral Change

A contemporary review of family therapy can argue that earlier theories actually focused on both perceptual and behavioral change. For example, reframing, as reviewed in Chapter One, is a technique aimed at facilitating perceptual change—that is, changing how a client views some aspect related to the problem. Structural, strategic, and brief therapy models all employ reframing in some way. Accordingly, despite the argument that intrapsychic insight is not "the royal road to change," many interventions in these models address the importance of the client's view or perception of the problem. While this is not the same as intrapsychic insight, it does involve an element that is internal to the client. Similarly, intergenerational therapies have had a greater emphasis on perceptual changes within the therapeutic session that are akin to insight, and yet much of the coaching toward objectivity takes the form of motivating and directing the client toward different interactional patterns with family members. Thus, these major schools, while claiming their distinctions, also have some important similarities that will eventually serve as a guide for the practitioner.

Two contemporary models of family therapy illustrate how the clinician might address both perceptions and behavior in the practice of family therapy. The Milan team makes use of questions and reframing to bring forth new information, as well as directives and tasks to bring forth new behaviors. The therapy of Michael White also integrates these elements by asking questions that bring forth exceptions and by assigning tasks that will amplify these exceptions into sustained and changed behaviors. The identified exceptions are often begun by a strategic reframing of some typical behavior that describes it in a new light. These newer models of family therapy illustrate what the brief and Ericksonian models describe as their goals of changing the "viewing" or "doing" (O'Hanlon & Weiner-Davis, 1989). Such evidence of integration can help the clinician to simplify therapeutic goals, rather than having to choose between multiple points of view.

Table 2.1

Type of Therapy	Role of Therapist	Type of Interactional Sequences	Primary Interventions	Theoretical Distinctions
Structural	Stage manager	In-session sequences	Track sequences Reframing Directives	Subsytem Boundaries Hierarchies
Strategic	Formulates directives	Parent-child sequences	Track sequences Reframing Directives	Parental hierarchies Cross-generational coalitions
Intergenerational	Coach or guide	Emotional sequences with family-of-origin, spouse, children	Questions Track sequences Directives	Extended-family patterns, myths, rules
Experiential	Modeling	Sequences between therapist and client	Track sequences Directives	Developmental environment for human growth
M.R.I.	Identify myths Identify successes	Sequences related to problem solving	Track sequences Reframing Directives	Attempted solutions
The Milan team	Hypothesizing Positive connotation of the symptom	Developmental sequences of how symptoms formed over time	Questions Track sequences Reframing Directives	Roles of symptoms in family Extended-family relationships
Michael White	Finds and emphasizes exceptions to the problem	Interactions related to overcoming problematic influences	Questions Track sequences Reframing Directives	Influences upon the presenting problem that are outside the family

With contemporary writers, we see increasing specificity in the similarities that are shared across modalities. By relating therapist behaviors and attitudes to the goals of perceptual and behavioral change, a metamodel—a framework that integrates the differences across schools of thought—begins to emerge. Table 2.1 summarizes some of the similarities and differences of various models discussed in this chapter. The common elements described herein serve as a basis for developing a therapeutic position in working with families. Clearly, the skills, attitudes, and goals described here can serve only as guides and not as a complete training program; practitioners who use them are obligated to add further expertise in developing treatment plans suited to their clients' needs. With this foundation, the interactional process of therapy can be explored in greater detail.

Chapter Three

Family Therapy: Developmental Processes

Stages of Family Therapy

The Referral Process

The Joining Process

The Therapeutic Contract
Levels of Communication
Expectations
Goals

Data Gathering
Content versus Process
Past, Present, Future

Hypothesizing

Formalized Interventions

Evaluation

Summary

T hus far, the basic elements of practice have been identified across the various models of family therapy. Some of these elements relate to skills, attitudes, or qualities of the therapist, and some relate to specific concepts. We have attempted to integrate areas of similarity among the theories studied. In this chapter, we continue this integration process, by reviewing the common interactional elements of these models in problem or symptom resolution. These elements are presented within a developmental framework, in which the therapeutic process is characterized as interactional, circular, sequential, and evolving over time. We outline this framework in the form of sequential steps or stages, to help the beginning family therapist manage the complexities of direct client contact. However, several of these processes can also occur simultaneously in microsequences of therapist-client interaction.

Stages of Family Therapy

Family therapy can be thought of as an interactional and perceptual process. One person, called a therapist, and one or more persons, called clients, interact together. Efran, Lukens, and Lukens (1990) suggest that:

> If psychological assistance is to be effective, it must take place in the very same space in which our living and our problems are enacted—in meaningful conversation. In other words, that which we have labeled "psychotherapy" must begin to be seen as a specialized form of dialogue—not as a medical treatment analogous to administering inoculations, performing surgery, or dressing wounds. (p. xv)

This "specialized form of dialogue" evolves through many different stages, some of which may be limited to a certain order, whereas others repeat over time to form a pattern. These stages, which we believe are found in every therapy experience, are

1. The referral process
2. The joining process
3. The therapeutic contract
4. Data gathering
5. Hypothesizing
6. Formalized interventions
7. Evaluation

While not every family therapy model addresses each of these processes consciously or explicitly, we suggest that each one occurs either simultaneously or consecutively as an influence on the larger process of therapy. These interactional processes, when combined with therapist skills and attitudes, form a macro framework from which to apply the other skills taught throughout the remainder of this book.

The Referral Process

Referral is the process in which a client enters family therapy. The context of referral is an interactional process, in which, generally speaking, someone decides that a problem exists and someone initiates the idea that therapy is a possible resource and should be sought. Important questions to ask are these:

Who first thought there was a problem?
Whose idea was it for you to seek therapy?
And when you began to think about seeking help, who or what gave you the
      thought that therapy might help?

With the increasing frequency of court-ordered therapy in the United States, it is important to explore and understand the step-by-step sequences of interaction that led the client to schedule an appointment or make a telephone call of inquiry. At the very least, the family therapist obtains information about who has taken the initiative. Ideally, the family therapist obtains crucial information about the family's level of motivation, their influential external relationships, and whether therapy is even appropriate in such circumstances. Obviously, a court-ordered case will have implications for the motivation of the client to do "traditional" therapy.

If one spouse is more motivated and one more reluctant to pursue marital therapy, the questions might be something like these:

When you thought about coming to counseling, how did you talk to him or her
      about it?
When she or he talked to you about counseling, what was your reaction?
Did you get dragged here against your will?

In this way, differences in motivation may be addressed during early stages of the therapeutic process. By asking these questions and tracking the perceptual and interactional process, the therapist gains information for subsequent use in developing mutually satisfying goals that are sensitive to individual needs.

In addition to court-ordered cases or public agency referrals, there are circumstances in private-practice settings where relatives, family members, clergy, and service providers have recommended or even initiated counseling, while excluding themselves from the process. For example, the parents of a young married couple may send them to marriage counseling and even pay for the process. The Milan team has consistently addressed the referral process in the case where therapy was initiated by someone who claims to be uninvolved in the life of the problem, such as a member of the clergy or a sibling (Selvini Palazzoli, 1985; Selvini Palazzoli et al., 1980b). They found that examining the relationship between the referring person and the family must take precedence over traditional therapy—that is, over merely examining relationships within the family or even exploring the problem itself.

In addition to the Milan team, O'Hanlon and Weiner-Davis (1989) address a similar concern by establishing who is the "customer" of therapy—that is, who is actually requesting that a change be made. Questions such as these can aid in establishing who is the customer:

Who first noticed that this was a problem?
How was it brought to your attention?
Do you agree or disagree with them that this is a problem?

On discovering that someone besides those in attendance actually developed the definition of the problem, the family therapist's goal is to clarify the relationship between the family and the parties who have defined the problem. This remains the focus of treatment until the appropriate role of the family therapist with respect to the parties involved is clear. As the Milan team discovered, when the problem is being defined by a sibling, in-law, or service provider, that party—or at least that party's opinion—should be included in the session in order to properly define what the problem is. Since the family may disagree with the person's opinion but still initiate therapy, the family may define the real problem as a difference of opinion with this outside influence.

In court-ordered cases, it is appropriate to involve caseworkers or probation officers until the problem can be defined in a way that will mobilize the clients' motivation (for example, "As family therapist, my job will be to help you develop a plan that will get the court system off your back"). While other models rarely address this aspect of the therapeutic process, it is our opinion that the beginning family therapist will encounter puzzling superficiality or courteous compliance without personal involvement unless the influence of the referral process is ruled in or out as a major issue.

The Joining Process

First used by Minuchin (1974) as he developed structural family therapy, joining is probably the most universal—or the most borrowed—of family therapy terms. Not surprisingly, the personal rapport or empathy that therapists develop with those they are trying to help remains the single most proven variable determining the effectiveness of psychotherapy (Garfield & Bergin, 1978). However, when a family therapist begins to grapple with this process from a larger systemic framework, the number of people involved may make this a significant challenge.

Minuchin and Fishman (1981) view joining as an attitude:

> Joining a family is more an attitude than a technique, and it is the umbrella under which all therapeutic transactions occur. Joining is letting the family know that the therapist understands them and is working with and for them. Only under this protection can the family have the security to explore alternatives, try the unusual, and change. Joining is the glue that holds the therapeutic system together. (pp. 31–32)

In contrast to the referral process, which can be thought of as an interactional and political event to be explored at the outset of therapy, the joining process can best be conceptualized as an interactional pattern that is repetitive throughout the entire course of family therapy. When a family therapist first becomes acquainted with the family, a certain formal stage may exist, but later stages of therapy require an understanding that is continually expanded as new information challenges the original perceptions of therapist and client alike. Therefore, it is helpful to think of joining as a process that pervades all the other stages discussed here. For example, by attending to the referral process described in the previous section, the family therapist may successfully join with the family through an astute sensitivity to political issues that are often overlooked by other therapists.

The following exemplifies how each school of thought in family therapy can also contribute to the family therapist's ability to join with family members.

Theories regarding the importance of ethnicity can help a family therapist join through an appreciation of the family's language, customs, heritage, or beliefs.

Theories regarding the life-cycle can help a family therapist join through identification with their age, empathy with their stage of life, or understanding of the dilemmas they face as various transitions approach.

Intergenerational theories help a family therapist join through a recognition of significant family members who may not be present in the session. Their nicknames, circumstances, and impact on present family members may lead the family therapist into the clients' private world.

Structural and strategic theories help a family therapist join through assessing the family's hierarchy and making sure that those in authority are sufficiently engaged.

Contextual theory encourages multidirected partiality, which is the art of consecutively siding with each member in order to develop trust and fairness in relationships (Bernal & Flores-Ortiz, 1991).

Ericksonian and constructivist theories are often noted for encouraging humor and playfulness. Also, they accept resistance as a helpful message about the client's uniqueness.

While these are not exhaustive, they are meant to stimulate the reader's creativity to find spontaneous and endearing ways of relating to family members that will contribute to trust and rapport. Many family therapists find it useful to join through the use of metaphoric comparisons from the client's world. For example, a therapist who routinely obtains a genogram and a relationship history provides a rationale to each client for the necessity of such information gathering. A young couple who likes to go boating were provided this rationale for an assessment:

> In order for me to help you, it is important for me to get to know you and understand something about the important people and events in your life. Marriage counseling is often like teaching someone how to sail. By

gathering information on your extended family, I learn something about what kind of boat you have, from the type of sail that it comes with, to its size and shape. Your families equip you with many skills for sailing through the waters of life. In addition, some of the experiences you have with your families help you to develop certain strengths in areas as you meet similar challenges along the way. By learning about your relationship history, I learn something about the weather conditions that you have sailed through in the past and in the present. In addition, the direction of the wind and the speed of the currents are important for the sailor to know about. A good sailor must learn to take many different factors into account while planning the journey. Once I understand something about the gusts of wind in your life and the many directions that your boats have taken you, I can help you to fine-tune your sailing skills for the current waters and your future life together. Your present complaint is likely to be a result of a coincidence between several of these elements, just as a storm might come up in the water and you must struggle to learn and master some new sailing technique.

In the above example, the therapist took into consideration the couple's stage in the life-cycle; this was a young couple in the first stage of married life. If the couple had been married 20 years, a different metaphor might have been more appropriate. A later stage in the life-cycle would suggest that these people have been struggling with the same problems for a longer time. What they may need is some new way to address their conflict, if the old ways have not worked in 20 years. Thus, a more appropriate metaphor for such a couple might involve a new mode of transport: learning to canoe or deciding to take the train.

The process of joining is closely related to therapist flexibility. Is the clinician a person who can modify his or her style to match that of the family? If they are boisterous, can the therapist join with them, rather than convey subtle disapproval? Has the clinician been influenced by theories that encourage stilted jargon, or is there room for a wide range of interactions—playfulness, empathy, firmness, and humor? The chemistry between the family therapist and the family will depend, in part, on the ability of the clinician to become comfortable with a wide variety of people.

During a period of training, it is sometimes most helpful for the trainee to spend as much time as possible with nontherapists in order to remain connected to the broader culture. In addition, the academic world can sometimes become an obstacle to the trainee's attempts to remain balanced and versatile. It may seem an ironic paradox, but nonprofessional leisure activities can often be the best teacher in providing a trainee with exposure to a variety of people, cultures, languages, and metaphors. The use of metaphor is especially effective when clients differ dramatically from the therapist in stage of life-cycle, values, economic level, and ethnic background, to name a few. If the client is a farmer, the family therapist might want to be compared to the County Extension Agent. If the client is a physician, the family therapist might want to be compared to a medical specialist, perhaps a cardiologist. If the client cares a great deal about physical appearance, the therapist might want to be compared to a hairdresser. By searching for metaphors and analogies that come from the clients' world, the therapist attempts to join clients in their world, rather than expecting them to fit into the prescribed world of the therapist.

The Therapeutic Contract

Although some schools of therapy never mention an explicit contract between family therapist and family, it is our belief that all therapeutic interactions are part of a spoken or unspoken therapeutic contract. This contract consists of expectations and goals transacted at two levels of communication: content and process. How clearly goals and expectations are communicated affects how cooperatively therapist and clients work together.

Levels of Communication

To use Bateson's (Ruesch & Bateson, 1951) terms, all communication has report (content) and command (process) levels: The report level is the verbal information transmitted; the command level is the nonverbal manifestation of how the sender is defining the relationship. Therefore, the family therapist and family each define the nature of the relationship, but neither may be communicating their expectations to the other. For example, the family therapist may have chosen a role as neutral negotiator vis-à-vis the family. Meanwhile, the family may have defined the therapist as a referee or even an ally. As these implicit expectations unfold through nonverbal behaviors (process), the implicit conflict may interfere with explicitly stated goals (content). Once the implicit information is brought forward, roles can be clarified in a way that enlists cooperation more fully. It may be helpful to think further about the therapeutic contract as it relates to negotiated expectations and goals.

Expectations

The family therapist and the family each bring a set of expectations to the therapy hour. These expectations relate to each party's role, the procedures that will be followed, and the conditions that each party expects to be met by the other. Perhaps the family has a media-related stereotype of a counselor, therapist, or social worker. Perhaps the family therapist has a desire to maintain a certain image with the family. What if the two sets of expectations don't match? For example, a woman once sought help from a family therapist and evolved into a pattern of bringing a different problem to therapy each week. Puzzled and frustrated that she was of no help, the therapist wondered about how the woman might be defining the role of the therapist. In the next session, the therapist inquired about the pattern and what it could mean. With prompting from the therapist, the woman was able to explain that involvement was more important to her than problem solving. She thought that, if she didn't bring in some problem to talk about each week, the therapist would discontinue involvement with her. Having clarified the relational aspect of her communication, they could decide a better way to structure the course of therapy. With this added information, the therapist could help the woman feel more in charge of therapy and how long it continued. Once the problem of involvement was solved, they could move on to more important issues.

Very often, families have unrealistic expectations regarding what a therapist can actually do for them. Sometimes they hope for a miracle; sometimes they may have hidden agendas that they are unable to make explicit. For example, an unfaithful spouse may come to marital counseling simply to assuage his or her guilt, having already decided to leave the marriage. Without ever intending to salvage the relationship, this client may hope that the therapist will become someone for their abandoned spouse to lean on. However, the client may be unable to disclose that intention unless the family therapist raises the possibility first. In another case, a single parent may seek family therapy for his or her child when the parent is still grieving the loss of the marriage. In the first case, the hidden agenda has a great influence on the course of therapy, especially if it remains unknown to the family therapist. If it can become known, it may become the focus of therapy, since it is actually the primary motivation for seeking services. In the second case, the hidden agenda may not greatly affect the course of therapy, since divorce adjustment work could be done in a way that simultaneously benefited parent and child, but it might be helpful for the therapist to understand the implicit expectations in order to intervene in a broad enough way.

In addition, families often have expectations regarding who will actually be seen in sessions (the child alone, each spouse separately, and so on), how the problem will be defined, and what topics will or will not be discussed. While it is difficult to second-guess all the possible expectations, the therapist can try to join sufficiently so that families feel comfortable in disclosing even their most sensitive agendas (for example, "I'm hoping you can tell me if my marriage is worth saving"). Sometimes it may help to make some tentative guesses about what clients may be expecting; other times it may only be necessary for the family therapist to provide an atmosphere that is comfortable for sharing all possible responses. When the therapist suggests an acceptance of the most unusual, the family will be more forthcoming with hidden agendas.

Deciding whom to include in sessions is often difficult for the beginning family therapist. While some pioneers were noted for their insistence upon seeing the entire family (Boszormenyi-Nagy & Framo, 1965; Napier & Whitaker, 1978), others were noted for seeing individuals (Bowen, 1978). With such apparent diversity, the following questions may be helpful to the reader:

• *Who is defining the problem?* If it is a spouse or parent not in attendance, involving that person is a priority.
• *Is the client living with significant others in the household or dependent on others in significant ways?* If so, involving them as sources of information and support should be strongly considered. It is important to engage spouses for such "individual" problems as depression, anxiety, and eating disorders. Many times

they are willing to come, but it simply did not occur to them to do so. At other times, they may need to know they are not being blamed but, rather, are considered a therapeutic influence upon the healing process.

 • *Does the client explicitly name others as a legal, psychological, financial, or relational part of the presenting problem?* To ensure a peaceful resolution, the client must believe that the therapist can remain on his or her side while also engaging the other party. If convincing the client of this proves to be beyond the skill level of the clinician, working systemically may involve playing devil's advocate, developing interactional strategies, or asking questions that provide multiple points of view.

 • *Has the person definitely decided upon a divorce?* If not, informed consent could involve the information that individual sessions may contribute to further distance in the marriage. Many times, one spouse who is reluctant to involve the other can clarify her or his own fears over including the husband or wife. Addressing these fears can become a preliminary goal until the person is assured that the therapist will be able to conduct conjoint therapy in a manner that is comfortable for the reluctant spouse. While the skill level of the therapist may be a factor in this issue, later chapters will address basic skills for conducting conjoint sessions.

 • *Are there significant others who appear to have ongoing knowledge of the day-to-day occurrence of the problem?* If so, a preliminary goal of gathering multiple points of view is important, even if those other parties are unwilling to attend. Many times, however, parties who are involved but not necessarily perceived as part of the problem may be willing to attend as consultants. When expectations can be addressed and respected, it is possible to involve a number of people as sources of information or support, as long as the clinician respects their position as nonclient—someone who was not asking for help or change.

 • *If others were involved in sessions, would the person seeking help become more or less alienated in the process?* Situations of violence, emotional abuse, and extreme alienation may be contraindications for involving other parties on whom the client may be dependent. The clinician's skill level, the client's goals, and other contributing circumstances will have to be explored in total to determine the most beneficial course to take.

 In clarifying expectations and making recommendations for the structure of therapy, it is important to remember Whitaker's (1986) assertion that "there is no such thing as a person without a relationship." However, in deciding on issues of structure, it is also important that the expectations of the client be fully known at the beginning, in order to negotiate effectively without coercion.

Goals

 Each individual (including the clinician) not only has personal expectations about the process of family therapy, but also brings goals—both stated and privately held. Although similar to expectations, goals concern the actual problem that becomes defined and mutually understood as the focus of the therapeutic process. While expectations can often involve personal needs related to the nature and structure of the process, goals relate directly to what problem or issue will be addressed and what is to be accomplished.

In the early years of family therapy, setting goals was a continual struggle. Clients would come in asking for help with a child's behavior or their own predefined mental illness, but family therapists, anxious to convert their client-families to systemic thinking, would be quick to persuade families to think of their child's behavior as a family problem or their mental illness as a marital problem. This approach only served to communicate blame to other family members, even though the intent of the family therapist was to develop a shared goal.

Today, many constructivist theories speak of cocreating the definition of the problem (O'Hanlon & Weiner-Davis, 1989) and integrative models such as the P.B.F.T. model speak explicitly about avoiding resistance and respecting the family's uniqueness. By asking families to clarify what they would like to see happen in family therapy, therapists have the opportunity to rid themselves of any hidden agendas that might prevent the negotiation of mutually agreed-upon goals. Many times, families come to counseling with a definition that has been cocreated by others in the system. As the therapeutic contract is negotiated, the therapist may be able to influence the definition of the problem away from a pathologized view. Sometimes families are relieved at this and are able to express their hopes and fears. However, if families feel strongly about a certain view of the presenting problem, family therapists must negotiate a cooperative relationship above all else, rather than one that unwittingly becomes subtly adversarial. If the family's definition of the problem becomes an issue for the practitioner, he or she must take care to understand fully the importance of their views before designing interventions for later stages of therapy that might have an influence on their perceptions. Consequently, in making the initial contract, the therapist explicitly accepts the family's definition of the problem, while implicitly exploring possibilities for future change. In these instances, the therapist must be flexible and trusting enough to grant the clients a certain wisdom that demands further understanding. The clinician can often gain this understanding by engaging in more systematic data gathering.

Data Gathering

The process of data gathering can occur in many formal and informal ways. Schools of family therapy provide a wide variety of distinctions regarding what type of information to gather and how to gather it. However, in keeping with our integrative theme, the goals of perceptual and behavioral change may be incorporated into the process of data gathering. From a systemic perspective, perceptual and behavioral change may be related to the levels of communication discussed previously: Perceptual data—how clients think about themselves, their family, and the problem—could be considered content; behavioral data—how clients behave relative to the problem—could be considered process.

Therefore, data gathering can be conducted through observations and through questions that elicit information on multiple levels of experience. In addition, the clinician must decide whether to gather such information from the past, present, or future.

Content versus Process

When family members come to therapy, they usually focus on the content of their concerns. Parents may say that their child will not come home on time or is hyperactive. A couple may describe their relationship as empty. The therapist listens to *what* family members say about each other (content) and is interested in *how* family members interact with each other (process). A distinguishing characteristic of family therapists is their interest in process rather than content alone. Therefore, the beginning practitioner must begin to gather data on multiple levels. Through observation, in-session interactions can reveal the nature of intrafamily relationships, as well as the nature of the therapist-family relationship. Through questions and sequence tracking, the clinician also learns about out-of-session relationships and personal perceptions. As information is gathered regarding perceptions and behaviors related to the problem, the therapist may begin to develop hypotheses about which area of change will be the most appropriate to target.

Communication theorists at the Mental Research Institute often look for myths or patterns of thought that may hinder problem resolution in the present. One of their concepts—the utopian syndrome—refers to problems that are defined as due to a client's idealistic view of how the world should be. For example, a widow hoping to cure her depression through therapy is helped to see that her depression is a natural response to loss and not a problem to be solved. It may actually be her response to her own grief that is the problem. Only in a utopia would humans fail to feel the impact of death and loss. To integrate with other dimensions, we can see that change might occur as a result of exploring the content of the client's thoughts and providing a new reality for her.

Another concept—the solution becomes the problem—suggests that some presenting problems grow out of proportion when an attempted solution has an exacerbating effect. In this instance, the therapist would discover this phenomenon by tracking interactional sequences and gathering specific behavioral information about attempted solutions for the original problem. On the basis of these concepts, therapists help the client analyze the content of thoughts and the process of problem solving in the present, so as to discover alternative solutions that were previously overlooked. Whether the clinician targets behavioral or perceptual change is often a matter of skill level and preference.

The Milan team's model balances attention to content and process. Their approach is based on the Batesonian concept that information regarding differences or comparisons within the family is information that can bring about change in family life (for example, the therapist might ask, "How are Mom and Dad different from each other?"). Some questions were designed as interventions to bring forth information (content) regarding the systemic functioning (process) of family members that was new or different from the family's normal way of viewing the problem—that is, to reframe the situation. Informational interventions can be thought of as eliciting systemic insight into the therapeutic arena, so that a family can view itself from a distance. This metaperspective, as articulated by the Milan team, often includes data gathering regarding family roles, rules, and beliefs that may be related to the life of the presenting problem. This information would then become the basis for hypotheses and directives that would effect out-of-session relational changes in a family group.

Past, Present, Future

Among the many decisions that a family therapist must make in conducting a session is whether to focus on the past, present, or future. Fleuridas, Nelson, and Rosenthal (1986) suggest that within each of these categories the therapist may examine "(a) differences or changes within the family between relationships, between beliefs or behaviors of family members, or between their family and other families; (b) agreements or disagreements between members; and (c) explanations of why relationships and interactions proceed as they do and the intended or perceived meanings of certain behaviors" (p. 119). While separate schools show some variation on the dimension of time, all family therapists focus on current relationships, although some give more attention to the past and future than others.

For many years, psychotherapy tended to focus primarily on the client's experience of the past. However, as family therapy began to offer new ways of thinking about mental and emotional problems, data-gathering strategies leaned away from focusing solely on past experience. Similarly, other therapists, such as Haley and Minuchin, recognized the importance of information regarding the family's current stage of the life-cycle and would focus observations on present, in-session behavior.

More recently, the historical approach has been expanded to include the integration of systemic thinking. For example, Framo's approach seeks information about past interactions and perceptions to understand the development of current relationships. Boszormenyi-Nagy gathers information about the past relationships between the child and his or her parents, in order to understand the unconscious needs of parents. Systemic therapists such as the Milan team are often interested in tracking the life of the problem from the past into the present, with interventions focused on the client's ability to impact the future (Boscolo, Cecchin, Hoffman, & Penn, 1987).

While the past and present provide background information regarding the context of the problem, the future becomes the stage for more flexible options. Herein lies another key concept for an integrated model of change. Regardless of whether data gathering focuses on past or present, the therapeutic direction is always future-oriented; the therapist facilitates hopeful connections between the original problem and future solutions. In later chapters, the reader will be helped to strike a balance between gathering information from the past and present. However, that balance must also include guiding families into "forward thinking"

(White, 1986), by gathering data about projected perceptions and behaviors in the future. Positive possibilities may be evoked by such questions as, "What would you imagine your life to be like when you no longer have this problem?" or, "What things would you like to be doing when this is no longer a problem?"

The process of data gathering illustrates how the family therapist is required to think about multiple levels of experience and to alternate between levels in order to gather relevant information about the family system that will contribute toward positive change. Data gathering can be thought of both as an ongoing process that pervades all other stages of the therapeutic process and as an early formalized stage in some cases. In later chapters, skills for data gathering will be discussed in detail.

As this discussion illustrates, the family therapist must be able to think broadly about families and about how to help them change—whether it is broadly about time or broadly about levels of content and process. This ability to think broadly is also exemplified by the process of hypothesizing.

Hypothesizing

This term, which was used by the Milan team as a formal part of their strategic plan, is found to best describe the individual and collective process by which conclusions are formulated about the data gathered. Hypothesizing comprises the way in which the individuals involved—both the family and family therapist—make sense of their experience; in other words, it encompasses what people think about what is going on and also the assumptions that they bring to the situation. As mentioned in Chapter One, specific theories often encourage family therapists to bring certain ideas with them to the therapeutic experience. However, these assumptions may limit their ability to see other possible realities. Just as data gathering can become theory-specific, so can the hypotheses generated by the therapy. Therefore, we want to encourage a style of hypothesizing that is creative and flexible, rather than limiting and rigid. Rather than being told what to hypothesize, the beginning family therapist should learn to formulate a hypothesis and then test it through additional data gathering. By asking the right questions—"How do you know?" or, "What brought you to that conclusion?"—students and trainees can examine and test hypotheses, rather than transform their hypotheses into unquestioned truths that may not fit their families' experience.

Campbell, Draper, and Crutchley (1991) describe this process:

> The hypothesis is described as a means of organizing the information available to the therapist in order to provide a guide to his or her activity in conducting a systemic interview. It is "neither true nor false," but rather "more or less useful" (Selvini Palazzoli et al., 1980b, p. 3). A hypothesis allows the therapist to search out new information, identify the connecting patterns, and move toward a systemic formulation of the family's behavior. In addition, an interview that is conducted from the basis of a systemic hypothesis allows the therapist

to hold on to a view of the family's behavior that is different from the family's simply by being "a difference." The hypothesis, as it guides the interview, will introduce information and structure (or negentropy) into the family system, which tends toward repetitive patterns of behavior and diminishing appreciation of differences. (p. 328)

The process of hypothesizing is also related to co-creating a definition of the problem. Certain theories generate certain static definitions of the problem. However, family members often have their own definition of the problem, whether private or public, that has a bearing on how the family responds to family therapy. More important than what the therapist thinks is what the family thinks and how the therapist will interact with them around these variant definitions. We submit that the majority of family therapy schools, while specifying certain assumptions about problem formation, become more unified in addressing the interactional process between family therapist and client. Therapist flexibility and the perception of client competencies become woven into the interactional fabric that ultimately determines which definition of the problem will become shared by therapist and family.

In addition, most schools of family therapy also share a basic hypothesis about physical and emotional problems. This hypothesis is relational in nature and assumes that some relationship within the family or with some significant other (even a teacher, employer, or neighbor) is possibly part of the problem or, at least, a potential part of the solution. This relational hypothesis leads to the identification of relationship conditions—rather than simply individual conditions—that are important to consider. The following case is a good example.

A man in his mid-50s sought therapy for depression. His wife agreed to accompany him in order to be helpful. In pursuing a relational hypothesis, the therapist pursued the client's own description of his internal process and the couple's description of how they each responded to his depression. Rather than attempting to convince them that depression is really an interactional problem, rather than an individual problem, the therapist chose to acknowledge the internal reality of the man's depression, while exploring the couple's attempted solutions and their own interactional process. This discussion eventually led to the identification of perceptual and behavioral sequences that all agreed were problematic. The wife thought of her role as his emotional caretaker. Each time he expressed his despair ("I feel lousy"), she tried to make him feel better ("Cheer up. Look on the bright side"). To him, these responses were implicit disagreements with his internal experience. Feeling misunderstood, he became more entrenched in his own position.

As the therapist helped them to examine and change this interactional pattern, the man was not robbed of his internal experience and his wife was not blamed for his depression. Instead, they both were directed toward a plan that could facilitate the healing process. In this instance, the end result was a lifting of the depression, as the spouses began to cooperate in a new way. However, had the depression persisted, the couple, equipped with new relational skills, could then pursue additional solutions with their relationship strengthened rather than strained. In this case, the hypotheses of the client were included in an expanded definition of the problem, which grew to include relational factors. Since the couple's hypotheses about the depression had included such things as the man's job change and a strained relationship with his only daughter, these were easily incorporated by becoming the content that their new relational process could address more effectively.

Another relational hypothesis deals with a universal concern for all therapists: the phenomenon of resistance. Interpreted as an individual issue, resistance is often described as client rigidity or lack of cooperation. However, a relational hypothesis of resistance would suggest an interactional definition that involves the therapist as a participant in the problem. Such a hypothesis helps the beginning family therapist to examine his or her own interactional process with the client, rather than merely indicting the client alone. Interactional hypotheses can help the practitioner change perceptions and behaviors that may have unwittingly elicited resistant behavior. Like the wife of the depressed man, many family therapists learn how to be more helpful by examining and changing their part of certain problematic sequences.

Formalized Interventions

Formalized interventions—therapist behaviors such as questions and directives—should not be thought of as the sole mechanism of change. It is our belief that all the stages of the therapeutic process discussed in this chapter are important and legitimate interventions in themselves. For example, the family therapist should avoid the temptation to think of the joining process as something that is done *before* treatment begins. Likewise, examining the referral process is not some preliminary adjunct to therapy but, in some cases, may become the focal point of many sessions to come.

It is helpful to conceptualize the earlier stages of the process as specific interventions to address specific issues, whereas formalized interventions represent a less strictly defined stage that might take many different creative forms as a logical extension of data gathering and hypothesizing. This process may then be understood as a sequence: Incoming information (data gathering) leads to certain assumptions (hypotheses), which lead to certain actions from the family therapist (interventions) related to the presenting problem. Simple interventions such as questions, directives, and reframing often require minimal data gathering and hypothesizing. Other interventions require more extensive data gathering and could be regarded as more elaborate directives: for example, experiential exercises, psychoeducation, conflict resolution, communication training, rituals, paradox, and perceptual or behavioral tasks. These specific skills, addressed in later chapters, are only a sampling of the choices that can be made as the clinician gains an understanding of the family's developmental level. We conclude this chapter by considering a process that is crucial in determining the developmental level and, ultimately, what will be most helpful to the family—evaluation.

Evaluation

This is another process that is informally taking place all the time, regardless of whether the family therapist provides the opportunity for the family to formally express themselves. As a process, evaluation can be thought of as each party's response to the larger question of fit: What will best fit this client? Implicit and explicit evaluations influence the therapeutic contract in order to clarify expectations and to develop mutually agreed-upon goals. The beginning family therapist is encouraged to seek explicit feedback from the family in order to avoid impasses and misunderstandings. Coleman (1985) makes the point that changes in goals that have not been negotiated cooperatively with families can sometimes lead to treatment failures. It is important for the practitioner to learn how to benefit from honest client feedback in order to make mid-course corrections. Clients' responses to an assigned task can always be an implicit message about whether the task was helpful or relevant to them.

As with many of the other stages of family therapy, this interactional process may occur in microinteractions, as the therapist asks clients, "When I said _____ just now, how did you take it?" Or it can occur as part of a crossroads in the course of therapy, as a therapist says, "We seem to have been discussing _____ the last few sessions. I'm wondering if you think this is helpful or whether we should consider a different direction." Such explicit initiatives toward evaluation respect the clients' role as the consumer, as the ultimate authority on their own lives, and reminds the family therapist that the ultimate evaluator is the clients' perception of helpfulness. While external evaluators such as court systems or schools may sometimes participate in the definition of a problem, the eventual progress made by families in therapy will be heavily influenced by the family's evaluation of the therapist's helpfulness. Once the beginning practitioner overcomes the fear of being evaluated, she or he will discover that eliciting the family's evaluation is also an intervention that can facilitate change.

Summary

These stages, while not strictly occurring in a consistent sequential pattern, nevertheless serve as a guide to help the beginning family therapist anticipate and initiate certain basic interactions that will maintain and strengthen the nature of the therapist-client relationship. The first three stages—referral, joining, and creating a therapeutic contract—can be thought of as being broken into smaller parts: data gathering, hypothesizing, intervention, and evaluation. Subsequently, these four processes can also be thought of as a progressive sequence that recurs throughout the middle and later phases of therapy.

It is our belief that many of these elements are overlooked in traditional literature because specific models often adopt the goal of educating the reader about a theory. Also, experienced theoreticians and clinicians often become intent upon illustrating specific techniques in isolation from the natural ongoing flow of the family therapy experience. Rather than dwelling on the specifics of concepts and theory, this overview of family therapy practice has been intended to review key processes that will help the reader through the remaining chapters on specific skill development.

To summarize, the practice of family therapy can be thought of as a series of interactional processes that take place between flexible, competency-based clinicians who employ four basic skills: questions, tracking sequences, reframing, and directives. Using these skills, they proceed through a relational process with individuals and families that targets behavioral and perceptual changes in the clients' personal lives. Like all relationships, the therapeutic relationship evolves through developmental stages, as clinician and family discover new definitions of their problem and corresponding new solutions. The family therapist organizes the structure of therapy, joins with each family member, and gathers information that focuses on the family's potential for change. As new information emerges, the therapist develops interventions that match the family's developmental level and the therapist's skill level. As these interactions unfold over time, each side of the transaction—family and therapist—is reviewing and reacting to the process, evaluating the impact and the results of their encounters. The following section, which pursues skill development, will help the clinician to master specific behaviors needed to successfully navigate each of the interactional stages discussed in the present chapter.

Part Two

BASIC FAMILY THERAPY ASSESSMENT SKILLS

Chapter Four

Organizing the Intake Process

Referral Information

Clinical Information

Previous Therapy

Family Information

Scheduling Information

Formulating Initial Hypotheses

T he gathering of intake information is crucial to the effectiveness of the initial interview. Wright and Leahey (1984b) pay specific attention to the telephone contact preceding the first interview, suggesting that this first contact can have great impact on the further course of subsequent contacts. The initial telephone contact has also been an issue of note for other clinicians, many of whom have developed guidelines and strategies for addressing systemic dynamics with the earliest possible contact (Brock & Barnard, 1988; Napier & Whitaker, 1978; Selvini Palazzoli et al. 1978). For family therapists working in agency settings, there may already be an intake process established, over which the practitioner has little control. If this is the case, the initial interview may serve as an opportunity to reconcile differences between the process recommended here and that of the practice setting. Another solution to this problem is for the clinician to make an additional telephone contact after the agency intake and before the first session; the family therapist can then provide important direction before the first meeting. For others who have the discretion to structure client contact according to their own preference, this chapter may serve as a step-by-step guide to the beginning stages of family therapy.

Colapinto (1991) further elaborates:

> Assessment begins with the information gathered during an initial telephone call or by reading an intake sheet. On the basis of simple, concrete information, such as the composition of the family and the ages of its members, as well as more subtle data, such as who makes the initial call and how that person describes the family problems, the therapist generates his or her first impressions about the family's "shape" and some of the possible strengths and weaknesses. These initial hypotheses are invaluable in guiding the first contacts of the therapist with the family, even if they may have to be discarded quickly at that point. (p. 431)

The intake interview is generally conducted by telephone and includes the following categories of information: (a) referral information, (b) clinical information, (c) previous therapy, (d) family information, and (e) scheduling information. Box 4.1 provides an overview for gathering intake information. After the information is gathered, the family therapist may begin to develop initial hypotheses regarding the nature of the problem.

Referral Information

It is critical to get full names, addresses, and phone numbers for each member of the family. A distinction should be made between the client of record (person who makes the call) and other family members (partner or children). This is particularly true in divorced and remarried families where members are living apart. If the family doesn't have a phone, it's important to obtain a phone number of a relative or neighbor who is in regular contact with the family. This information will help to identify who else is involved with the family.

Box 4.1 ***Steps of the Intake Interview***

Referral Information
1. Specify names, addresses, and phone numbers.
2. Identify referral source and the relationship between family and referral source.

Clinical Information
3. Get a brief description of the problem and any recent changes in the family.
4. Ask how the problem is affecting other family members.

Previous Therapy
5. Ask if any family members have been involved in previous therapy.
6. Are there other informal helpers who have positive or negative effects on the family?

Family Information
7. Identify family members and others who are related to the problem.
8. Are there additional extended-family members who have strong feelings about the problem?

Scheduling Information
9. Ask for additional relevant parties to attend the first session (for example, spouses, additional children, referral source, extended family, significant friends).
10. Specify date, time of appointment, and location of facility.

Referral sources should also be identified. Family therapists may receive referrals from various sources, including school counselors, psychologists, social workers, previous clients, and family members involved in the problem (self-referral). When a family is referred by an outside agency (for example, a court or school), they may be suspicious and less willing to attend the initial session. This is particularly the case when families are forced to attend therapy by a probation officer or the court (Boyd-Franklin, 1989b). If professional referral sources (for example, social workers or school counselors) make the initial contact, they should be made aware of the family therapist's role and how to make a referral. If referral sources are aware of overt conflict between their view of the problem and the family's view, they should be encouraged to develop a collaborative understanding with the family before making the referral. If they consider the difference of opinion irreconcilable, referral sources should be encouraged to emphasize the family therapist's independence, in order to minimize client defensiveness. In such cases, the role of the family therapist may involve resolving conflict between the family and the larger system. That role can be carried out effectively only when family therapists establish a stated position of neutrality with respect to the referral source and of support with respect to the family.

When interacting with the referral source, therapists should gather information about the problem and the referral source's attempts to alleviate it.

Weber, McKeever, and McDaniel (1985) suggest that it is important to determine what the referring person is requesting (for example, consultation for self or therapy for the family). The following dialogue illustrates these issues with professional referral sources:

Social worker: I need your help with a family our agency is involved with. Can I talk to you about them?

Family therapist: Sure. What seems to be the problem?

Social worker: Well, the husband attends our Adult Day Center and has Alzheimer's. I've been trying to get his wife to start planning for his long-term care needs, but she says they're doing fine and she doesn't need anything like that. She's really in denial.

Family therapist: What type of help did you have in mind? Are you looking for a consultation for yourself or therapy for them?

Social worker: I really think they need therapy. We just haven't gotten anywhere with them.

Family therapist: Have you discussed this idea with them?

Social worker: Yes, the wife said she would be willing to talk to you.

Family therapist: OK. Tell me what you said to her and the reasons you gave for recommending that she come here.

Social worker: I told her that I was concerned about her future with her husband's illness and I thought it would be a good idea if she talked to someone about her options.

Family therapist: How did she respond to this?

Social worker: She said, if I thought it was necessary, she would be willing to come.

Family therapist: Did you mention earlier that you don't think you've gotten anywhere with them?

Social worker: Yes, she just won't look at the future.

Family therapist: Well, I wonder if we could think of this as a difference of opinion between the two of you. You want her to look at the future and she doesn't want to.

Social worker: Well, I suppose you could say that.

Family therapist: If this is the case, she may respond to me in the same way she has been responding to you, unless I'm able to establish a position with her which is independent of yours. Do you think you could raise the issue of this difference between you and explain that I will be a neutral third party?

Social worker: Yes, I can do that. I told her I'd call her back after I talked to you.

Family therapist: Good. Why don't you describe me as someone who is interested in her point of view? Then, you and I should come to an understanding about my role. I've found that I can often help people reach a resolution by increasing their understanding of each other. Would you be open to additional information that might help alleviate your present concerns?

Social worker: Oh yes. If you can just get her to open up, that would really help.

In this instance, the family therapist should be prepared for the client to be cooperative but not necessarily motivated to pursue the social worker's agenda. However, because the social worker has been prepared for a new agenda—that of increasing their understanding of each other—the family therapist will not be hindered by the previous misunderstandings between referral source and client. Very likely, the goal the client will be most motivated to pursue is one that enables her to feel more support from the social worker and more freedom to manage her life as she wishes.

When callers are family members, the therapist should determine what role the referral source might have in the definition of the problem. The Milan team recommends that family members who call as the referral source be considered as the client of record. If the family member wants to be excluded from the initial interview, the therapist should refuse to see the family (Selvini Palazzoli, 1985).

With self-referrals, it is recommended that others (referral sources, care-givers) who are related to the problem be asked to attend the initial session to present their view of the problem. However, if the client is uncomfortable with this suggestion, the family therapist can seek a release of information from the family in order to communicate with the person making the referral. If the referral source does not attend the initial session, the therapist can make permitted contact to (a) understand the source's perception of the problem; (b) clarify what the source wants to see happen; and (c) clarify how information should be provided to the referring source (Weber et al., 1985). Likewise, significant others (for example, friends and relatives) who are concerned about the problem and who can provide support to the family should be encouraged to attend the initial session.

Once information about the problem has been gathered, an agreement should be reached about how treatment information should be shared. Court referrals often require periodic reports summarizing the progress of treatment. School counselors and teachers may want to know how the child is progressing so that they can support these changes. In many cases, families may request a report or evaluation of their progress. If the case is court-ordered, the family must be informed regarding the therapist's responsibility to the court. However, in cases where there is no legal obligation to report, the intake worker should advise the referral source that the family has legal control over what information is shared. The intake worker should make a note of this issue, instructing the therapist to discuss these questions with the family.

Clinical Information

It is important to get a concise statement of the problem. When family members call, they are giving their view of the problem. Often family members will express concern through the use of labels. For instance, they may state feelings of "depression" or "anxiety," or refer to a child as "out of control." While these labels offer a general indication of the problem area, they have different meanings for different people. Therefore, it is important to get concrete examples for each label. For example, "out of control" may mean that the child "doesn't come home on time."

Likewise, the intake person should ask how the problem is affecting other family members. For example, if a mother calls and reports that her teenage son is "out of control," it is important to determine how his behavior is affecting her or, if she is married, her relationship with her husband. For example, she may report that she and her husband "disagree about how to handle this problem"; she may report that her husband is the only one who can handle him. Finally, it is important to summarize the referring family member's view of the problem ("So you see the problem as your son being 'out of control,' that he won't come home when you tell him, and that you and your husband don't agree about how to handle him").

A brief dialogue illustrates how intake information can be gathered from the referral person.

Intake worker: Can you give me a brief description of the problem?

Referral person: My husband and I are not getting along.

Intake worker: Can you tell me what is going on that makes you feel that way?

Wife: We never go out . . . we just don't seem to have anything in common since Laura, our daughter, left for college.

It's important to note that the intake worker questioned the referral person *immediately* following her description of the problem. *Therapists should train intake workers to get a quick and concise description of the problem.*

It is also helpful to obtain information about previous marriages, divorce dates, recent deaths, illnesses, and any other significant changes that have occurred in the family system. This information may be useful in formulating hypotheses, particularly if a marriage has followed soon after a divorce, or there have been other significant changes in rapid succession.

Previous Therapy

Assessing previous therapy will help determine what works and what doesn't work. Noting prior therapy on the face sheet will alert the therapist to ask about those experiences. This information will help the therapist determine how the family viewed the previous therapy. If a family left therapy because the therapist wanted to focus on the marriage rather than the child, the therapist knows he should not focus on the marriage; that is, this information will assist the therapist in not making the same mistakes as previous therapists. In addition, if any family members are currently in therapy, the therapist can ask the family to sign a release, so that information and services may be coordinated.

After determining the effects of previous therapy, family therapists should ask about others who may have offered help or opinions about the problem in the past—friends, neighbors, clergy, or extended-family members. What suggestions have they made? How does the family feel about these informal helpers? If such parties have significant influence with the family, it may be wise to ask about the possibility of their inclusion in the first session.

Family Information

Family information includes names of the client of record and partner or spouse, birthdates, level of education, and place of employment or school. Blank lines are also included for the children. It is critical to determine who is living in the home, as well as those who are related to the problem. This information will help to determine who will attend the first session. All family members who live in the household should be asked to attend the initial session. If the contact person is unwilling to bring the whole family to the initial session, then treatment options may vary. Therapists could meet with family members who are most concerned about the problem, or they may insist that all family members must attend therapy. However, when significant others are excluded from the process, family therapists must ask questions during the assessment process to bring to light information about the missing parties' point of view and how much influence they have on other family members. Then, as understanding increases about each person's position in the system, the therapist should look for opportunities to address the exclusion of key family members and negotiate their subsequent inclusion. Such strategies will be addressed in Chapter Five.

Scheduling Information

It is helpful to know scheduling requirements (times available to be seen) and who will be attending the first session. Intake workers should be instructed to encourage all family members living in the home to attend the first session. Once this information is gathered, an appointment date should be set for the family. The date, time, and location of counseling should be provided. Families should be instructed when to arrive and given all relevant information about the intake procedure and fees. The family should also be made aware of the cancellation policy, if there is one.

Often, family members making the appointment may be hesitant to invite others to the first session. They may report that their spouse's work schedule prohibits attendance or that they are reluctant to impose upon extended-family members not living in the home. As mentioned previously, some may also sense an adversarial relationship with the referral source and refuse to include that person. In these instances, family therapists should prioritize the various parties who could be included. All family members living in the household are the highest priority; next would be influential extended family; and last would be referral sources. If the client of record has objections to all three possibilities, household members should become the primary focus. When the client is a single adult living alone, it is often best to proceed with the initial interview individually. During this time, the clinician can determine who are the significant others and how others might be successfully included (see Chapter Five).

The following intake dialogue illustrates how the interviewer might address the reluctance to include other members of the household:

Intake worker: Is your husband willing to attend the first session with you?

Wife: Well, . . . I don't know. He told me that he is perfectly happy and that it's my problem.

Intake worker: What do you think about his assessment?

Wife: He's probably right. He usually is.

Intake worker: So, what do you think would happen if you asked him to come?

Wife: I don't think he would come.

Intake worker: Have you ever been afraid that he would become violent with you?

Wife: Oh, no! He would never do anything like that. He's just stubborn.

Intake worker: Let's think about some other issues for a moment. Even if he agreed to come, can you think of some ways that you might be more uncomfortable if he was included?

Wife: Well, . . . I guess I would probably clam up. I don't like to make him mad and every time I bring up how I feel, he gets mad.

Intake worker: So you're afraid that things would go just like they do at home?

Wife: Yes.

Intake worker: I see. . . . You may be right. I'm wondering if you might be able to tolerate that possibility in order to get the very best help?

Wife: What do you mean?

Intake worker: Our family therapists generally find their greatest success when they are able to hear all sides of the question. Even if your husband thinks the problem is yours, it would help the therapist to understand your husband's point of view. That way, since you plan on staying married, she could give you the kind of direction that would be good for you and your relationship. Sometimes, therapists give suggestions that seem good for the person, but which turn out to threaten their marriage in some way.

Wife: But I don't know how to make him come in.

Intake worker: Would it be possible for you to simply quote me? You could tell him, "The intake worker at the agency says your opinion is important to the process, to help me with my feelings. He knows you're not seeking any help right now, but he'd like to know if you would attend a session and give your opinion about what you think my problem is. He says it's customary for the therapist to meet the person's spouse before proceeding with individual work. Would you be willing to attend the first session with me?"

Wife: OK. I'll try. What if he still won't come?

Intake worker: Let us know what happened and we'll ask your assigned therapist to contact you for further direction.

In this dialogue, the intake worker explores the reluctance from the husband's and the wife's point of view. Although the wife was focused more on her husband's reluctance, her own unspoken reluctance may be a significant factor as well. Without trying to change the husband's mind (something the wife may do repetitively), the intake worker suggests a rationale that meets her overall goal (help) without escalating the conflict between them. If the intake process reveals the presence of violence in the relationship or the wife's intention to follow through with divorce, the initial interview may be conducted individually, unless the therapist has advanced training in how to engage violent men in therapy (Jenkins, 1991).

Formulating Initial Hypotheses

The information gathered from the initial telephone contact helps the therapist to formulate initial hypotheses. Initial hypotheses can be formulated by assessing whether the family's evolving structure (organization) is appropriate for their particular developmental stage. For example, a young couple seeks therapy, each complaining that the other places their career above their marriage. The following hypotheses are all possible views of the problem:

1. They have not learned to negotiate closeness or distance in their relationship—a major developmental task of the beginning family.
2. They did not successfully clarify beliefs, roles, and expectations—a developmental task of courtship and mate selection.
3. Over time, there has been some structural change in their relationship, which they cannot understand or resolve.
4. Their communication and problem-solving styles have not brought about successful conflict resolution (more of the same or the solution becomes the problem).

The therapist can pursue each of these hypotheses until concrete information eliminates or verifies them. In addition, the system can be assessed as to whether interactional change (the way they behave) or cognitive change (the way they think) will be the focus of the therapist's interventions.

In addition, hypotheses about the nature of the problem can be generated:

1. Is the problem chronic, developmental, or situational?
2. Does the family need help in solving a specific problem ("We're fighting constantly") or in tolerating an uncomfortable time in their life ("We just filed for bankruptcy and both of us must work longer hours in order to catch up").

By approaching the initial session with an array of questions to be answered, the family therapist can be directive in providing a structure for the interview, while remaining tentative enough to allow the uniqueness of the family to emerge.

Box 4.2 is a sample intake interview form. Box 4.3 presents sample case material on the intake form. From the information in Box 4.3, the following hypotheses can be generated prior to the initial session:

1. A rapid remarriage may have left no time for the new marital subsystem to successfully organize parenting responsibilities or for the biological parents to resolve custody and visitation issues.
2. There may be divorce-adjustment and grief issues lingering for Robert and his mother.
3. There may be conflict between Jerry and Robert.
4. There may be some historical interactions between Robert and his mother that have become an ongoing pattern.

While there are additional possibilities, these serve as examples of developmental, structural, and interactional hypotheses that family therapists can use to begin their exploration of the family. These hypotheses provide a sense of direction until other information is available. Once the initial interview occurs, these hypotheses may be eliminated or expanded with additional information. For example, in the first session, the therapist may discover that Jerry works many evenings, leaving little opportunity for conflict with Robert. However, when he is home, Robert seems to respond more obediently to Jerry than to his mother. This information may eliminate hypothesis 3 and strengthen hypotheses 1, 2, or 4.

Whereas the family therapist gathers much factual information from the intake interview, the initial interview, which we consider next, is an opportunity for more personal and involved interactions between therapist and family.

Box 4.2   *Intake Form*   Date _____

Referral information

Client of record   Last _____ First _____ Mid. _____

Partner/spouse   Last _____ First _____ Mid. _____

Street _____ City _____ State _____ Zip _____

Phone #s: Home _____ Work _____

Other _____   Phone _____

Referral source: Org. _____   Name _____

Phone _____   Status _____

Clinical information

Problem description _____

_____

_____

Previous Relationships: Client of Record _____   Dates _____

Partner/Spouse _____ Dates _____

Current marriage date: _____

Previous therapy

Name	Org.	Address	Dates
____	____	____	____
____	____	____	____

Family information

First name	Last name	Birthdate	Ed.	Employ./School
____	____	____	____	____
____	____	____	____	____
____	____	____	____	____
____	____	____	____	____

Scheduling information

Appointment date _____   Time _____   Therapist _____

Box 4.3 *Completed Intake Form*   Date 5/13/95

Referral information

Client of record   Last Russell   First Barbara   Mid. S.

Partner/spouse   Last Russell   First Jerry   Mid. L.

Street 2553 Hawthorne Avenue City Batesville   State IN Zip 47006

Phone #s: Home 451-8484 Work (his) 897-3333

Other Barbara's wk.   Phone 276-3533

Referral source: Org. Hawthorne Elem.   Name school counselor

Phone ____   Status inactive case

Clinical information

Problem description Mrs. Russell stated that her son, Robert, is failing the 4th grade. He also resists rules at home. This started after her remarriage last year. She thinks Robert is depressed about being away from his biological father who moved out of state last year.

Previous Relationships: Client of Record widowed Dates wife died 3 yrs ago

Partner/Spouse divorced Dates married 1980, div. 1991

Current marriage date: October 1991

Previous therapy

Name	Org.	Address	Dates
Mrs. Russell	The Family Ctr.	1337 W. Main St.	May, 1990, 2-3 sessions

Family information

First name	Last name	Birthdate	Ed.	Employ./School
Barbara	Russell	9-1-43	H.S.	Sec., Ford Motors
Jerry	Russell	10-5-40	H.S.	Sales, Lincoln Ins.
Robert	Starks	10-10-82	4th grade	Hawthorne

Scheduling information

Appointment date 5-20-95   Time 4 pm   Therapist Jim Austin

Chapter Five

The Initial Interview

A review of family therapy literature reveals that several approaches share some common elements of the initial interview. Breunlin (1985) noted a beginning phase of family therapy in which the therapist organizes the referral system, convenes the family, begins the helping relationship, assesses the family, and develops a definition of the problem. Haley (1976a) described the initial interview in four stages: social, problem, interactional, and goal setting. According to Segal and Bavelas (1983), the goal of the initial interview is to gather specific behavioral information regarding the nature of the complaint and the client's attempted solutions; this resembles Haley's interactional stage. The general pattern for many schools of thought involves the evolution of the therapeutic system where family and therapist come together in an exchange of information to determine the who, what, where, when, and how of family therapy. The key elements discussed here include joining, exploring the referral process, deciding whom to involve, defining the problem, negotiating goals, and contracting.

Joining

The process of joining begins with the first family contact and continues as the foundation for effective family therapy. Rather than an event, it is more a process of understanding and building rapport with each member of the family. While some family members may be more central than others, an understanding of all members is often necessary if family therapists are to be successful. General psychotherapy models share the goals of empathy and positive regard for clients; however, family therapy integrates these goals with systemic thinking. The result is a type of systemic empathy, in which the clinician is able to identify and describe the unique roles and dilemmas experienced by each family member.

Methods of Joining

The methods therapists use to join a family are often just beyond their conscious awareness and appear to be much like those used in ordinary human relationships. The past few decades of pop culture have produced several expressions to describe the phenomenon: The slang expressions "on the same wavelength," "in the same groove," and "on the same track" all refer to joining. Each family has a unique blend of characteristics that serve as interpersonal cues to family identity. Additionally, each family has a complex structure that provides rules for its interactions among members and with the outside world. Family therapists place a high priority on being attentive and responsive to family members.

If workers are to be effective with the family in this context, they must connect with the family. Connecting is both an attitude and a skill. To connect with the family, the family therapist must convey acceptance of family members and respect for their way of seeing and doing things. It is critical to validate each family member and acknowledge their experience and actions. The therapist must let family members know that they are understood and their views are important. Family members must be encouraged to express their feelings and views and to understand that these feelings are normal. The therapist can join with family members in the following ways:

1. Greet each member of the family by name.
2. Make friendly contact with each member. The therapist should ask each member what she or he does and where they live; share information about the children; and so on.
3. Respect the family hierarchy. The therapist must begin with the parents when asking each member about his or her view of the problem.
4. Acknowledge each member's experience, position, and actions. ("So, Ms. Brown, you think your son ran away because he was angry at you.")
5. Normalize experiences, views, and actions. ("It is common for people in your situation to feel the way you do.")
6. Validate positive things you can say about a family member whenever possible. ("Ms. Jones, I know you have tried your best to help your son. It shows how much you care about him.") Reinforcing or validating a family member will often confirm that individual and help other members to view the problem differently.

In some cases, the therapist may join with the family by connecting with one of its members. This process is called selective joining (Colapinto, 1991). The therapist may often choose to affiliate with the most peripheral member in the family; or, in some cases, the therapist will make special efforts (mimesis of language and tone of voice) to get closer to the family member who will most likely bring the family to therapy.

There may be occasions when the therapist is unable to join with a family. It may be difficult to join with a family in which members have values different from the therapist's (for example, parents who abuse their children) or in which members have hostile or detached personalities. While these feelings are understandable, therapists must find some way to engage the family if they are to be effective in altering the situation. Milton Erickson developed a process called utilization to address this issue (Erickson & Rossi, 1979). He learned to use, rather than challenge, a person's way of relating. For example, he would think of hostility as honesty and would encourage the client to use it in solving the problem. He would reframe a detached personality as cautious or careful and would search for a context in which this behavior would be advantageous. Family members must feel that the therapist is supportive and understands them before they will change the way in which they interact with each other.

A recent trend in family therapy facilitates the joining process by helping the therapist identify family strengths in spite of the severity of the problem (Karpel, 1986; Zeig & Lankton, 1988).

Identifying Family Strengths

A good relationship with the family focuses not only on problems but also on the family strengths. Knowledge of family strengths will help the therapist to understand how families cope with problems and how they promote growth and development. Assessing a family as potentially healthy—rather than adopting a deficit (problem) model—gives the family hope that they can solve their own problems. While this may seem obvious to most clinicians, it is frequently overlooked when family therapists become more intent on solving the family's problem, rather than developing a good relationship with them.

Focusing on the family's strengths and resources contributes to the development of self-confidence, inspires hope, and enhances growth within the family. Each family has unique strengths that may be buried or forgotten. The therapist must explore and probe to discover these strengths. Family members must be encouraged to discuss how they have coped with problems. The following guidelines will help beginning clinicians to join with the family by identifying their strengths:

- *Emphasize positive statements reported by family members* (for example, "My mother listens to me when I have a problem"). It is also important to observe behaviors that reflect sensitivity, appreciation, or cooperation between family members.
- *Encourage family members to share their story about themselves.* Pay particular attention to those aspects of their story that reveal how the family has coped successfully with problems.
- *Note family interactions that reflect strength and competency* (for example, "I like the way you help your daughter find her own answers to the problem"). Underscoring positive family interactions helps the interviewer to identify other strengths and competencies.
- *Emphasize those times that family members enjoy together.* What are they doing? What makes it enjoyable? These questions offer opportunities to discuss strengths and capabilities.
- *Reframe problems or negative statements in a more positive way* (for example, "Your anger shows how much you care about him"). Reframing consists of changing the conceptual or emotional viewpoint so as to change the meaning of the problem without changing the facts. The situation doesn't change, but the interpretation does.
- *Emphasize what families do well.* All families have areas of strength (such as patience, skills, and coping behavior). By asking questions, the therapist can learn how families utilize these strengths to solve problems (for example, "What works best with your child?" "Tell me about the times you were able to get him to _____. What did you do?" "How were you able to get him to _____?" "What does that say about your ability to get him to do that in the future?").

If the family therapist thinks of joining as the primary task of the initial interview, then it is possible to see each stage of the interview as an opportunity to join with them and develop rapport. Each of the following sections represents specific content to be covered, generally through the systematic use of questions. As the interview progresses, the clinician may develop a rhythm that follows this general pattern:

1. Therapist inquires with questions.
2. Family responds with verbal and nonverbal messages.
3. Therapist responds to family's responses by identifying strengths, reframing problems, validating feelings, or asking more questions.

Exploring the Referral Process

The referral process will often include interactions within the family and between the family and other systems. Understanding these interactions can help the clinician to answer the following questions:

1. Which relationship should be the central focus?
2. Which parties are most relevant to a successful outcome?
3. Who is the most motivated participant in the therapy process? Who is most reluctant?

These questions, which can be answered indirectly through conversation with the family, direct the family therapist toward an exploration of the referral process. When individuals are being interviewed alone, it is important to assess whether their motivation for counseling is internal, or whether they have been sent by family or friends who want them "fixed." The therapist can inquire directly:

1. Whose idea was it to seek outside help?
2. Who agrees or disagrees with the idea of seeking outside help?
3. How did you know to come here?

When it is discovered that an outside party has suggested counseling, it is likely that the definition of the problem will have to focus initially on the relationship between those being interviewed and the referral source. This might be the family versus another system or the individual versus family, friends, or employer. Thus, if a family has sought therapy because the school is concerned about Johnny's behavior, the family therapist must decide how much the family agrees or disagrees with the school's perception of Johnny. Also, if a husband has come alone for counseling because his wife has given him an ultimatum, the therapist must determine who has defined the problem and whether the husband agrees or disagrees with her point of view. He may want to save his marriage, but he may be unable to fully represent his wife's point of view. The intricate politics that have led to her exclusion from the session must also be investigated: Does she have her own therapist and feel that he should take his turn? Has she already privately decided on divorce and identified the therapist as someone her husband can turn to when she "lowers the boom"? Does she think he is totally to blame for the marriage? Has he been violent, so that she has had to separate in order to capture some degree of control over her life? Detailed questions about the referral process will often help the family therapist to expand the definition of the problem. When it is not feasible for the referring person to be included in sessions (as in the case of court workers and abused or abusing spouses, for example), the problem can still be defined as an issue between the client(s) and the outside party.

If intake information has noted previous experiences in therapy, these should also be explored as part of the client's problem-solving history. Work with other therapists may be related to this current request for help. However, even if previous therapy seems unrelated, the current therapist should always explore the effects of these other experiences on family members, by asking:

1. What was your experience like with Dr. _____?
2. Was there anything uncomfortable about your work with him?
3. What things do you remember being helpful?
4. Why didn't you return to him for help with this problem?

These questions often facilitate the joining process with families, by revealing how other types of help have influenced them. Do they think their current therapist will be just like the last one? Are there certain things that make them drop out of therapy? Can the current therapist discover what fits for this family by listening to their descriptions of past therapy? This information is often crucial to future successes with any client who has had previous helpers. In fact, the same questions can often be asked about informal helpers (friends, family, co-workers) with equally fruitful results. Sometimes, informal helpers become unrecognized influences on the course of therapy, unless they are identified during such a discussion.

This focus on the referral process often provides a macro view of diverse relationships that may have some bearing on the problem. As this larger context is taken into account, the clinician should then pursue more specific questions regarding the potential structure of subsequent therapy sessions.

Deciding Whom to Involve

Certain questions provide the family therapist with the information necessary to determine the structure of the therapy process. Are significant people absent from the session? If so, their absence can be addressed by exploring the client's expectations for service and whether including others would conflict with the family's perception of help:

1. How did you decide who would participate in today's session?
2. Maybe you are more comfortable without _____ here. Are there some reasons why you would prefer to leave them out?
3. What do you think might happen if _____ was invited?
4. If I became insistent about inviting them, would it be so uncomfortable that you might consider dropping out of counseling?

The answers to these questions help the family therapist determine whether to insist on others' attendance. Certainly, there are many situations in which a person's own framework for help would be violated and such an insistence would be inappropriate. Conversely, there are times when a family therapist will consider the attendance of others to be essential to a positive therapeutic outcome. To resolve this dilemma successfully, the family therapist should conduct a self-evaluation on these issues:

1. Have I elicited and acknowledged fears the client has about inviting others to join us?
2. Have I reassured the client that I can orchestrate a constructive outcome when others are included? Do I know enough about these other people, and do I have the skills necessary, to set goals that guarantee the outcome of such a meeting?
3. Am I ignoring messages (verbal or nonverbal) from the client about what is essential to them?
4. Am I operating out of a model that narrows my perception of how I can be helpful? Does the client have important information to which I should defer, rather than insisting on a certain structure?

The answers to these questions can help the practitioner weigh priorities and skills. In some cases, clients can be shown how inclusion of others will be helpful. Of particular value is the work of a research project in which family therapists helped drug abusers to involve their family of origin in therapy (Van Deusen, Stanton, Scott, Todd, & Mowatt, 1982). Sometimes the invited people become motivated clients in their own right if the therapist helps them to personalize what they may gain from the process. At other times, they may come and provide helpful information without agreeing to further involvement. Still others may come and be successfully enlisted as consultants as long as the family therapist refrains from overt or covert attempts to make them into the client. However, if clients are still opposed to inviting others after they have explained their reluctance and they have been given reassuring explanations, it is imperative that the therapist accept the clients' position.

Meanwhile, the family therapist can take this as important information that can invoke the influence of the larger system without actually including the additional parties. A subsequent discussion can be conducted about why it is best to meet alone, so that the family therapist gathers important information about specific sensitivities in significant relationships. Identifying these specific obstacles can lead the clinician to an understanding of a client's personal reality. Accepting this reality enables the therapist to begin the joining process successfully. Some family therapy is conducted with only one person present in the room. This can be done effectively when these macrodynamics are incorporated into the content of therapy.

However, as therapy proceeds with an individual or a family group, it is also important to develop greater specificity about the problem. Therefore, if the client context, agency context, or therapist skill level does not permit the inclusion of others, the beginning practitioner can focus on systemic characteristics through a careful definition of the problem that includes interactional, familial, and organizational (structural) dynamics.

Defining the Problem

The definition of the problem ultimately governs the goals and process of family therapy. Historically, the various schools of family therapy have adopted problem definitions such as "undifferentiated ego mass" or "diffuse boundaries," which are outgrowths of specific theoretical concepts. While they might be seen as problems through the eyes of a specific theoretician, rarely are these definitions written in lay terms consistent with a client's language and experience. Such discrepancies have become stumbling blocks for beginning practitioners. Suppose that a family comes in seeking help for a chemically dependent member. If the family therapist suggests that the problem is really a family problem, the family is likely to leave the session thinking to themselves, "But we still think the problem is *his* drinking!"

Such instances underscore the importance of developing a problem definition that includes diverse opinions. If an individual has come to the session alone, the definition of the problem might evolve from questions not only about the individual's opinion but about his or her significant other's. If a couple or family has come for family therapy, the definition might incorporate each person's opposing view of the problem. For example, if a husband says the problem is too little sex and his wife says the problem is too little communication, the family therapist might suggest that the problem is the couple's inability to meet each other's needs. The newly formulated problem definition must include the diversity expressed by the client(s).

Ultimately, this stage must evolve from an exploration of the client's definition of the problem toward a more systemic and interactional perspective. This can be accomplished through questions that focus initially on family members' opinions and then move toward the tracking of interactional sequences.

Assessing Clients' Definitions of the Problem

To begin a dialogue about the problem with a family or individual, the family therapist might ask the following questions:

1. What brings you here?
2. What would be helpful for us to discuss?
3. Who first noticed the problem and how long ago was this?
4. What led you (or another person) to conclude that this was a problem?
5. Who else agrees or disagrees that this is the problem?
6. Who else (inside or outside the family) has an opinion about the problem?
7. Have you or anyone else thought of any other possibilities regarding what the problem might be?
8. Are there times when the problem isn't occurring? What is going on at those times?
9. What are the differences between times when the problem does and doesn't occur?
10. What would happen if things don't change?

It is important to accept the family members' description of the problem without criticism or premature advice. It is also essential to validate the importance of each member's contribution ("That's a very good point. You seem to have thought a lot about this issue"). If family members interrupt each other, remind them that they will each have an opportunity to express their views.

As these questions are pursued, the client information that begins to emerge will guide the therapist in two possible directions. In cases where outside parties have heavily influenced the definition of the problem and the referral process, the therapist should remain curious and ask specific questions regarding how those other parties are involved. Such information can lead to a hypothesis that defines the problem within that specific relationship. In cases where the problem has become defined within the microenvironment of those attending the session, the therapist should help each family member reduce the size of the problem.

In either case, family therapists must be prepared to ask questions that bring about greater specificity. Clients will often express global concerns through the use of labels (depressed, angry, nervous, and so on). While labels offer a general indication of the problem area, they often mean different things to different people. For example, a family member may say she is unhappy, which really means, "I don't want to go to school." A therapist might use the following questions to help each family member clarify the problem:

1. What do you mean by _____?
2. Give me some examples of _____?
3. Describe a situation when you _____?
4. How does this affect you now?
5. How does _____ affect you?
6. Tell me the last time _____ happened.

The goal is to help each family member to be specific and concrete, so that the problem defined will become more solvable.

Often, a family member will present several problems. In such cases, clinicians will need to clarify the problem by providing questions that prioritize the person's concerns:

1. What needs to be changed now?
2. So the first change we need to make is _____?
3. What might happen if _____ doesn't change?
4. What do you think would happen if _____ occurred?

The therapist will also want to focus on times when the problem is not occurring.

1. When are the times that you are able to handle the problem?
2. What are you doing differently in these situations?
3. What seems to be different when you are able to manage?

Understanding when they are able to manage the problem helps family members to get in touch with their strengths and resources. As the family members share their views, therapists can use this information to further clarify the interactional sequences that surround significant family experiences.

Tracking Interactional Sequences

The approaches used in tracking a family's communication are similar to relationship techniques derived from client-centered therapy (Rogers, 1961).

The therapist's open-ended questions, ability to reflect content and feelings, and attentive demeanor to help establish a supportive relationship with the family. More complex techniques of tracking center on the therapist's efforts to "listen with a third ear." The therapist responds to thoughts and feelings that family members may be unable to acknowledge. When family members begin to talk, they usually describe the *content* of the problem. For example, a parent might say that a child "won't come home" or "won't do what I tell him." While therapists may listen to what family members say about each other (content), they are mainly concerned about the *process*—how family members interact with each other. Do family members talk for each other? When the child speaks, does Mom or Dad interrupt him or her? The therapist who focuses only on the content will not be able to assess the interactional pattern that contributes to the problem.

Colapinto (1991) states:

> Following the content and the process of the family interaction, like the needle of a record player follows a groove, is the basic structural procedure to collect information on the family map. As the therapist listens to and encourages the contributions of family members, observes their mutual dances, and asks for clarifications and expansions, he or she begins to draft first answers to structural questions: Whether family members can converse without being interrupted, whether they tend to interact in age appropriate ways, how they organize each other's behaviors, how they deal with or avoid conflict, what alliances they tend to form. (pp. 431–432)

In some instances, the therapist may use metaphors to represent patterns of communication. The therapeutic use of metaphor helps to reframe a family's reality by simply tracking the family's communication from the content to the process level. Minuchin (Minuchin & Fishman, 1981) is a master of such tracking skills, using metaphors for family process as diverse as, "You're wired to one another"; "You're his alarm clock"; or, "You're her memory bank." Often he will derive a metaphor from a family member's occupation. With an electrician (content), he might say, "You are wired to each other" (process); with a mechanic, "You need a tune-up." If there is a point of family pride, as with a family whose policy is "never a late payment," he might say, "You are indebted to each other." When illustrating a family rule, as with a family that has a strong work ethic, he might say, "Play time should never be done slipshod!" Tracking is a form of accommodation because it is effective only when therapists are able to tune themselves in to the family language rather than imposing their own.

When a family member begins to describe a problem, the therapist must explore with whom this problem exists and how the sequence unfolds. The following dialogue illustrates how this may be accomplished.

Mother: He won't listen to me.

Therapist: Who won't listen to you?

Mother: My son, Eric.

Therapist: What does he do to indicate that he doesn't listen?

Mother: He just sits silently and watches TV when I tell him to do something.

Therapist: And what do you do when he does that?

Mother: Sometimes I go in and make him listen to me.

Therapist: How do you do that?

Mother: I go in and shut off the TV to get his attention.

Therapist: And then what happens?

Mother: He usually throws a tantrum.

Therapist: So what happens next? How does your husband get involved?

What is important here is that the therapist is thinking about the pattern of interactions that surrounds the problem. By assessing this pattern of interactions, the therapist begins to decide who needs to speak to whom in resolving the problem. The therapist might assess such patterns of interaction by asking the following questions:

1. When do you first notice the problem? What is going on? Who is talking to whom? Who notices first?
2. Where does the problem take place? Where is she or he when this happens?
3. What next? What does he or she do then? What does he or she say then?
4. How do others get involved in the problem? What does your husband (your wife) do when you say that to your son? How does your mother get involved?
5. So what happens after he leaves the house? How long is he gone? What happens when he returns? Who agrees or disagrees with you that this is a problem?
6. Has it always been this way? When was it different? What else was different then?

The family's interactional description of the problem tells us who should be talking to whom about it. For example, can a mother and stepfather discuss the problem in the presence of their child? Rather than reporting about the problem, the family shows how they respond, thus verifying the interactional sequence before and after the problem. The therapist probes the family by asking the following questions:

1. How have you (for example, mother and son) tried to handle the problem?
2. When you're arguing with your son, what does your husband do?
3. Is that normally the way you talk to each other?

When the therapist asks specific family members to discuss the problem, the hierarchy and family structure often begin to emerge. For example, a grandparent may be responsible for a child and complain about the mother's irresponsibility. If the therapist asks the mother to take responsibility for the child in the interview and the grandparent interferes, then the interactional sequence around the presenting problem (the process) becomes clear: While the grandparent complains that the mother is irresponsible, she interferes when the mother takes responsibility.

A typical sequence of communication that may occur with this type of organization is as follows:

1. Grandmother is responsible for the child while complaining of mother's irresponsibility.
2. Mother withdraws and grandmother continues to be responsible for the child.
3. Child misbehaves.
4. Grandmother is angry with mother because she should not have to discipline child.
5. Mother moves in to take care of the child.
6. Grandmother criticizes mother for not being competent and moves in to rescue child from mother.
7. Mother withdraws, allowing grandmother to be responsible for child.
8. Child continues to misbehave.

Another common interactional sequence involves one parent who is overinvolved with the child while the other parent remains peripheral. The typical sequence of interactions that often occurs with this type of organization is as follows:

1. Mother is overinvolved with the child.
2. Child acts up, expressing symptomatic behaviors.
3. Mother calls in father to assist.
4. Father deals with the problem ineffectively.
5. Mother criticizes father for not dealing with the problem appropriately.
6. Father withdraws.
7. Mother and child continue to be overinvolved until they reach another impasse.

This interactional sequence consists of an overinvolved parent-child dyad (a cross-generational coalition) and an underinvolved or peripheral parent. The child's misbehavior thus serves to trigger an interactional sequence between the parents.

Enacting the Interactional Sequence

In some cases, the therapist will need to decentralize his or her participation and direct the family members to enact rather than describe the problem sequence. Here the therapist is creating a context for functional and dysfunctional interaction. The therapist might ask the family to "discuss the problem with each other" or to "continue last night's argument." The therapist must be specific, such as, "Tell your son what he must do to gain your trust." After the directive has been given, the therapist should pull his or her chair back and observe how family members resolve conflict. The therapist observes the family and attempts to get information to the following questions:

How is the message delivered?
Does the family member talk firmly?

Does he or she make eye contact?
How does the other family member respond?
Does he or she get angry?
Does he or she acknowledge the other family member's point of view? How?
Are any of the children pulled into the discussion?
When do they get pulled in?
How do they get pulled in?
Does the therapist get pulled into the interaction? When? How?
When do members change the subject?
How does the interactional sequence end?

The answers to these questions will help the therapist assess the interactional sequence. Focusing on these sequences begins to transform the definition of the problem from an individual attribute (for example, "He's depressed") to an interactional definition ("When he's depressed, we don't agree on the solution"). Special attention should be given to repetitive behavioral sequences that occur around the problem. As these sequences and the relevant family members become identified, family therapists can integrate this information with referral information in deciding whom to involve in therapy. As the definition of the problem becomes more interactional in nature, therapists will begin to develop a therapeutic plan—that is, an understanding of who would be invited to participate in subsequent sessions.

Goal Setting

The goals pursued in family therapy should develop from information gathered about how the family defines the problem, what made them seek help, and who will be the primary participants. While many schools of family therapy have goals that are theory-specific, an integrated set of goals will usually involve behavior change, perceptual change, or a combination of the two (O'Hanlon, 1991). Ultimately, negotiated goals must address the client's definition of the problem. Additionally, the initial interview should produce a problem definition that is clearly stated in behavioral or perceptual terms. When this does not occur, the clinician will need more sessions to evolve a clear and concrete problem definition. In the interim, therapist and client must agree on some preliminary goals—process goals such as exploration, clarification, and experimentation.

These goals are aimed at developing a more specific definition of the problem. For example, if an individual states the goal as, "I want to stop hating my father" or, "I want to have a better relationship with men," the therapist may pursue present-oriented interactional information only to discover in later sessions the existence of childhood sexual abuse. Therefore, if the problem definition is still vague at the end of the initial interview, family therapists are encouraged to negotiate a process goal in order to maintain a sense of direction with the client. An example of this follows:

> Mary Ann, it sounds like there are many factors that enter in to your desire to "stop hating" your father, and I want to make sure I fully

understand your relationship with him before we develop more specific goals. You've been very helpful today and I'm wondering if we could take another session to explore all of your feelings about this issue. If you decide to return, I would like to continue clarifying this situation until we are able to develop specific problem-solving strategies for you to try.

In this way, the therapist helps the client anticipate a two-step process of problem resolution: clarification of context and development of strategies.

When a family or couple is being interviewed, the process will be similar. Families are usually so intent on getting results that they have become oblivious to their own process. This is why certain situations can benefit from a shift to process goals. Such goals can be explained to the family as a first step toward eventual problem resolution, to be followed by a second step in which strategies for change are developed. In the first step, focusing on the perspective of the family, the therapist can ask questions that begin to associate specific behaviors and perceptions with the description of the problem. This microinformation can then be used to develop specific goals and strategies for change in the intervention phase of therapy. The family therapist might negotiate such a two-step agreement by stating the following:

It sounds to me like you have an idea about what the problem is but are struggling with how to go about resolving it. In the past, I've found it useful to help people develop a very specific understanding of the behavior, thoughts, and feelings that they would like to change. After that, it's much easier to help them develop solutions. If you decide to return, I would want some time to explore more details about the problem [perceptual change], so that all of us can come to some agreement about what should change. After that, if you're satisfied with the direction we're heading, we can pursue a specific plan of action [behavioral change].

If clients already have a clear set of behavioral goals when they enter family therapy, the negotiated goals may be determined by whether the practitioner has a clear sense of direction at the end of the first session. This sense of direction is usually related to the therapist's skills and the model of change adopted. Breunlin (1985) notes that structural-strategic family therapists are comfortable intervening on the basis of a partial assessment of family functioning, whereas therapists using other models prefer a more thorough assessment before developing interventions. It is our belief that both methods are of value. Thus, in the initial interview, if a beginning family therapist is ready to interrupt certain interactional sequences and assign tasks, she or he may negotiate a behavioral goal such as experimentation. That would signal an emphasis on a quick strategic turnaround rather than a longer developmental process such as clarification or exploration.

Because the type of goal is tied to a certain sense of timing as the practitioner moves through the stages of family therapy, process goals also become closely tied to the type of working contract that the family and the family therapist develop.

Developing Therapeutic Contracts

Contracting is a form of structured bargaining that specifies clearly what is expected. In its most basic form, the contract for family therapy services is an explicit understanding between the therapist and family members about the specifics of the treatment process.

Contracts help families to be good consumers of services. Personal services are most effective when families have the opportunity to take responsibility for the terms under which the services are rendered. Would the family prefer a long or short assessment period? What are the pros and cons of each? Do they want insight or only results? What constitutes informed consent when a person or family sees a family therapist? These questions are quite unorthodox compared to current norms of practice; however, even in court-ordered cases, service delivery can be administered more cooperatively if the practitioner will review the setting and determine what elements of the process can be presented as choices for family members to exercise. For example, a violent husband who has been ordered into treatment as part of a deferred-prosecution agreement may not have a choice about frequency or duration of sessions, but there may be some element of the content or process that he can influence, such as the topics to be discussed (violence, patterns, relationships), the role of the therapist (director, guide, consultant), and goals (behavioral change, perceptual change, or both).

When a contract is negotiated between therapist and client, it will largely be a commitment by both parties to participate in an initial treatment plan. One type of contract might be a request to include certain people as sources of information during the assessment process, with the expectation that a different type of contract will be agreed upon for treatment. Another type of contract could define the role of the therapist as a consultant rather than a referee in the case of a highly emotional couple. Still another contract with an individual seeking help for depression might formalize the client's choice regarding which topic to pursue: family-of-origin influences having a bearing on the client's depression; or strategies for day-to-day coping with the depression. In order to account for the essential elements of a therapeutic contract, the clinician should review these questions:

1. Do I know what the client's initial expectations were for the therapy process?
2. Have I provided a rationale explaining why the process may depart from their expectations?
3. Does the client have an understanding of what specifically will occur from session to session and how these activities will address their presenting problem?
4. Have I explained the process goals of family therapy (assessment, exploration, experimentation, and so on) and explained the role of each family member?
5. Have I enlisted each member in the process and addressed their objections or questions?

Developing a contract is a process of sifting information related to the definition of the problem, the decision to seek therapy, the likely participants, and their expectations for treatment. As this sifting takes place, the nature of the therapeutic process begins to evolve from the important elements that surface. The result is a contract that specifies the role of the therapist, each family member's role, intermediate and long-range goals, and an initial plan for achieving the goals. While these initial roles, goals, and plans may be changed many times throughout the therapeutic process, grappling with them in a systematic way during the initial interview helps the family therapist begin the process in an organized manner. As the therapeutic contract evolves, the therapist should help the family anticipate the experience by describing the process.

Describing the Therapeutic Process

Once therapists have begun to develop a contract, they should start orienting the family or individual to the process of therapy—that is, the staff involved and the specific techniques employed to pursue the goals. It is important at the outset to provide at least a minimal structure of the therapeutic process. Just as a travel agent might provide an itinerary for a family vacation, the therapist might provide an overview of the therapeutic process in the following way:

> If you decide to see me, we'll talk about things that concern you (your family) and discuss what you want to do about them. Maybe we can pool our ideas and come up with some things you can try. I usually spend a few sessions learning everything I can about what works best for you. After that, we start to develop a plan of action. If you try something and it doesn't work, we'll talk about it and try to figure out what else might help.

The description of the therapeutic process will vary depending on the family's previous experience in therapy. Families who have not been to therapy or who are uncertain of what to expect will require more specificity. On the other hand, with families who have had previous therapeutic contact, it will be important to explore their expectations for service. After hearing about the family's previous experiences with counseling, family therapists may need to describe the current process, in order to clarify how it may be the same or different from that of other practitioners.

One of the questions clients may ask is whether the therapist will reveal what is said in the session to others (for example, parents, a probation officer, a social worker). Before the question arises, family therapists should say that what is discussed will be held confidential except under certain conditions. A promise without this qualification can prove frustrating. There are cases where it is in the clients' best interests that the information be shared. There are also laws in many states that mandate reporting under certain circumstances. If clients find their statements have not been confidential when the therapist promised total confidentiality, the trust is damaged and the therapist loses effectiveness. Consequently, these qualifications should be included. For example, the therapist may say:

> I will try to keep what we talk about between the four of us, but if one of you said you were planning to do something that would be harmful to you or someone else, I probably would tell someone else and try to keep

anyone from getting hurt. I promise that I'll let you know if I'm going to tell anyone what we've talked about. And sometimes, if I think it would be helpful for someone to know something you've told me, I may ask you if it's okay for me to mention it. For example, if you told me you were having trouble in school, I might ask you if you minded my discussing it with your teachers. It is also important for you to know that the law also requires that I disclose information in certain cases. These include . . .

Questions concerning the therapist's role or the therapeutic relationship may come up throughout the therapy sessions and should be answered as they arise. What's crucial in explaining the therapeutic process is to relieve initial anxieties that clients may have, to give them some expectations about what is likely to happen when they come, and to help them feel at ease in the therapeutic situation.

Finalizing the Contract

A practitioner's setting may influence whether a therapeutic contract is written or verbal. Fees, liability, releases of information, and other legal aspects of therapy are usually written in order to become legally binding. In some instances, clients are provided with statements regarding their rights to obtain records or to file grievances. In addition to these considerations, the following checklist is provided to help beginning practitioners achieve a satisfactory understanding with families about the process of therapy:

1. Who will attend? (referral source, extended family, others)
2. What will each person's role be? (consultant, client, provider of information)
3. What are the goals? (assessment then treatment, further exploration to define problem, specific behavioral changes)
4. When will sessions be held? (frequency or pace)
5. How will sessions be conducted? (in-session directives, circular or systematic questioning, out-of-session tasks, genograms, specific interventions, psychoeducation)
6. When will the terms of this contract be renegotiated?
7. What resources, space, time, and help are needed?
8. Who else needs to be made aware of the contract?
9. Are there any barriers or costs to the contract?

It is empowering for clients to know that the therapist expects to renegotiate and to evaluate the process on the basis of the client's personal experience. Too often, therapists develop expectations that clients will blindly participate in the process without holding the therapist accountable for their part of the contract. When no-shows occur in clinical settings, it is an indication that the terms of the contract had not been mutually agreed upon. Many consumers are more compliant when they are in crisis, only to find later that they need to renegotiate but are too intimidated to do so. Dropping out of therapy becomes the most expedient option.

Beginning practitioners sometimes try to maintain client commitment in indirect ways—by persuasion or lectures about why clients should return for treatment. At other times, therapists may expect clients to continue attending and paying for sessions in spite of lingering reservations. These situations may be avoided by thoroughly exploring and validating the concerns and reservations that clients express in the first session. By assuming a one-down position, the clinician is able to empower the client to feel a sense of entitlement when it comes to dictating the terms of therapy. The clinician always has the right to refuse to see a client, but the client must also be allowed the same right when services do not seem helpful.

Summary

Box 5. 1 summarizes the key questions from each portion of the initial interview. In some instances, the time allotted for an initial interview may not allow the therapist to cover each section adequately. In such cases, the therapist may want to explain the initial stage of therapy as one of exploration leading to an initial treatment contract. Then, the second session can be used to address remaining topics before an initial plan is proposed. In other cases, the therapist can propose a contract that allows for an assessment period with recommendations from the clinician. At the end of this assessment period (from one to four sessions), the family can decide whether they would like to continue.

As beginning practitioners prepare for the first session, they may review Box 5. 1 and the intake information in Chapter Four to decide what aspects of the outline they should emphasize. If initial hypotheses have been formed, they can determine which aspects of the initial interview will best address these hypotheses. As the interview proceeds, the outline can serve as a guide for the practitioner to know when to move on to the next section.

In addition to this outline, there are questions that beginning family therapists often ask as they approach their early clinical experiences. These questions represent common clinical situations that may have a significant impact on the course of therapy. The following section provides some initial guidelines to help practitioners address such issues.

Questions That Clinicians Often Ask

1. How Should I Handle the Issue of Alcohol If I Suspect It Is a Part of the Problem?

When family members identify alcohol as part of the presenting problem, this issue must be addressed if therapy is to be successful. The therapist must assess the function of alcohol and its relationship to the problem in the family. Is the family concerned that one of its members is abusing alcohol? How has the family dealt with this problem? How are family members affected by the alcohol

---

Box 5.1   The Initial Interview

I. Joining
    A. What common ground can I share with the family?
    B. What family strengths can I identify and validate?
    C. How can I address issues of race, gender, culture?
II. Exploring the Referral Process
    A. Whose idea was it to seek help?
    B. How do you feel about the idea of getting help?
    C. How did you know to come here?
III. Deciding Whom to Involve
    A. How did you decide who would come to today's session?
    B. What would happen if other people were invited?
IV. Defining the Problem
    A. Clients' definition
        1. What brings you here?
        2. Who first noticed the problem and how long ago?
        3. How was this conclusion reached?
        4. Who agrees/disagrees with these opinions?
    B. Tracking interactional sequences
        1. When you first noticed the problem, what was happening?
        2. Who says what to whom?
        3. What happens next?
        4. How do others get involved?
        5. What does each person do or say?
V. Goal Setting
    A. Exploration (creative discovery or cognitive change)
    B. Clarification (reframing or cognitive change)
    C. Experimentation (behavioral change)
VI. Developing Therapeutic Contracts
    A. Address client expectations
        1. What are you hoping a therapist can do to help?
        2. What did you think would happen in counseling?
    B. Negotiate the role of the therapist (related to process goals)
    C. Provide a rationale for the goals and roles
    D. Explore each person's motivation/commitment to the process
        1. Is there anything that doesn't fit for anyone?
        2. What would have to happen for the process to be more
            beneficial?
    E. Address issues of informed consent (confidentiality, and so on)

---

abuse? Do those affected family members have a plan for addressing the issue? Treadway (1989) suggests that, if therapists are therapeutically joined, they may raise issues of chemical abuse. He emphasizes the importance of remaining allied (joined) with the substance abuser and remaining neutral about the chemical-dependency problem. The beginning therapist should understand that discussion of the alcohol use will provoke resistance on the part of the client unless those two objectives have been achieved.

Phrases such as "problem drinking" or "alcohol use" are preferred to "alcoholic." Treadway also suggests that the therapist and client should develop a controlled-drinking contract (for example, time-limited abstinence). If clients are unable to comply with this plan, they should be referred to Alcoholics Anonymous (AA) and a chemical-dependency assessment. If other family members object to this type of plan, the clinician can use their objections as an opportunity to intervene with the family and to begin encouraging the new patterns of thought and behavior that will be needed for successful recovery in the future.

When the therapist suspects alcohol is contributing to the problem but family members do not identify it as part of the problem, the issue should be considered as a preliminary hypothesis that must be explored and validated before deciding to focus treatment in that direction. Tracking interactional sequences and exploring the referral process can elicit information about the evolution of the presenting problem. As this is done, the practitioner can assess alcohol use by asking if any member was using alcohol or drugs before, during, or after the sequences described. Steinglass, Bennett, Wolin, and Reiss (1987) encourage clinicians to make a distinction between families who have become organized with an alcoholic identity and those who happen to have an alcoholic member. Their research sheds much light on various types of "alcoholic families," suggesting that the stereotype of a dysfunctional family does not represent the diverse levels of competency and strength that may exist among families affected by alcohol.

2. How Should I Deal with a Suicide Threat?

A suicide threat brings with it tremendous responsibility. The first step in dealing with a suicide threat is to understand the extent of the client's thinking. Do such clients have a well-thought-out plan for conducting the suicide? What keeps them from completing this plan? What effects does the suicide threat have on the family? What message is the client trying to send by expressing this threat? Is the suicide threat linked to other losses in the family? Is the client attempting to help another family member avoid a painful transition? Beginning therapists may be tempted to offer the person advice or to argue against suicide. At the beginning of a conversation about suicide, it is important to explore and ask the preceding questions with concerned curiosity. If the therapist takes too strong a position, the determined client may decide to go underground and withhold information in order to maintain personal control. If the therapist remains concerned and exploratory at the outset, the client is more likely to share fully regarding the extent of his or her progression toward an actual attempt.

Once therapists have listened and explored the client's experience, they may proceed toward an intervention strategy. If the danger of suicide presents itself during an individual session (due to previous attempts or the presence of a specific plan), therapists should discuss a no-suicide contract that will stay in force until a family or network intervention can be organized. Family members and significant others should be notified immediately. The family and others (for example, referral person, agency personnel, or physicians) should be convened, in order to build a coalition to cooperate around therapeutic goals. One group of family therapists developed an in-home crisis intervention strategy that avoided hospitalization in 42 of 50 cases (Pittman, DeYoung, Flomenhaft, Kaplan, & Langsley, 1966). Madanes (1981) provides guidelines for addressing suicidal adolescents, and Scalise (1992) reports the successful structuring of a family suicide watch in the case of a suicidal adolescent. In the case of suicidal adults, the family therapist should engage spouses, significant others, or extended-family members in discussions regarding any significant life-cycle transitions or changes in family roles that might assist in understanding how the suicide threat may be a response to some unrecognized problem (Pittman et al., 1966). Efforts should be made to involve the network in treatment. Making sure that *all* the members of the therapeutic system (family, friends, caseworkers, and so on) commit to the goals and the successful completion of treatment is a critical feature of this therapy (Landau-Stanton & Stanton, 1985).

3. What Should I Do If I Discover Family Violence?

Increased awareness of family violence has drawn the attention of family therapists to their responsibilities in this area. The therapist must be aware of behaviors that indicate physical abuse. For example, a mother may appear depressed although seeking help for her children rather than herself. Families often feel shame that makes it difficult for members to discuss the abuse. Most therapists are legally bound to report violence to the appropriate agency (for example, adult protective services) if they suspect it. It is important to properly inform clients of this legal responsibility early in the initial interview so that, if abuse or violence becomes apparent, clients will not feel betrayed by the therapist.

As the issue of reporting is addressed with clients, family therapists should explain the procedure as it is carried out in the given community. In some communities, if clients are already voluntarily seeking therapy, the consequences of reporting may be minimal, with little disruption to the family or their therapy. However, in other cases, there may be more formal involvement with the legal system. In view of this diversity, beginning practitioners should thoroughly investigate local procedures under a variety of circumstances in order to be as accurate as possible in explaining the process to families. In addition, it is important for practitioners to understand the legal definition of abuse in their community in order to avoid unnecessary reports.

In all cases, it is best to maintain a position of partnership with all family members, with special emphasis upon maintaining an empathic bond with the abuser. The process of reporting can then be an opportunity to join with the family by highlighting the courage it takes to discuss the violence and by suggesting that many people are never able to muster the courage to do so (Jenkins, 1991). By emphasizing what courage has already been shown, the therapist can lay a positive foundation for the reporting process.

In some cases, therapists are able to persuade clients to personally make the call in the office as a manifestation of their commitment to improving the relationship. By speaking directly with authorities, clients are able to take greater control over their lives and, correspondingly, they often feel empowered and respected. They receive information directly from social services and do not have to be dependent on the therapist for interpreting the process. Families who remain reluctant to participate in reporting may be helped by encouraging an anonymous telephone call for information, followed by the actual report. If danger is not imminent, it may also be possible to delay the report until the clinician and family can agree upon how the report will be made. In those cases, however, the issue should not be confused; the question is not whether a report will be made, but only *how* the report will be made—who will call, what will be said, and so on.

In defining the problem, the therapist must view the violence as the problem rather than as a symptom of something else. While other dynamics such as gender socialization, communication patterns, or faulty belief systems may encourage violence, family therapists must remain firm in defining the initial problem as violence, with the hope of creating a safe foundation for examining the related dynamics. However, without addressing the safety issues first, a climate for further growth cannot occur.

4.   How Should I Handle Family Secrets?

Family secrets usually become an issue in two ways. First, there are times when family members or referral sources want to disclose information about other people to the therapist (thereby forming a covert coalition). Second, there are times when family members disclose information about others in individual sessions that they are unwilling to discuss in the presence of those involved.

Such revelations need not be disruptive, if the therapist takes a few precautions. One is to decide how such information may affect the therapist's relationship with other family members. For example, Keith and Whitaker (1985) give an account of a young practitioner who received a telephone call between sessions about a family member's alcoholism. He decided to share the information with the family. Subsequent sessions were preempted by a suicide attempt on the part of the identified patient. Keith and Whitaker suggest that families have their own wisdom about how much information they can tolerate. In this case, they argue, the clinician violated the family's threshold for emotionally charged information. These professionals suggest that it may be unnecessary to reveal secret information if the therapist abides by the family's intuitive judgment on such issues. They make the assumption that there is no such thing as a secret in families because members know at some covert level and have merely agreed not to address it openly.

The Milan team has chosen to avoid receiving disclosures altogether (Selvini Palazzoli & Prata, 1982). Instead, they maintain a strict rule that, if the discloser must share the information, it will not be kept confidential and they must be willing to be exposed as the source of the information. In receiving between-session phone calls, they begin by stating that anything disclosed will have to be discussed in the next session. Then, callers have the opportunity to decide how much they will say. If family members are unwilling to change their rules of communication, the Milan team is unwilling to become part of a covert coalition. With this approach, maintaining the neutral position of the therapist (process) takes priority over gaining additional information (content).

These examples illustrate issues of context and therapist bias. However, in cases where individuals share personal information that is difficult to share in conjoint sessions, family therapists must make decisions about structure that will depend on the stage of the therapeutic process. Since we are discussing the initial interview, the therapist should take into account whether a client's spouse will eventually be engaged and how the therapist will delay the potential alignment with the client until both parties are present. When individuals come in without other family members, the order of the initial interview presented here is designed to help the therapist stay away from detailed and intimate content until the structure of the individual's significant relationships can be identified. Also, it is helpful if the therapist explains to the client that the order of the initial interview leaves the most detailed information for last in order to obtain a general picture of the client's relational world. Then, if an individual is willing to invite a partner, the therapist can suggest that the details of problem definition be saved for the next session. In later stages of the therapeutic process, clients may request individual sessions in which they begin to disclose information on a different level from that shared in conjoint sessions. The therapist must assess family and couple dynamics to determine how these disclosures should be handled, given the current goals of the therapeutic process.

When the information disclosed concerns abuse or safety issues in the current relationship, therapists must assess whether their relationship with the abuser is strong enough to confront the abuse directly without escalating danger for the spouse. In the worst case, more individual sessions with the victim might be required to develop an initial safety plan. Sheinberg (1992) has addressed treatment impasses at the disclosure of incest by integrating constructionism and feminism into strategies that respect all sides of three major dilemmas: social control versus therapy; pride versus shame; and loyalty versus protection. Her work makes an important contribution in addressing secrets of this nature.

If the information disclosed is important but not related to physical or sexual safety, it is best for the therapist to go slowly, taking the time to understand the complex issues of secrecy, privacy, and confidentiality. In particular, family therapists should consult a collection edited by Imber-Black (1993), which makes a detailed study of the topic. In this work, she encourages clinicians to understand their own biases about the sharing of information and to grapple with the complexities that make many situations unique and call for careful understanding from the professional.

Chapter Six

Models of Family Therapy Assessment

Gender-Sensitive Models
> When to Focus on Gender
>
> Implications for Treatment

Models Related to Race and Culture
> When to Focus on Culture
>
> Implications for Treatment

Intergenerational Models
> When to Focus on Intergenerational Issues
>
> Implications for Treatment

Life-Cycle and Developmental Models
> When to Focus on Developmental Issues
>
> Implications for Treatment

Structural Models
> When to Focus on Structure
>
> Implications for Treatment

Individual Models
> When to Focus on Individual Dynamics
>
> Implications for Treatment

I n family therapy, the assessment process can be thought of in at least two ways. First, whatever information the therapist seeks should be related to intervention—to what will eventually bring about change. Second, gathering information is, itself, a type of intervention that can often bring about change. Thus, when beginning practitioners develop their own model of assessment, they should begin by asking themselves what they believe to be the information most related to effective change in therapy. In addition, it is important to take into account how the assessment process itself might be impacting clients.

The primary sources of information for most models of family therapy are therapist observation of self and the system, family members' responses to therapist directives, and family members' answers to therapist questions. Since questions are often at the center of therapeutic dialogues, this chapter will review the major family therapy models primarily in terms of the questions that shape the assessment process. Our review will include suggestions regarding when each model can be helpful and how these questions can be used in the development of successful interventions.

The contributions of each school of family therapy can be organized along a continuum that proceeds from larger to smaller spheres of observation. These differences are sometimes referred to as macro- versus microviews of family process. At the macro end of the continuum are broad social factors that affect family process such as the influence of gender, race, and culture. As the view narrows slightly, intergenerational and extended-family relationships become additional influences upon the nuclear family. At the nuclear family level, it is possible to look at the family's life-cycle progression and structural interactions. Finally, within the nuclear family, the individuals can be studied as systems in their own right—as a combination of thoughts, feelings, behaviors, and intentions and, in tandem with their psychodynamics, also as a collection of biological subsystems that operate at all times. Like a camera with a zoom lens, the family therapist must maintain a flexible viewpoint in order to examine different angles and multiple levels of process. To begin, models of family therapy assessment will be reviewed along a continuum from macro- to microlevels of observation.

Gender-Sensitive Models

At the most general level, all families are influenced by patterns of socialization that lead to rules and roles governing family process. Gender-related roles and rules are the most fundamental of these patterns. Goldner (1988) has argued that gender is not a special topic in family therapy, but is "at the center of family theory" (p. 17). Because gender influences structure in the family, it should be a fundamental element in family assessment.

In a pioneering article on the subject, Hare-Mustin (1978) offered suggestions for implementing gender-sensitive family therapy:

> My purpose in what follows is not to analyze family therapy techniques, per se, but rather to consider certain areas of intervention in

which a feminist orientation is important. These areas are: the contract, shifting tasks in the family, communication, generational
boundaries, relabeling deviance, modeling, ownership and privacy,
and the therapeutic alliance with different family members. (p. 185)

Of the areas cited by Hare-Mustin, the contract has already been covered in the
initial interview. To begin the assessment process, the following questions pose
possible hypotheses that address each of the other areas:

1. Could role inflexibility regarding tasks be related to the problem?
2. Are communication styles disempowering to the females in the family?
3. Have generational coalitions developed as a result of disempowerment in the
   marriage?
4. Can disempowering stereotypes ("nag," "passive-aggressive") be relabeled
   to account for the context of powerlessness?
5. Can the female therapist model more egalitarian relationships with males in
   the family and can male therapists affirm female strength within the family?
6. What are family rules around females' personal development and autonomy
   outside the family?
7. What will each family member need from the therapist in order to feel
   understood and accepted?

As family therapy proceeds from the initial interview to the assessment
process, these questions can be considered by the therapist as the definition of
the problem is explored in greater depth. Then, during the assessment process,
it may be useful to explore each person's point of view regarding gender
development and how they arrived at their current position. An initial set of
questions posed to clients might be:

1. What are some of the differences between how you each grew up as a female
   and male in our society?
2. How does your family address the differences that exist between females and
   males in our society?
3. Are there certain traditions in your family that are more closely related to
   either women or men?
4. How do you feel about these traditions and practices?
5. Are there any ways you think these ideas and traditions might be related to
   _____ (the presenting problem)?

Such a line of questioning acknowledges gender differences in a neutral,
exploratory way. While the ultimate goal may be to correct gender imbalances,
beginning with neutral questions allows families to describe themselves without
feeling a pressure to change. As exploration continues, family therapists can
decide which issues might be targeted for change at a later point in the process.

Some clinicians provide suggestions for therapeutic dialogue that combines assessment and intervention. For example:

1. "What best explains your not wanting to tell me too much: that I am white,
   female or highly educated?" (Goldner, 1988, p. 29)

2. "Should you accommodate to prescriptions for men's greed and expediency or defy these prescriptions and insist that wisdom influence your decisions?" (White, 1986, p. 15)
3. Would you prefer a life where you are a slave to tradition, or would you prefer a life where you are free to develop new views of people and relationships? (White, 1990)

While these questions are generally employed after extensive groundwork to establish the relationship and develop empathy, they illustrate the creative use of questions that not only assess readiness for change but motivate families to consider change.

When to Focus on Gender

General questions about gender differences should be incorporated into all assessments. Each person's experience should be heard. In cases of marital conflict, gender differences are often the core issue and should be identified. For example, Jacobson, Holtzworth-Monroe and Schmaling (1989) have found that women often complain more than men about their current relationship. Indeed, women often desire greater involvement and closeness from their husbands, while husbands prefer to maintain the status quo and create greater autonomy and separateness for themselves. Moreover, women are more likely to seek therapy and push for an egalitarian relationship, whereas men are less likely to seek therapy and are inclined to maintain traditional gender roles.

Frank Pittman (1991) notes that a therapist must remember three things when working with men:

1. A hypermasculine display indicates the man is frightened of his own inadequacy. The show of hypermasculinity is an effort to scare off whoever is coming to measure his shortcomings.
2. Men who suffer from hypermasculinity cannot tolerate female anger, they will wet their pants and run away, or do something hypermasculine, as if they think every angry woman is their mother come back to take their puberty away.
3. Hypermasculinity is armor, just a protective coating, a shell—like mussels, or clams, or lobster, or shrimp. Just beneath the shell the meat may be sweet. It's there you'll find the beautiful, vulnerable boy. (p. 23)

Hypermasculinity can often contribute to domestic violence and child abuse. In such cases, it is critical that both survivors' and perpetrators' beliefs and traditions about gender be explored in detail. Current trends in the treatment of abuse suggest a focus on both cognitive and behavioral change. Exploring beliefs and attitudes about gender differences is an important step toward identifying which beliefs and behaviors will be ultimately targeted for change.

Implications for Treatment

The client's understanding of how gender relates to the presenting problem should dictate whether the therapist addresses gender directly or indirectly. When families are not ready to address gender differences directly, the practitioner should refrain from direct confrontation and address the issues in more indirect ways. For example, child and adolescent problems may be an opportunity to explore the impact of gender on developing children, thus confronting parents more indirectly with their own limitations.

Sheinberg and Penn (1991) list three categories of gender questions:

- The first category examines the "norm" the man or woman aspires to and the relational consequences of changing it . . .
- These questions can be followed by hypothetical questions: ideas about the relational consequences of changing these norms . . .
- Questions that identify norms to which the couple's parents aspired: how those affected both the couple and their parents . . .
- Once the family considers different possibilities of gender behaviors, future questions address the potential for establishing new norms as well as altering how the problem continues (pp. 36–37)

Marital partners may be highly sensitive to discussions regarding gender if they feel criticized. For example, men may be sensitive about being labeled "chauvinistic," and women may be sensitive about being labeled "just a housewife," when a therapist begins to explore issues of sex-role stereotypes. Practitioners should maintain a curious but hopeful position as they explore and identify patterns of thought and behavior related to gender differences. A lack of readiness on the part of families to discuss gender directly suggests the need for a more thorough assessment of the family's experience before choosing an intervention strategy.

Another set of issues that family therapists must address in their practice concerns race and culture.

Models Related to Race and Culture

While gender is undoubtedly the first element that distinguishes human beings from each other, race and culture must rank second. Although race is similar to gender, in that it is biologically determined, it will be considered with culture in this discussion because of its cultural influence upon social and family groups.

The first family therapists to review ethnicity in a broad way were McGoldrick, Pearce, and Giordano (1982), who surveyed diverse ethnic groups in terms of their history, values, and other distinguishing cultural characteristics.

> Italians rely primarily on the family and turn to an outsider only as a last resort . . . .. Black Americans have long mistrusted the help they can receive from traditional institutions . . . . and Puerto Ricans . . .

and Chinese . . . are likely to somatize when they are under stress and may seek medical rather than mental health services . . .. Likewise, Iranians often view medication and vitamins as a necessary part of treating symptoms, regardless of their origin. (p. 11)

In addition, these authors explored the process of family therapy for each group, with particular attention to ways in which therapy could be respectful of cultural norms and values. Often a family's cultural heritage is overlooked as an important resource and strength that may be at the center of the family's ability to overcome their current difficulties.

In addition, the social class and background of therapists can be a critical factor in how they draw conclusions about the family. Spiegel in McGoldrick et al. (1982) summarizes some typical therapeutic values:

Middle-class therapists, no matter what their ethnic origins, have been socialized in terms of mainstream values. The therapist will be future oriented, expecting clients to be motivated and to keep appointments punctually. He or she will also expect families to be willing to work on therapeutic tasks (Doing), over reasonable periods of time (Future), with the prospect of change before them (Mastery-over-Nature). All this is to be done while taking a pragmatic view of moral issues (Neutral), and at the very least the therapist will expect to help clients to distance themselves from any overwhelming moral burden or intense feelings of shame. And clients will be expected to separate themselves from enmeshment in the family structure and to develop increased autonomy (Individual). (p. 46)

Thus, ethnicity—a sense of shared identity that has developed over many generations—can be a critical variable in understanding client families and mobilizing their strengths. If clinicians are not aware of differing worldviews and values, they are apt to be critical rather than complimentary of differences exhibited by families out of the mainstream.

In addition to acknowledging differences between cultural groups, it is also important to avoid stereotyping. The practitioner's intent should be to strike a balance between understanding the common ground of general patterns and clarifying distinctions and variations within the larger group. Boyd-Franklin provides valuable help in this area with African-American families. Summarizing the fundamental premises of her book, *Black Families in Therapy* (Boyd-Franklin, 1989a), she lists the first five as these:

1. There is a great deal of cultural diversity among Black families that is often overlooked or misunderstood.
2. Black Afro-American culture represents a distinct ethnic and racial experience that is unique for a number of reasons, including: history; the African legacy; the experience of slavery, racism, and discrimination; and the victim system.
3. The illusion of color blindness or the "class not race" myth needs to be challenged as both misguided and counterproductive.

4. There are many myths about Black families in the social science literature that have painted a pejorative, deficit picture of Black family functioning.
5. There is a need to clarify and understand the strengths of Black families, which can serve as a foundation for therapeutic work. (p. 5)

When family therapists serve minority families, they can prepare by referring to Boyd-Franklin (1989a) or McGoldrick et al. (1982) for helpful specifics related to many minority groups in the United States.

In developing an assessment process that will account for the effects of culture, the questions in Box 6.1 may be used. Regardless of which questions the practitioner chooses, it is important to acknowledge and respect any differences that may exist between family and therapist. Then, families can be invited to teach therapists about the significant parts of their cultural identity. As clinicians pursue this type of assessment, their role is similar to that of the anthropologist who lives with the people and understands them while being a participant in their process. Such a role is in contrast to the physician or scientist who analyzes, categorizes, and treats people from a distance.

A cultural critique of the social service system by Minuchin (1984) illustrates that cultural conflicts can often be central to the definition of a problem. In reviewing selected court cases from British Social Services, he describes the plight of Mrs. Obutu, a Ghanian mother rearing her family in London. After her daughter, Sylvia, was arrested for shoplifting, Mrs. Obutu was summoned to the police station and was observed beating her daughter with a stick. Court proceedings determined that Sylvia should not return to the family home. After the mother's poignant objections, Minuchin provides this commentary:

Box 6.1   *Questions for the Assessment of Racial and Cultural Factors*

1. How does your racial/cultural/religious heritage make your family different from other families you know?
2. Compared to other families in your cultural group, how is your family different?
3. What are the values that your family identified as being important parts of your heritage?
4. At this particular time in your (family's) development, are there issues related to your cultural heritage that are being questioned by anyone? By whom and what?
5. What is the hardest part about being a minority in this culture?
6. When you think of living in America versus the country of your heritage, what are the main differences?
7. What lesson did you learn about your people? About other peoples?
8. What did you learn about disloyalty?
9. What were people in your family really down on?
10. What might an outsider not understand about your racial/cultural/religious background?

The magistrates return, looking upset. Not because Mrs. Obutu roared in pain; in their many years on the bench, pain has become a frequent witness in the chamber and they have learned how to deal with it . . . No, they are upset because their sympathies are with Mrs. Obutu. They understood, because all of them are parents, that Mrs. Obutu is a Ghanian mother trying her best with her English daughter. Cultural gaps are familiar to them. But they were caught in their own legal structure. Nobody protected Mrs. Obutu from giving evidence against herself. Nobody defended her because she wasn't accused . . . Nobody represented Mr. Obutu. And certainly it didn't occur to anybody to have Mrs. Obutu and Sylvia talk to each other in the court to put in evidence for the magistrates the conflicting sets of loyalties, affection, care, frustration, and rage that characterized their relationship. Just as in all families. (p. 130)

When to Focus on Culture

As the preceding example illustrates, cases that involve families of an immigrant or minority culture will invariably have cultural issues to which the clinician should attend. With these families, the focus on culture is an important part of the joining process. As clinicians invite families to teach them about their culture, the opportunity to join emerges in a context that is familiar and comfortable for the family. In this way, the family becomes the expert and the therapist becomes the learner.

If the joining process does not evolve into a comfortable collaboration, family therapists are encouraged to invite a native consultant into sessions—someone who can provide support for the family and a voice of clarification regarding the cultural differences between therapist and family (Waldegrave, 1990). This consultant might be an extended-family member who is bilingual, a professional from the native culture, or anyone else of the family's choice who could serve as a bridge between cultures. Such an effort on the part of the practitioner will nonverbally communicate an acknowledgment of differences, a respect for his or her limitations, and a desire to tailor the therapeutic process to fit the family's unique circumstances.

With respect to families who appear mainstream, it is recommended that family therapists still ask one or two basic questions about culture, race, or religion, because many subcultures in the Western Hemisphere are not set apart by physical or biological characteristics. For example, military families form a subculture in the United States characterized by certain patterns of mobility and a degree of patriotism not found in many nonmilitary families. In addition, certain religious groups have histories of persecution that may leave members with a heightened sense of alienation from the dominant culture. While on the surface such families might appear to be white, middle-class, and protestant, questions about the effects of military life or religion could alert the therapist to the family's uniqueness and relevant cultural differences.

Implications for Treatment

As mentioned earlier, therapist inquiry into culture facilitates the joining process. When specific personalities clash or the clinician is having difficulty joining, attention to culture can overcome difficulties that might arise at the micro-level of the therapeutic relationship. This is because an inquiry into the world of the family moves the therapist away from a hierarchical position ("Do what I want you to do") and into a collaborative position ("Teach me what is important for me to know about you"). As this exploration shifts practitioners into a macrolevel of experience, the new information broadens their perspective about the interpersonal impasse.

Constructivist therapists such as White (1990) use gender and culture as concepts to define the problem so that the family can be helped to externalize blame and minimize shame while assuming more responsibility for solving the problem. Working on the assumption that socialization impacts an individual's internal experience, these practitioners come to understand interpersonal dynamics through the lens of socialized cultural practices.

In addition, as therapists learn about the client culture in detail, rituals, tasks, directives, and their rationale can be couched in language and practices that are comforting and empowering. Very often, seemingly mainstream clients feel alienated from some part of their world on account of the problem that brings them into therapy. This alienation may be addressed as a cultural problem in order to acknowledge the family's pain and isolation. As treatment proceeds, the family therapist can assist the family in feeling more connected to their world by a process known as normalizing—helping them to see their similarities with others. One way of accomplishing this task is to explore intergenerational patterns.

Intergenerational Models

The family is not only the usual vehicle for socialization within a given culture but it also evolves more specific traditions, roles, rewards, and obligations that bind family members together. Each family's history shapes unique patterns of belief and interaction, analogous to cultural practice. These patterns often take the form of nonverbal rules (shoulds) that shape attitudes, communication, and intimacy.

Many family therapists have recognized previous generations as a major influence on family life in the present. Bowen (1978) conceptualized multigenerational transmission as the process by which dysfunctional patterns of coping are passed from one generation to the next. Boszormenyi-Nagy and Spark (1973) focused on loyalties or transgenerational obligations, suggesting that these were represented by symptoms in various family members. Ferreira (1963) discussed the significance of family myths, those beliefs that go unchallenged within the family and enable members to maintain a certain image of themselves. Other family therapists applied object-relations theory to family life, theorizing that we unconsciously attempt to change intimate relationships on the basis of those in our past, either by making them familiar or by making them fit our fantasies of idealized relationships that would compensate for past rejections or abandonment (Framo, 1976; Jacobson, 1984; Sager, 1981).

Recent trends in intergenerational family therapy include a wide range of issues. Williamson (1981) focuses on how an individual can develop a sense of personal authority within the family-of-origin. Kramer (1985) resolves generational conflicts through an emphasis on acceptance of differences rather than approval or agreement on the issues. Boszormenyi-Nagy (1973) assists family members to explore their invisible loyalty or debts and to find appropriate tasks by which to balance the ledger of indebtedness to the previous generation. Anderson and Bagarozzi (1989) explore family and personal myths on the grounds that they give meaning to the past, define the present, and provide direction for the future. These developments represent attempts at integration that work to resolve historical conflicts in multigenerational families.

In assessing intergenerational dynamics, the therapist might ask questions regarding past family issues, current extended-family relationships, and future hopes and expectations for these relationships:

1. What stories from your own life would best describe your development in your family of origin?
2. What stories from your family's history are still having an influence on the thinking of family members?
3. What family members have strong feelings about this situation?
4. Are there family members who have tried to help you with this situation?
5. Does this situation seem similar to any other situation that you recall in your family of origin?
6. Have other family members had experience in resolving a similar situation for themselves?
7. With which extended family members do you feel most comfortable? Least comfortable?
8. What are the emotional debts in the family?
9. What are the issues of loyalty?
10. What past experiences trigger current problems?

For couple interviewing, Wamboldt and Wolin (1989) have developed a structured interview that incorporates questions such as these:

1. How did you meet?
2. What is the state of your relationship now?
3. What are some of the important challenges that the two of you have made it through?
4. What are some of the most important similarities and differences between you and your family members?
5. What do you most want to conserve from your family background?
6. What do you most want to change from your family background?

7. Given the family you grew up in, is there a reason that your partner is a particularly good or meaningful choice? Is your partner ever too much that way? What is that like?
8. What do your parents think about your relationship? How do they react?
9. Is there anything I haven't asked that you think is important?

When to Focus on Intergenerational Issues

Unattached adults who are not in significant relationships can benefit from intergenerational exploration, since the intensity of family-of-origin relationships has not been diminished by relationships in a family of procreation. For clients whose goal in therapy is to understand some aspect of their lives, an intergenerational assessment will often lay a foundation for later discussions of self-understanding. Additionally, adults who would normally seek individual counseling for the healing of traumatic childhood experiences can benefit from an intergenerational perspective, which encourages reflection on past experience as a springboard for future change.

Frequently, clients will seek family counseling for a marital or child-rearing difficulty. In these cases, questions about present extended-family relationships may alert the therapist to historical family issues that may be restraining the change process in some way. For example, the therapist might assume that the family member has an internalized critical voice that keeps telling him he is incapable of changing his problem or his perception of the problem. In addition, problems related to aging and the elderly must often be put in the context of relationships that have evolved through the generations, in order to assist adult children to make necessary transitions with their parents.

Implications for Treatment

Erickson and Rossi (1979) suggest that change can be brought about in individuals by facilitating "an inner resynthesis of past experience." Analogously, it is also possible for families to change their views and behavior toward each other by identifying restraining myths, exploring unconscious patterns of communication, and detaching from their current experience in order to develop a broader and more hopeful perspective with positive possibilities.

Durrant (1988) illustrates such a case, in which intergenerational messages are identified for a female client and used as an externalized influence over which she was helped to triumph. Because the intergenerational process was used as the definition of the problem, blame was not personalized to any one person, but was assigned to tradition. In this way, motivation for change is facilitated, but clients do not need to feel disloyal to parents. Even in cases of painful abuse, an intergenerational perspective can often help families and individuals to explore the historical issues without becoming weighed down with unproductive introspection. Because intergenerational therapy maintains a focus that is interpersonal, clients can be helped to focus on interactions rather than internal pain alone and to discover important insights while also claiming the necessary strength to heal. By addressing stories, myths, rules, and roles from their family of origin, clients can also gain a sense of moving through time, just as the generations of their family have evolved over time. This opportunity for a sense of temporal movement can be enhanced by reflecting upon life-cycle issues that may have influenced the transmission of intergenerational dynamics.

Life-Cycle and Developmental Models

The critical timing of traditional nodal events or transitional periods for each stage of life was first undertaken by Evelyn Duvall (1977). She conceptualized the family as passing through eight stages, with developmental tasks for each stage. While there are many variations to Duvall's eight stages, all of them emphasize nodal events: entering and leaving the family, birth, parenthood, children leaving home, retirement, and death (Carter & McGoldrick, 1989b). Hiebert, Gillespie, and Stahmann (1993) have paid particular attention to stages of marital relationship and the interactional and psychological nuances that occur during each of the important nodal events.

Nodal events often require a reorganization of rules and roles in order for the family to remain functional. This reorganization can be thought of as a set of developmental tasks for each life-cycle stage. Box 6.2, adapted from Hiebert et al. (1993), outlines assessment questions that can be used to understand family functioning at each stage of the life-cycle. For some cases, questions from the current stage will be all that is needed. For other cases, a complete review, with a sampling of questions from each stage, may be needed to fully understand the family's lived experience.

Newly married couples have the task of solidifying their relationship and placing family of origin second to the marriage. When this task is not negotiated successfully, in-law conflicts may be chronic. In the next stage, the family must renegotiate rules and relationships to allow for the entry of children. Parenting roles must be established, and the relationship with the extended family must be redefined to include parenting and grandparenting.

The adolescent stage begins when the first child enters puberty. The primary task during this stage involves increased autonomy for adolescents in the household. Parents must continually alter their relationships and rules to allow the adolescent to move in and out of the family system. At the same time, the parents are facing mid-life decisions and emotions. The way in which critical tasks of communication and boundary negotiation have been resolved in previous stages will affect the resolution of challenges in this stage.

To the degree that previous developmental tasks have been mastered, the family can move into the launching stage. It is at this stage that the parents and the adolescent are, one hopes, in a position to attain greater independence from one another. Parents must develop adult relationships with their children and renegotiate their marital relationship without children. Stress occurs when parents are alone for the first time in 20 to 25 years and must renegotiate their time, new careers, and other issues.

Box 6.2   *Questions for Nuclear Family Interviews*

I.   Stage One: Between Families
     When did you meet? What year?
     Who introduced you to each other?
     Who initiated further dates?
     Were you dating other people at the time?
     When did this relationship become exclusive?
     What did you like about each other?
     What did you discover? How were you different from each other?
     What didn't you like?
     How did your families react to each of you during dating?
     When did each of you say on the inside, "You're for me"?
     When did each of you say to the other, "You're for me"?
     When did you get engaged? How did that happen?
     Did the relationship change after the engagement?
     How did you determine the wedding date?
     How did you determine who was to be at the wedding?
     Were you sexually involved prior to marriage? Were you able to talk about
          sex?
     Did you have any serious disagreements before marriage? How did each of
          you know that the other was angry?

II. Stage Two: Marriage
     How did the wedding go? What were your expectations?
     How did the honeymoon go? What kinds of expectations did you have?
     When did the first difference of opinion come about?
     What kind of social life did the two of you have at the beginning of this
          relationship? Who initiated it? How were decisions arrived at
          in regard to what you would do? Who were your friends? His,
          hers, both?
     How did the two of you decide to handle your money? Who decided that?
     Did anybody have veto power?
     How much could each of you spend without asking the other?
     When did the two of you first begin your sexual experiences? Did you
          discuss it before it happened?
     How did you each experience the first time?
     Who initiates now?
     How did each side of the family feel about the marriage?
     What were early relationships like between each of your families?
     How were disagreements handled between in-laws in the early years?
     How did you each define happiness?

III. Children
     How did the two of you go about deciding whether to have children?
     Did you talk about contraception and family planning?
     What were your different attitudes and ideas about it?

(continued)

Box 6.2 *(continued)*

How did your husband react to the pregnancy?
How did your wife respond to the pregnancy?
How did the pregnancy go? How was the delivery?
What kind of changes took place after the coming of the child?
Did you notice any differences developing after the birth of the child? How did you resolve these?
What attitudes from your families of origin have influenced your child-rearing relationships?
What percentage of your time is spent taking care of your marriage as against taking care of your children?
Who do the children turn to for support? If they want something fixed? If they want to play?

IV. Families with Adolescents
Who do the children think is more strict, more lenient, more moody, and so on?
How do Mom and Dad feel about school? Friends? Other issues?
What privileges do your teenagers have now that they did not have when they were younger?
How do you think your parents will handle it when your younger sister wants to date?
Will that be different than when you wanted to date?

V. Launching Children and Moving On
How did your parents help you to leave home?
What is the difference between how you left home and how your children are leaving home?
Will your parents get along better, worse, or the same with each other once you have left home?
Who, between your Mom and Dad, will miss the children the most?
Did you confide in one or more of the children if you were having difficulties with each other?
What effect did the children's leaving home have upon your marriage?
Have either of you thought about goals for yourselves after the children leave home?
What type of support do you need from each other to adjust to the children being away?
Are there any unresolved issues between you that can be traced back to an earlier stage of development?
Have you discussed this time as an opportunity to resolve those issues?

VI. Families in Later Life
As you see your child moving on with a new marriage, what would you like your child to do differently than you did?
If your parents are still alive, are there any issues you would like to discuss with them?

(continued)

Box 6.2   *(continued)*

When you look back over your life, what aspects have you enjoyed most? What has given you the most happiness? About what aspects do you feel the most regret? What was the one thing you wanted but did not get from the children?

Have there been any changes in the way you and your children relate since they have become adults?

How does your family deal with the effects of illness and advanced age?

How do you maintain a zest for life as you get older?

Have you discussed issues such as death, living wills, and life supports with your children and each other?

Do you have a plan for resolving conflicting feelings over any of the above?

Source: Adapted from Hiebert, Gillespie, & Stáhmann, 1993.

The postparental family must deal with its own declining health. Spouses must reassess their own life structures and explore new ways of living. At this stage, they may have to deal with the loss of a spouse or loss of vitality and fears concerning senility and death, both their own and their spouse's. These developments will also affect all the other members of the family.

Box 6.3 contains interview questions for divorcing and remarried families. The divorced or remarried family goes through additional stages of development. Like the stages of the family life-cycle, the stages of divorce and remarriage include developmental issues that can guide the clinician and family toward the most beneficial adjustment. It may be more difficult for divorced and remarried families to complete developmental tasks than it is for the original nuclear family. Remarried families may have role models for parenthood but lack such models for single parenthood or stepparenthood. While society focuses on the joys of family living through advertising and television, the divorced and remarried families have difficulty adjusting to this pattern. Moreover, at the time of remarriage, spouses must deal with many of the issues unresolved in the previous marriage.

In addition to the traditional life-cycle transitions and tasks that have been conceptualized for white, middle-class families, each family and individual also has a particular developmental path that evolves from the different settings where development occurs, "including each family's construction of its past and present" (Falicov, 1988). Nodal events such as untimely deaths, chronic illnesses, or other unusual circumstances may affect the course of the life-cycle and the completion of various stage-related tasks. Also, many other types of transition may occur for unmarried adults, gay and lesbian couples, adoptive families, and family groups from nonmajority cultures.

The level of stress is much greater for families today than for those of past generations. The increasing divorce rate, the women's movement, and sexual and technological revolutions have had a profound impact on families moving through the life-cycle. The vast amount of change produced by these events puts

---

Box 6.3

Questions for Divorced Family Interviews
Have you accepted your inability to continue this relationship?
How do you and your ex-spouse deal with the issue of custody? Visitation?
    Finances?
What do your parents think about the divorce?
What do you miss from your old family?
How are things different for you now?
What do you like about your new life? What don't you like about it?
Do you ever wish you were back together?
Have you developed any new relationships? Activities?
What kind of relationship do you have with your ex-spouse?
How did you tell your children about the divorce?
What have you learned about yourself in this process?
What kinds of problems are your children having?
How are you responding to those problems?

Questions for Remarried Family Development Interview
When did your last marriage end?
Do you think you had enough time to finish your first marriage?
What kind of communication do you have with your ex-wife? Ex-husband?
How are each of your children getting along?
How do each of them feel about your marriage?
How often do they see their mother/father?
How do your children get along with your wife/husband?
What do you do to help them get along with your wife/husband?
Which of your children has had the most difficulty with the new marriage?
How do your children get along with their stepbrothers? Stepsisters?
Do your children accept your wife/husband?
How do you expect your wife/husband to relate to your children?
Who is mostly in charge of the children?
What kind of help do you get from your wife/husband for your parenting role?
Are each of you responsible for disciplining your own children?

---

a great deal of stress on families today. Job loss or divorce often precipitates a crisis that sends the family to therapy. However, if therapy focuses only on the symptom or the interactional patterns at the time of crisis, the therapist may be missing information from a macroview that will help to normalize the current difficulties, thus making them easier to overcome.

To trace a family or individual's development over time, the family therapist must understand traditional and alternative patterns of evolution through time. Carter and McGoldrick (1989b) do this by enlarging upon Duvall's work and discussing stages of divorce adjustment and remarriage. Howard (1978) researched related and nonrelated family groups, discovering that high satisfaction was related to the following aspects of family life:

1. Good families have a chief—someone around whom others cluster.
2. Good families have a switchboard operator—someone who cannot help but keep track of others.
3. Good families are hospitable.
4. Good families deal squarely with directness.
5. Good families prize their rituals.
6. Good families are affectionate.
7. Good families have a sense of place.
8. Good families find a way to be involved with children.
9. Good families honor their elders.

In diverse and nonrelated family groups, these aspects can be considered as developmental tasks that lead to relational satisfaction over time.

In adopting a developmental view, the practitioner becomes aware of sequences and processes that evolve over time. The result is a perspective that identifies family and individual problems according to their developmental place in time:

1. What stage of relationship is the family/individual in now? What other major life transitions have they lived through? What will the next stage be?
2. How did things come to be the way they are now?
3. Has the problem always been this way? When did it change?
4. When were things better than now? When were they worse?
5. Does the family view their current life situation as part of a temporary stage or part of a permanent problem?
6. Does the family therapist have a view of the problem that uses time as a dimension of hope or as an indictment of despair?
7. Does the use of parental control fit the developmental needs of the individual?
8. Does consideration of differences allow developmentally appropriate autonomy?
9. Are there signs that tasks of previous stages have not been successfully accomplished?
10. Is each person in the family attaining his or her needs in a fashion that helps the parents maintain control?

When to Focus on Developmental Issues

Many family-therapy theorists focus on developmental issues in some way (Haley, 1980; Hoffman, 1983; Minuchin, 1974; Selvini Palazzoli et al., 1978). Most commonly, client populations with children, adolescents, and elders are best served by focusing on life-cycle issues because common life transitions can be easily implicated as part of the problem. In addition, individuals and nontraditional family groups can benefit from an assessment that helps them to identify and label their unique developmental progression, giving them a sense of movement through time. That sense of movement through time helps create a positive context for targeted changes.

Implications for Treatment

The advantage of a life-cycle perspective is that it offers the family therapist increased options for defining the problem. Rather than seeing a problem as a permanent condition, the therapist is able to view behavior and symptoms as a response to a unique transition in the person's life (Haley, 1980). If a couple's marital conflict became serious after the birth of their first child, that developmental stage can be explored for circumstances that might have prevented the couple from developing problem-solving strategies. These developmental circumstances (such as isolation, poverty, or in-law interference) can be labeled as the problem and the couple can then be invited to join together to overcome this problem, rather than blaming each other and remaining adversaries (White & Epston, 1991).

When a person or a family does not proceed through traditional life-cycle stages, the problem brought into therapy can be thought of as an opportunity for clients to pioneer a new societal pattern, or as an opportunity for the therapist and the clients to collect information from their unique experience to share with others. In a developmental interview, the family therapist might ask participants to talk about what they perceive as the major stages of their life thus far and, more specifically, to reflect on perceptions of self and others and also the challenges and abilities that characterized each stage. Erickson and Rossi (1979) suggest that therapeutic change occurs when a person undergoes an inner resynthesis of their past experience. By focusing on developmental milestones in family and individual history, the family therapist can conduct an assessment that will invite the process of change to begin.

As the therapist assesses the developmental process, information begins to emerge about the interactional process between family members—that is, the microprocess that accounts for small, specific behavioral sequences in families such as who started the fight or who stole the last cookie from the jar. Interactional process within the family is generally assessed as an indicator of family structure.

Structural Models

The study of family structure is primarily concerned with interactions within the family that determine its organization. According to Minuchin, this organization must be modified to meet the developmental tasks for each stage of the family life-cycle. The concepts of hierarchy, boundaries, subsystems, and coalitions are invoked in describing family structure.

The structural approach to family therapy evolved from the work of Salvador Minuchin and associates with families of delinquent boys at the

Wiltwick School. These practitioners began to theorize that patterns of delinquency are related to the degree of disorganization in the family (Minuchin, Montalvo, Guerney, Rosman, & Schumer, 1967). This disorganization is characterized in terms of hierarchy—the pattern of leadership and power manifest in the family. Within families, hierarchy is often expressed by the pecking order, by shared perceptions of who is the boss, and by interactional patterns that indicate who gets the last word.

The family organism, like other social organizations, carries out its functions through an internal organization of subsystems (couple, parental, and sibling). When the functioning of subsystems breaks down, the family is unable to provide support and autonomy to meet the developmental needs of individual members. Thus, the family therapist must ask: Does the family's structural organization at this time, in this particular social context or culture, sufficiently meet the needs of all its individual members? Families who are not able to meet these needs often lack models for sufficient functioning and thus seek treatment.

A breakdown in the parental subsystem occurs, for example, when one parent joins in a coalition with one or more children against the other parent. Such a coalition is often indicated if the therapist notes critical discussions about a parent who is absent, if one parent confides in a child about marital discord, or if one parent openly sides with a child against the other parent. In structural terms, parent-child coalitions are thought of as a violation of the boundary between the parental and sibling subsystems, since it changes the role of the child from one of dependent to one of confidant or emotional peer.

Questions to assess family structure include:

1. How much time do you spend with each other? Who does each family member spend the most time with, and what things do they do together?
2. How do you decide what gets accomplished within the family? What is the process of decision making and who is involved?
3. Who is close to whom? Who is most alike and most dissimilar in the family?
4. How are mother and father different from each other?
5. How is each sibling different from the others?
6. Who agrees and disagrees with stated views about the problem?
7. Do you feel your wife/husband doesn't care what is going on?
8. How do you decide the rules for your children?
9. Do you feel your wife/husband is too easy with your son?
10. Who seems to be most upset by this problem?
11. What are some things you have tried to do to solve this problem?
12. Which of these seem helpful to you? How are they helpful?

The therapist assesses family interaction by observing various kinds of behavior. Useful nonverbal clues include tone of voice, facial expressions, or eye contact with other family members. It is important to take careful note of who speaks for whom and when. The therapist may also probe other family members to assess their view of the family problem. Using these data, the therapist formulates hypotheses about the family problem and the underlying structure of the system.

When to Focus on Structure

It is a basic practice in family therapy to assess the power structure of each family and to develop a collaborative relationship with the family members who have the greatest ability to influence family life. Thus, a structural assessment is recommended for all cases, since treatment is maximized when it is aligned with the family's hierarchy. In addition, information about structure is important in order to assess specific interactions in the family and who is actually involved in problematic sequences.

Implications for Treatment

While structural assessment is most closely associated with the clinical work of Minuchin, Haley's strategic therapy also makes use of structural concepts in defining child and adolescent problems. Structural-strategic forms of family therapy routinely emphasize the goal of strengthening the parental subsystem and addressing parent-child coalitions. These goals are often pursued by tracking interactional sequences in detail and intervening in these interactions to change a targeted relationship. In addition, the Milan team and other practitioners have developed circular questions designed to elicit information about family structure and family politics: Who is close to whom? How did the family come to their conclusions about the problem? Whose opinion has the most influence? What purpose might the symptom be serving? What is the exact sequence of events when the problem is occurring? As these questions are answered, the therapist can describe the structure of the family and note, in particular, how family interactions are influenced by the personal dynamics of each individual.

Individual Models

Despite the tendency in the field of family therapy to deemphasize the analysis of intrapsychic dimensions within the individual, many approaches provide very helpful information related to how a family therapist would address individual concerns. In fact, even those approaches that may overtly discourage attention to psychodynamics eventually reveal that they have not totally thrown the baby out with the bath water. For example, although Watzlawick has long been an advocate of analyzing failed solutions, rather than analyzing people (in the traditional psychoanalytic sense), he suggests that, in finding solutions, "the tactic chosen has to be translated into the person's own 'language'; that is, it must be presented to him in a form which utilizes his own way of conceptualizing 'reality' " (Watzlawick, Weakland, & Fisch, 1974, p. 113).

Thus, without a framework facilitating empathy for each person's position—each person's hopes, fears, dilemmas, motivations, and so on—the family therapist will likely not be able to successfully elicit trust and cooperation from the significant parties involved. The following review will illustrate the variety of views related to understanding individuals from a systems perspective.

1. *Self-esteem.* Experiential family therapy focuses primarily on individual growth. As an extension of this emphasis, experiential theorists have conceptualized self-esteem as the result of interpersonal processes. Virginia Satir (1972) was particularly interested in teaching others about the impact of family functioning upon the self-esteem of the individual. Satir was noted for therapeutic interventions in which she adopted a nurturing role with clients while coaching them toward more honest, open, and accepting communication with each other. In a statement (Satir, 1972) that she called "My Declaration of Self-Esteem," Satir envisions the potential of every person to become an aware, self-responsible, growth-oriented person.

Satir also had an influence on other personal growth theorists who were interested in interactional models based on self-awareness and communication. One such model, developed by Miller, Nunnally, Wackman, and Miller (1988), integrates the study of interpersonal interaction with humanistic psychology and family studies. Known as the Couples Communication Program, this approach begins with five basic elements of self-awareness that can be taught to a student or family member so as to enhance the self-awareness and communication skills needed for personal satisfaction in relationships. These five elements are now considered in turn.

2. *Senses.* Information from the five senses is the initial link between the individual and the outside world. Sensory information—the words that people hear, the actions that they observe, physical or touching sensations, smells, and tastes—is present at the beginning of all human life and continues through to the end, as part of an interactional cycle. Sensory data are regarded as factual; carefully assessed, they yield a limited but verifiable truth. For example, if a wife hears her husband's voice raised, this is an objective fact, distinguishable from her subjective response, which may be the thought, "He's mad." Only her husband can really verify what his emotion is at that moment, even though family members commonly consider their subjective information to be fact.

3. *Thoughts.* This category includes interpretations, assumptions, opinions, beliefs, and the conclusions that an individual makes in response to sensory information. Often the result of history and experience, thoughts become a frame of reference that influences a person's actions, feelings, and intentions. In addition, assumptions are distinguished from objective facts in that they are constructed by the person in response to sensory data. If a wife says, "I think you're angry," the statement legitimately communicates a fact about what she is thinking and distinguishes her thought process from what her husband's emotion might really be. In addition, self-esteem in individual family members will often be related to their beliefs or thoughts about themselves, as well as what they perceive to be the beliefs of others about themselves.

4. *Feelings.* This category encompasses the physiological and behavioral responses associated with feeling a certain emotion. Common feelings include sadness, anger, happiness, fear, shame, and hurt. However, there are hundreds of words in the English language that label an even wider range of emotional states. Self-awareness entails individuals' ability to label their emotions, whether pleasant or unpleasant, and to accept them as part of being human.

Self-esteem involves an acceptance of emotions as important information about the self and an ability to act responsibly upon those feelings. When individuals are not able to tolerate their fears or anxieties, they develop controlling or addictive behavior intended to numb unpleasant emotional states.

5. *Intentions.* These are personal and general goals, hidden and open desires, short-term and long-term needs, motivations, dreams, and hopes. They can involve both the self and others and are related to an individual's thoughts and feelings as they evolve over time. Behavior is viewed as always having purpose; thus, intentions provide a personal context for actions. For example, when family members have an intent to please others as much as possible, they may develop behavior patterns that are consistently accommodating to others and not assertive on behalf of self. In other cases, intentions may underlie symptomatic behavior that serves a function in the family, as in the case where a child's problem interrupts parental conflict. While the intention in young children may not be conscious, adolescent and adult family members are often able to identify their systemic intention when the therapist asks, "How might this problem actually be preventing something worse from happening in the family?"

6. *Actions.* These are behaviors that can be communicated with verbs. The authors suggest that an individual can increase self-awareness by becoming aware of actions. Sitting, smiling, talking, shifting eye contact, listening, shouting, initiating, waiting, breathing, and walking are examples of actions that are related to the individual's feelings, intentions, thoughts, and senses. When the clinician begins to track interactional sequences, it is helpful to begin by focusing on actions, since family members often move quickly to their subjective experience before weighing the facts related to another's actions:

Therapist: Tell me exactly what happened.

Client: Well, he was trying to get me to do his homework for him. [a description of intentions, not actions]

Therapist: No, I mean what was he actually doing when you had that thought?

Client: Well, . . . I guess he was sitting on the couch, watching TV. [sensory data—"I saw him sitting"]

Therapist: What else was he doing that made you think he was trying to get you to do his homework for him?

Client: He doesn't have to do anything else! He knows that if he hasn't already started working on his homework before I get home, then I will do it when I come in! [statement of assumption—thoughts]

Therapist: Now, how do you think he knows that?

Client: He knows because I've told him time and time again that I want his homework done before I get home so I won't have to worry about it. [action statement]

Therapist: So, aside from what your son may think, you have a desire that you put into action when you walk through the door, is that right?

Client: Yes, I want to know if he's done his homework and, if he hasn't, I want him to get busy right then. [statement of intention]

Therapist: Is this pretty predictable behavior for you? I mean, does it happen nearly every night?

Client: Well, lately, yes, because he's been getting so bad.

Therapist: Well, we might want to start by seeing if we can help you to become more "unpredictable" in your son's eyes! Sometimes, surprising behaviors help kids change their minds about things.

Taken together, the five elements of self-awareness—actions, senses, thoughts, intentions, and feelings—represent the individual as a system of interrelated parts. These parts interact with each other to form an individual's contribution to a relationship, regardless of whether the relationship is with self or others. Interactional patterns are comprised of sequences that use all five elements:

Actions: Wife is fixing dinner in the kitchen.
Senses: She notices her husband coming up the driveway.
Thoughts: I wonder if he's still thinking about the argument we had this morning.
Intentions: I hope he isn't still mad at me.
Feelings: I'm afraid he won't be happy.
Actions: Husband comes in the door. He is frowning.
Feelings: He is tired and embarrassed about a traffic ticket just issued to him on the way home.
Intentions: He wants to save face; he wants his wife to think well of him.
Senses: Wife sees his frown.
Actions: She says, "Are you still mad about this morning?"
Thoughts: He thinks, "She's criticizing me and belittling my feelings."
Actions: Husband says, "Why do you always think you can read my mind?"

By paying attention to all five dimensions of experience, the clinician is able to track a sequence while also understanding the individual's experience as it evolves in the interaction. Then, as the therapist helps the couple to clarify and accept their emotions, both their own and their partner's, they are able to increase intimacy by understanding each other's intentions and emotions—especially their particular sensitivities. If each person had begun their part of the interaction with a statement of intent (for example, "I want you to be happy" or, "I want your approval") or with a statement of feelings (for example, "I'm afraid" or, "I'm embarrassed"), the interaction might have taken a different turn. When family members feel most vulnerable, their intent will be to protect themselves from anticipated psychological or emotional hurt.

In addition to experiential family therapists who focus on communication and self-esteem, social constructionists focus on communication and personal belief systems. These new theoretical frameworks have been greatly influenced by theorists such as Jean Piaget, George Kelly, and Kenneth Gergan. They posit that personal belief systems are an evolving set of meanings that continue to emerge from interactions between people. However, unlike traditional psychologists, who view the individual as a reactive being, the constructionist asserts that personal meaning (beliefs) derives from the individual's perception of what occurs in their interactions with others (Mahoney, 1991). For example, if a young unattached man characterizes himself as "weak" and "dependent," this may be because he has neglected those aspects of his life that are incongruent with his self-image of helplessness. The individual may have ignored those times when he was able to overcome his helplessness. Likewise, through his interactions with his family, he may allow them to describe him as helpless, which will likely influence the way they interact with each other. In this case, personal narratives become an internalized set of conversations ("I must depend on others for help") that are consistent with our behavior (acting in ways that elicit help from others). Thus, for constructionists, the meaning that family members attribute to an event determines their behavior.

Related to this view, the influence of Milton Erickson has brought a new understanding of the unconscious. For Erickson, the unconscious was an untapped reservoir of positive resources, not a complex stockpile of repressed anguish (Erickson & Rossi, 1979). As he put his own belief system into operation, he was able to help his patients begin to use their perceived deficits as strengths and assets. In a later section of this book, some of his techniques relevant to the practice of family therapy will be reviewed.

Although the term was not widely used in family therapy literature until the later 1980s, Erickson is regarded as a constructionist by the constructionists themselves. Evidence of his similarities with other constructionists can be seen in the way he views the formation of individual or family problems.

> Patients have problems because of learned limitations. They are caught in mental sets, frames of reference, and belief systems that do not permit them to explore and utilize their own abilities to best advantage. Human beings are still in the process of learning to use their potentials. The therapeutic transaction ideally creates a new phenomenal world in which patients can explore their potentials, freed to some extent from their learned limitations . . . As the therapist explores the patient's world and facilitates rapport, it is almost inevitable that *new frames of reference and belief systems are created.* This usually happens whenever people meet and interact closely. (Erickson & Rossi, 1979, p. 2)

Thus, Erickson considered the belief system of the patient and the meaning attributed to the ongoing flow of the person's life to be a critical factor in problem formation and problem resolution.

An intergenerational approach that addresses personal beliefs in a slightly different way is the contextual family therapy of Ivan Boszormenyi-Nagy

(Boszormenyi-Nagy & Krasner, 1986). In this approach, exploring a person's beliefs about the give and take in relationships helps the clinician to understand how an individual experiences fairness and equity within the family. These family therapists suggest that human beings carry with them a subjective family ledger, consisting of personal beliefs about how much they have contributed to family members and how much they are entitled to receive in return. According to Boszormenyi-Nagy and Krasner (1986), this concept of relational ethics is based on an innate sense of justice or fairness that exists within people. This approach suggests that dysfunction occurs within families when relational imbalances lead to a lack of trustworthiness or the development of "destructive entitlements" that involve individual symptoms (actions) developed in response to beliefs (thoughts) about unfairness within the family.

When to Focus on Individual Dynamics

Although many family therapy models address behavioral change before perceptual change, those cases that do not respond to behavioral interventions most likely need a greater focus on personal dynamics that may be restraining behavioral change. Therefore, cases where behavioral interventions are not successful can benefit from a shift to an exploration of personal dynamics (self-esteem, self-awareness, personal beliefs, or feelings of entitlement). In addition, when the joining process seems stalemated or the practitioner begins to notice subtle power struggles with clients, it is very important to step back from the normal operating procedure and explore personal dynamics, in order to understand and affirm clients' beliefs about their process and about the process between therapist and clients.

Too often, clinicians forget to focus on their *own* personal dynamics. How is their work related to their sense of self-esteem? Are they aware of their own hidden agendas that may be incongruent with what clients have stated as their priorities? Do clinicians have certain beliefs that may lead them to harbor critical or condescending views of their clients? Is their sense of entitlement such that they pursue unrealistic goals for their clients in family therapy? A focus on individual elements on both sides of the therapy experience often helps the clinician develop goals and expectations that match the developmental level of the family.

It is also appropriate to focus on individual dynamics in cases where the client goal is more process-oriented than problem-oriented (for example, "I need help getting over the death of my daughter"). When the client goal is related more to coping, growth, or adjustment to some transition, focusing on individual dynamics will also fit better with client expectations of the therapy experience.

Implications for Treatment

While many models of family therapy have deemphasized traditional Freudian views of individual psychodynamics, all models use some newer understanding of personal dynamics. Whether it is the structural therapist joining with the family, or the strategic therapist looking for a directive that will be accepted by the client, or the intergenerational therapist who seeks to help family members with unfinished business, the ability to understand personal dynamics is a clinical imperative in the practice of family therapy.

Falloon (1991) takes a stronger position by suggesting that the individual goals of every family member should be targets for treatment. He states:

> At times, these goals may be highly personal and inappropriate for intergenerational problem solving. For example, the resolution of sexual difficulties between parents, obsessive-compulsive rumination, or prophylactic drug therapy for schizophrenia. Such problems may be addressed in an individual or a marital context, where this seems most appropriate. (p. 79)

There seems to be increasing evidence that individually oriented strategies work best within a systemic framework. This is particularly so when the presenting problem involves major mental disorders, such as phobia, severe depression, or schizophrenia (Falloon, 1991).

Returning to the continuum of macro- and micro-models of family assessment, an emphasis on microdynamics facilitates therapeutic effectiveness as a complement to all other models of assessment. By starting with a larger view of life—for example, a focus on gender, race, extended family, life-cycle, or family structure—and evolving to an exploration of personal dynamics—for example, how do gender dynamics relate to self-esteem? What personal beliefs may perpetuate gender imbalances? Are individuals' beliefs about themselves constrained by societal norms for women and men?—family therapists are able to fluctuate between macropositions that minimize personal shame and blame and micropositions that liberate clients to think of themselves and their relationships in new ways.

Each model of assessment presented here can be thought of as a different reality or lens from which to view families who seek treatment. Each lens has its own set of issues and questions; they range from larger societal views of human problems to smaller dissections of personal and interpersonal process. The beginning family therapist can learn flexibility by using different lenses to view panoramas or get to the heart of the matter, depending upon clients' needs and the types of problems. Taken individually, each model provides a sense of direction to explore issues in a more complete way. In the next chapter, strategies for using these models will be discussed, with an application to case material.

Chapter Seven

Integrating the Assessment Process: Skills

Genograms

Circular Questioning

Tracking Interactional Sequences

Tracking Longitudinal Sequences

The Wilsons

I n conducting an assessment, the family therapist must move from theory to practice and from concepts to actual dialogue with families and individuals. In this chapter, we will review specific techniques that can be used to conduct an assessment and to organize the information obtained. Then, we will illustrate how these techniques can be incorporated into the initial stages of family therapy.

Historically, the field of family therapy has not focused on any one procedure for conducting assessments. Bowen (1978) popularized the use of genograms for collecting family-of-origin information. Structural and strategic therapists engage in tracking interactional sequences as a way of learning about common relational patterns (Minuchin, 1974). Constructionists inquire about the evolution of the family over time, as told in stories that the family relates (Boscolo et al., 1987; Sluzki, 1992; White and Epston, 1991). Since most family therapists use some form of these techniques in their work, we will review each of these procedures and illustrate how they may be systematically employed to gather micro- and macroassessment data.

Genograms

In the early days of family therapy, Bowen began to diagram a person's family-of-origin by means of a three-generational family tree that came to be known as the genogram. This genogram would start at the bottom of the diagram with the identified patient's generation, including siblings, and move up through the generations to each parent's family-of-origin, including parents and siblings. As the field progressed, numerous practitioners from a variety of orientations have adapted the genogram to their use. As McGoldrick and Gerson (1985) note:

> In family therapy, genogram applications range from multigenerational mapping of the family emotional system using a Bowen framework, to systemic hypothesizing for Milan-style paradoxical interventions, to developing "projective" hypotheses about the workings of the unconscious from genogram interviews, to simply depicting the cast of characters in the family. (p. 4)

The genogram is a diagram of a three- or four-generation relationship history of the family. The genogram includes family members (and their relationships to one another), ages, dates of marriage, death, divorce, and adoption, and places of residence. Women are symbolized by circles and men by squares (Figure 7.1). Vertical lines connect parents and children, and horizontal lines are used for

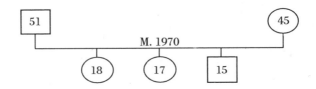

Figure 7.1

marriage and dates. For detailed instructions on the conventions of genograms, consult McGoldrick and Gerson (1985) or Carter and McGoldrick (1989a).

In Figure 7.1, we can see that the husband is 51 and the wife is 45, and they were married in 1970. They have three children—two daughters, 18 and 17, and a son, 15. The two-generational family can be expanded to include the grandparents on each side of the family (Figure 7.2).

The double slash in the line joining the paternal grandparents indicates they were divorced in 1968; the grandfather remarried in 1969, to a woman whose daughter is currently 49. The grandfather and his wife live in Louisville, KY. The paternal grandmother remarried in 1972 and currently lives in Monticello, IN. The maternal grandparents were married in 1947. The maternal grandfather died in 1980 and the maternal grandmother currently lives in Indianapolis. Box 7.1 provides a summary of suggested questions that can provide the family therapist with information at both micro- and macrolevels of family functioning.

We suggest that genograms be constructed with the family as a type of public note taking, which can help the family begin visualizing their own system. Since a family therapy model seeks to expand the area of focus regarding the presenting problem, a genogram is helpful in expanding the interpersonal area of focus from individual to family and from family to extended family. As the family therapist becomes aware of certain relationships that are important to the client of record, relevant areas of discussion can be determined through the construction of a genogram and potential sources of family support are usually identified. In family sessions, the genogram helps family members consider where the presenting problem fits into the larger context of their three-generational heritage. In individual sessions, the family therapist learns to understand clients through a knowledge and understanding of their families. When the practitioner wants to know "where a client is coming from," the genogram becomes a vehicle for such an understanding in a most literal way, since most clients come from a family with a tradition and a history.

To make successful use of a genogram, the family therapist must be able to articulate a rationale for its construction that is meaningful and reassuring to the client. In cases where the presenting problem may seem unrelated to family or extended family, practitioners can explain that a diagram of the family helps them understand significant relationships that might be a resource in addressing the presenting problem. With African-American families, the genogram should be

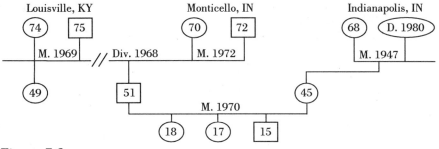

Figure 7.2

Box 7.1   Questions and Guidelines for Genograms

Roman numeral entries are questions to clients. Alphabet entries are directions to the therapist.

I. **How is your family different from other families you know?**
   A. Begin writing brief words on the genogram that represent the responses to this question.
   B. Use public note taking as a form of acknowledging each person's comments.

II. **How are Mom and Dad different from each other?**
   A. List adjectives near the corresponding person on the genogram.
   B. When negative labels are given, try to reframe in a neutral, positive, or empathic way.
   C. Use these questions as an opportunity to tease, joke, and set people at ease.
   D. Many people will be privately fearing judgment, criticism, and psychological analysis; therefore, the less "therapeutic" the environment, the better.

III. **How is _____ (each child) different from everyone else in the family?**
   A. List adjectives near the name of each person.
   B. As the interview continues, make small notes and diagram any information that will help in answering the general assessment questions of this section.

IV. **Who is most like Dad? Who is most like Mom? What makes you say that?**

V. **How does your family express affection?**
   A. What do they do to communicate positive feelings to one another?
   B. How do they know when a given family member is feeling positive toward them?

VI. **Who gets the most angry? How do you know when _____ is mad?**
   A. Reframe anger as pain or feeling overwhelmed.
   B. Ask who else gets angry besides _____. Ask what they get angry about.
   C. Whenever the family characterizes any member as being an extreme in any way, follow up the comment with, "Who is the next most _____?"

VII. **Who runs the family? Who gets the last word?**
   A. Give each member a chance to respond.

Source: Adapted from Hiebert (1980).

constructed after a period of joining has occurred, so that the family will be reassured that the genogram will not invite criticism of diverse extended-family structures. With these families, it is best to preface the genogram with an explanation such as:

> In order to help you, it's important for me to understand something about the significant people in your life and what they mean to you. It's my usual practice to diagram family and personal relationships so that I can get the big picture of a person's life. I think African-American families often have unique strengths in their families because of the variety of family relationships that exist and because they often have endured much hardship together. Would you be willing to let me get acquainted with that part of your life?

In cases where clients were adopted or transferred through many foster placements, the genogram can be adapted to depict the multiple settings and relationships that have become the norm for their development. However, even with early disruptions, some clients may still have a desire to know and understand their family roots. Thus, the main objective of a genogram may be either to chart biological patterns of behavior and relatedness or to discover and diagram the nature of any interpersonal patterns that shaped the development of family members, including thoughts, behaviors, and values that were imbedded in significant relationships. In either case, the end result will be a visual representation of important relationships, in which similarities and differences are identified. These patterns are used to target attitudes or behaviors that may be involved in perpetuating the presenting problem. Often, such details will be elicited through the use of circular questions.

Circular Questioning

Although the Milan team were the first to speak of circularity and circular questions, family therapists from a wide range of models now use the latter term generically in referring to questions that make "connections among actions, beliefs, and relationships of individuals within the system" (Campbell, Draper, & Crutchley, 1991, p. 346). Box 7.1 offers examples of circular questions that seek out perceptions of difference in family life. Systemic therapists find that circular questions elicit a broad range of information about family dynamics, including individual roles that make family members unique; marital patterns of power, communication, and intimacy; and coalitions among subsystems within the family. This "information about differences," as Bateson (1972) once labeled it, becomes the family therapist's foundation for understanding the family as a social system. As this understanding evolves, hypotheses and interventions are formulated.

Fleuridas, Nelson, and Rosenthal (1986) provide guidelines for teaching circular questions at each stage of the therapeutic process. The authors state the following:

> This form of questioning serves as an efficient process for soliciting information from each member of the family regarding their experience of: (a) the family's presenting concern; (b) sequences of interactions, usually related to the problem; and (c) differences in their relationships over time. This provides the family and the therapist with a systemic frame of the problem, thereby enabling the therapist to generate hypotheses and design interventions (or additional questions) which interrupt dysfunctional cycles of interrelating and which challenge symptom-supporting myths or beliefs (cf. Minuchin & Fishman, 1981; Papp, 1983; Selvini Palazzoli et al., 1978, 1980b). (p. 114)

In addition, circular questions may compare people across generations ("Who is most/least like the identified patient?"), developmental time periods ("Has it always been this way? When did things change? What was it like before?"), and meanings ("Who agrees/disagrees that this is the problem?"); explore differences in perceptions of relationships ("Who is closer to Mom, your brother or your sister?") or differences of degree ("On a scale of one to ten, how were you able to solve problems this week?"); focus on before and after distinctions ("Did she get angry before you told her or after you told her?"); and pose hypothetical possibilities ("How would things be different if you spent more time together?") (Boscolo et al., 1987). These questions help to track family members as they evolve through different experiences, developing beliefs and attitudes about family life as they go. This evolution can be explored on both micro- and macrolevels, by using some questions that focus on sequences of interaction and other questions that focus on sequences of important changes.

Tracking Interactional Sequences

As a genogram is constructed, the family therapist may discover certain relationships at the microlevel that seem to have ultimate importance in the client's mind. When these relationships are discussed, the therapist must gain a description of facts, not merely assumptions (O'Hanlon & Weiner-Davis, 1989). This can be done by tracking interactional sequences that occurred during important moments in the relationship:

Therapist: How would you describe your relationship with your father?

Client: I'd say it's strained.

Therapist: [Draws a line on the genogram between father-daughter and writes "strained"] How is it strained?

Client: Oh, it goes way back. . . . He always tries to make me feel guilty. I can never do anything right.

Therapist: [Writes "guilty" on the genogram next to daughter] When you say he always tries to make you feel guilty . . . what does he do or say that gives you that impression?

Client: Well, . . . when we talk on the phone, he'll say something like, "I sure would like to see you more often," implying that I don't visit him enough. Then, if I do come to visit, he complains that I haven't stayed long enough.

Therapist: [Writes "wants to see her" on the genogram next to father] So, when you're on the phone with him and he says he wants to see you more often, what do you say back?

Client: I try to explain to him that I'm busy and can't just pick up any ol' time to travel all that way.

Therapist: And then what does he say?

Client: He usually starts to lecture me about how families ought to be close.

Therapist: And then what do you say?

Client: I don't say anything . . . I just let him go on and on.

Therapist: So you clam up?

Client: Yeah.

Therapist: And you're probably thinking to yourself . . . what?

Client: Here we go again!

Therapist: O.K., so this is a familiar pattern with the two of you?

Client: Oh, yes!

Therapist: Well, let's backtrack for a minute. . . . When he first says he'd like to see you, what is going on right before that part of the conversation? Anything in particular?

Client: Mmm . . . usually just talk about what he's doing and what I'm doing.

Therapist: So in the earlier part of the discussion, you're talking and interacting with him, telling him about yourself, and then it changes when he makes his statement?

Client: Yes. It usually starts out OK and then goes downhill.

In this discussion, the client is making an assumption about her father's intention based upon what he says to her. The therapist does not challenge her assumption at this point, but merely seeks to illuminate the facts—in this case, what he actually says to her. Then, as the facts become known, they are put in sequence with her responses, and the entire sequence is placed in the larger context of their conversation and how it evolved over time. In the same interaction, the therapist could also follow up on the client's statement that her father complains when she comes to visit. The word "complain" could be written on the genogram and explored in the same way, since it connotes a negative intent on the part of the father. By gaining microinformation about what is actually said and what happens before and after his statement, the facts and assumptions begin to separate.

As the facts are described, the clinician can start to identify patterns of thinking and assumption that may be hindering the development of a new pattern. The daughter believes that her father wants her to feel guilty. If the therapist has developed a supportive relationship, it might be appropriate to begin challenging her assumption during this phase of an assessment (for example, by saying, "Is it possible that your father is trying to send you a different message besides wanting you to feel guilty?"). However, the decision to intervene must be based on what the presenting problem is and whether the client perceives the intervention as relevant to the presenting problem. If the presenting problem was a child-focused problem, genogram discussions and the tracking of interactional sequences may provide information to help the clinician develop a broad understanding of the client's relational patterns, but interventions should be related to the problem (for example, "Do you ever find that your son 'tries to make you feel guilty' like your father? How does he do that?"). Then, as similarities and differences are identified, the client's responses can be indicators of whether she is ready to consider alternative views.

If the presenting problem was directly related to the father-daughter relationship, the therapist may still want to complete the genogram, learning about the nature of other family relationships and tracking other important sequences before deciding on a treatment strategy. Sometimes, clients respond to the genogram with their own ideas about what is the best way to address the problem or who in their three-generation system could be most helpful with the problem. At other times, more developmental information may be needed to put a presenting problem into the context of the life-cycle. This may be done by tracking longitudinal sequences.

Tracking Longitudinal Sequences

In gathering information about developmental progress through the life-cycle, it is often helpful to diagram a horizontal timeline that illustrates the family's story during significant time periods or provides a chart of their life at the macro-level of observation. Hiebert, Gillespie, and Stahmann (1993) use a timeline for marital and premarital counseling, as a means of tracking the interpersonal dance of each couple and identifying the developmental roots of their presenting problem. Stanton (1992) uses a timeline to discover clues as to what might have triggered the family's problem. Both these applications adopt the premise that the identification of developmental patterns of interaction is an important step in developing hypotheses that are born out of client experience and that will address nodal events related to key patterns.

Other family therapists also emphasize assessments with a historical element. Hargrave and Anderson (1992) conduct life reviews based on questioning to validate an older person's life history, but without the use of a visual chart. Fleuridas et al. (1986) provide examples of time-oriented circular questions exploring changes and transitions in the past that may be affecting the present. In these cases, the focus on historical information helps family members reflect upon significant experiences that may stimulate their own natural abilities to heal or change.

The advantages of using a visual timeline are similar to those of using the genogram. Because families often feel stuck in a problem when they enter family therapy, a chronological account of important transitions can restore an element of movement and flow to the family's self-perception. If a genogram has already been constructed, it is a logical transition to take information already recorded there and to begin putting the significant events in sequence. The in-session process thus transforms awareness from the family as a system to the family as a larger story that extends beyond the presenting problem. Marriages, births, deaths, illnesses, job changes, graduations, and other significant events often cluster at certain time points in a family's life story. These clusters may be developmental times at which certain themes in the family developed. By tracking the sequences of these events through the life-cycle, the therapist is able to broaden the family's perception of how they came to be stuck and to summarize important information in a graphic manner. Consider the following example.

> When an adolescent boy was placed in a residential facility, his family was given an opportunity to reflect upon significant changes in their family history. A major loss was the death of the boy's paternal grandfather, who had been the center of the three-generational family. Shortly thereafter, the boy's mother took her first job outside the home, and his school phobia began almost at once. In a period of progressive discouragement over the ensuing five years, the family had no opportunity to stop and reflect upon the impact of these circumstances. Finally, in the residential facility, they responded to the construction of a timeline by developing a grieving process that allowed the identified patient to identify his own experience of his grandfather's death. Together, the family began to reclaim the parts of family life that had been lost since that time.

The timeline was a concrete representation of the family's life together, as well as a vehicle to help the family therapist focus on critical events that shaped the family's attitudes and feelings. As the timeline was constructed, the therapist highlighted family strengths and tracked interactional sequences for significant events, such as the parents' courtship and marriage and the onset of the son's phobia. As the timeline brought therapist and family up to the present day, it provided the clinician an opportunity to reflect upon the courage and endurance demonstrated by the parents in caring for their son, as well as a context for affirming the family's ability to overcome obstacles in the future. Since a timeline shows progression over time, it becomes an unspoken voice for the inevitability of change.

For the beginning practitioner, three things are important in constructing a timeline. First, creating a sense of movement along the continuum is the primary goal. Therefore, it is important to develop a different rhythm for each family or individual that will capture the uniqueness of their movement through time; in some cases, lengthy discussions will occur at some points along the timeline and only superficial coverage will be necessary at other points. However, the clinician must make sure that certain emotional points in time do not derail the discussion before it reaches the present; otherwise, the sense of movement may not be achieved.

One of the advantages of using a timeline is that it helps the family therapist keep a sense of direction during stages of exploration when emotional issues may be raised before a therapeutic direction has been explicitly defined. It becomes understood, through constructing the timeline, that both therapist and family are moving forward, from past toward future. The timeline allows an emotional issue to be explored in its original context, as a point along a continuum rather than an end in itself. In this way, microinformation generates empathy; macroinformation generates perspective.

Second, it is not necessary to write details or complete sentences on a timeline; key words, themes, or events with the month and year are adequate. Too many details can clutter the family's visual perception of their movement over time and leave them feeling just as overwhelmed. Therefore, if the clinician helps a couple to have a lengthy discussion about a misunderstanding that occurred 15 years earlier, when their first child was born, it is enough to note the event, together with important reframings, questions, or alternative views that emerge from the discussion.

Third, clinicians must provide a rationale and description for the timeline that emphasizes their neutral point of view and their desire to understand how the family came to be in its present position. The following sample rationale could be used in an initial interview to develop the contract.

> Listening to your account of the problem that brings you here, I have been impressed by your sincere desire to solve it. In spite of your best efforts, things have not changed, and you seem to be stuck. When people try as hard as you have to solve a problem, but to no avail, there is usually something missing in their understanding of what the problem is. I can usually help people solve this puzzle by reviewing the experiences they have been through together, each person's point of view, and how they have come to this point. By looking at the big picture of their life, we are able to discover some new direction that proves successful. I would like to propose a few sessions in which you give me the chance to review important experiences with you. Then, we can see what solutions will best fit for you in view of your unique experience.

For couples and families, the usual starting point for a timeline is the point at which the couple first meets, with progression from left to right through courtship to the birth of each child, and so on. For individuals, the usual starting point is at birth, unless the presenting problem is child-oriented or work-related, in which case the timeline may start at some significant marker in the sequence of a person's life—college graduation, divorce or marriage, or some other important change. To illustrate how the timeline can be integrated with genograms and circular questions, the following case study will provide an integration of the assessment process.

The Wilsons

The Wilsons were a white, middle-class family who sought family therapy after their son, Bob, 15, was caught smoking at school twice and was subsequently dropped from the basketball squad at school. Bob's parents were John, 42, and Kristin, 39. He also had a sister, Sue, 14, who attended the first session. John was a hospital social worker and Kristin was a nurse. They had been married for 19 years. Both were raised in small rural communities. They met and married while attending college.

First Session:
Intake and initial interview

Joining process: Therapist uses this information to identify with their particular life-cycle stage.

Defining the problem: Everyone is asked to comment, but the therapist notices that Kristin is the most verbal and Bob is the least verbal during this stage of the process.

During the initial intake, the family therapist asked both parents about themselves, their place of work, and their level of education. The children were asked for their ages, dates of birth, and year in school.

After some initial small talk, the therapist asked, "What brings you here?" The family responded with various accounts of Bob's recent problems at school and how each family member felt about the recent progression of events. He was caught smoking at school twice, was suspended for three days, and was dropped from the basketball team after playing in the first two games. John and Kristin expressed their concern and stated that they wished Bob would "open up."

Tracking interactional sequences: How did you find out about Bob's smoking?
What did you do when you found out?
Bob, what did you do when your Mother confronted you?
Sue, where were you and what were you doing while all this was going on?
John, how did you find out and what did you do?

With the focus upon present events, the therapist investigated interactional patterns of the family as the problem developed. Information came forth about Bob's tendency to withdraw, John's tendency to lecture, Kristin's tendency to interrogate, and Sue's tendency to stay busy when there is conflict.

Precipitating events: Attention is shifted away from the topic of "What did Bob do?" (present-oriented) to the topic of "What has been happening to Bob?" (recent past). This shift diminishes his shame and provides a developmental perspective on how problems evolve over time from a sequence of events.

Since Bob appeared reserved and uncomfortable during this part of the discussion, the therapist decided to engage him in conversation, which might be less threatening. "It seems unusual for a guy of 15 to already be starting on the basketball team. How were you able to do this?" At this point, Bob opened up and told the story of how the coaches noticed his unusual height and coordination while he was still in middle school. Anxious to have him, they began to encourage him to try out for the team the summer before he started high school. He began attending practices and easily made the team. However, as the season approached, he began to feel bad, although he couldn't explain why. His parents also stated that they did not understand why he would be feeling bad when things seemed to be going so well. However, they believed that he had negative feelings about himself and quoted him as saying, "Things don't matter. I wish I could fry my brains out."

Goals: All members are able to agree on the same goals. This is acknowledged by the therapist as a strength.

The therapist asked what the family would like to see happen. The parents stated their goals for therapy as wanting Bob to feel better about himself and wanting to improve communication and intimacy in the family. Bob and Sue both agreed that these would be good goals.

Contract: Since the family's goals are abstract (intimacy and communication) at this point, rather than concrete behavior goals, the therapist suggests an interim process goal of exploration, which will produce more concrete goals to work on during the intervention stage.

At this point, the family therapist responded to the family's story by describing the assessment process and clarifying expectations for change: "It sounds as if all of you care about each other and want to solve the puzzle of how to help Bob. It also sounds as if no one is certain about what the real problem might be. In view of this, one possible direction would be to take a couple of sessions to explore the problem in greater detail. Once we have a definition of the problem that we all feel comfortable with, our efforts at developing solutions will be more effective and we can move on to developing a plan of action. How does that sound as a starting place?" The family agreed to a plan for three assessment sessions, after which subsequent sessions would be devoted to developing a plan for helping Bob.

Data-gathering phase (genogram): The family is invited to shift their attention away from the immediate problem in the present to a discussion

With time left in the first interview, the therapist explained that it would be helpful to understand the family relationships most important to them as a

about general family relationships and extended-family influences.

group and how grandparents may have solved similar problems. Drawing a genogram with John and Kristin's marriage as the central relationship, the therapist proceeded to sketch a skeleton genogram that included Bob and Sue as the youngest generation and both sides of the extended family. Listing only the names, ages, deaths, and hometowns of the parents, the therapist had time afterward to ask circular questions regarding individual differences in the nuclear family and how the parents would describe their experience in their own families of origin (see Figure 7.1).

How are family members different from each other?

John is quiet; Kristin is more expressive, suggesting a possible complementary marital relationship. She stated, "We have a hard time expressing gut feelings." Bob watches a lot of TV and stays home more. Sue is immersed in school activities and homework.

What was each parent's experience in his or her family of origin?

Kristin expressed regret that her own family did not care more about her, and told the story from her younger years of how her family, hard-working farmers, never came to see her perform when she was a cheerleader.

John described his family as very controlling of him, and recounted an important experience: his decision to finally assert himself with his parents and change majors in college. As Kristin and John shared their experience, Bob expressed surprise at his father's account of standing up to the grandparents. Bob and Sue described their grandparents on both sides as "old fashioned." John also explained how he had been a "98-pound weakling" as a youth and therefore couldn't understand why Bob was not enjoying his enviable athletic ability; John would have given anything to have had the height and strength that Bob has. At this point, Bob was silent, eyes looking at the floor.

At the end of the session, the family therapist thanked them for their openness in sharing information about their family and indicated that the next session would be an opportunity to explore the development of their family and what events might be related to Bob's current feelings.

Second Session:
Tracking longitudinal sequences.

In this session, the family therapist constructed a timeline of the family's life together over the 19 years since John and Kristin married. The rationale provided was that Bob's difficulties could possibly be related to various changes —recent or past—that may have affected him in ways no one was aware of. Thus, it would be helpful to the therapist if the family could describe the various transitions they had been through together.

What does the family consider to be the major changes that they have experienced together in the areas of personal development, job experience, and family roles?

The timeline on the Wilson family began with their marriage in 1967 and continued to the time of their family therapy experience in 1986. When they married, John had recently graduated with a Master's degree in social work (M.S.W.). Kristin graduated with her nursing degree in 1970; Bob was born in 1971, Sue in 1972. Kristin reminisced about Bob's early accomplishments and how she enjoyed his first steps of independence and progress. The parents reported success as a beginning young family: They were happy with each other, John's work, and their young children.

From 1972 to 1974, there was some stress in the family. Sue developed a serious fever as a baby; Bob broke his arm when he fell off his bicycle; and Kristin began to work part time so they could buy their first home. The family

The horizontal timeline is divided into major time periods and labeled as the family discusses each stage (e.g., 1980: relocation). One-word descriptions note important issues as the chart moves from left to right, from past to present (see words in bold). Family members may be included by placing parents' experience above the line (e.g., Dad: depression) and children's experience below the line (e.g., Bob: verbally abused). As the timeline progresses toward present-day concerns, the therapist uses the visual diagram to stimulate a reflection and reconceptualization of the problem as developmental-interactional in nature.

weathered these challenges through hard work and sacrifice.

*In **1980**, John got a better job offer, and they contemplated a major **relocation**. Soon, they were reestablishing themselves in a new city, with new jobs and a new school for the children. From this time forward, life proved more **difficult**. John's job required many more hours, and he was assigned patients with terminal illnesses. In addition, the salary increase he was promised after three months was put on hold because of the financial instability of the hospital. He became depressed and sought individual counseling for his **depression**. After two years, rumors were prevalent about possible mergers, layoffs, and terminations because of the hospital's continued financial difficulties. John reported that his main way of coping was to tell himself that things would get better if he could only **work harder** and get a promotion. He found himself trying harder, but with **no results**.*

*In the meantime, Kristin was hired at a different hospital and was assigned to a critical care ward. She worked with patients whose conditions were listed as serious or critical. Bob remembered his mother talking about her work and how anxious she felt about the **stresses** there, but was completely unaware of his father's depression. Sue also indicated that she was unaware of her father's depression.*

*Kristin reported that John talked a great deal to her about his depression, to the point that she remarked, "I wish someone would **worry about me** once in a while."*

In the last four years, the children had become more involved in school activities: Bob played hockey and basketball in middle school and

Sue developed her hobbies and musical abilities. The parents stated that time spent with the children during this stage was usually after dinner and on some weekends when Kristin was not working.

*John and Kristin also said that their time together was usually when the children were busy or early in the morning. It had been years since they had scheduled any **regular time** for themselves.*

What were the main differences between various life-cycle stages for this family?

The therapist notes nonverbal clues as to the impact of the assessment process on the family: Bob becomes more verbal and involved.

*Asked how their past had been different, all the family members agreed that the period before 1980 had been much happier for everyone. Bob was very active in this discussion, reminiscing that his **Dad** had been **more involved** with the family during those days. He also defended John in some surprising ways, given the fact that he had a great aversion to his father's lectures. The family agreed that Kristin was more involved with the children during the week, and John was home on the weekends but uninvolved with the children while Kristin worked.*

The therapist uses the assessment process to identify and emphasize family strengths, while externalizing the problem away from Bob: Life got hard. Patients at the hospital were struggling with life-and-death issues, and everyone at home began to feel the effects of each parent's stress. Assessment begins to overlap with intervention.

The therapist ended the session by commenting extensively on the life-cycle transitions, reflecting back for this family a picture of themselves that included many successes; their closeness and caring as a family; the unexpected stresses after 1980; and the unintended consequences of these stresses as John's depression and Kristin's anxiety began to shape family interactions.

Third Session:
A return to the presenting problem, with an exploration of cultural issues, interaction patterns, family structure, and the meaning of the symptom.

The therapist began with a discussion about Bob's smoking and how he had taken up the practice. It emerged that he had started during the summer that the coaches began recruiting him for the team. When asked about the summer practices, Bob related experiences in which he felt **verbally abused** *by the coaches and thought about quitting. When asked what he thought might have happened if he had quit, Bob said he knew his Dad would have been disappointed. John indicated that he had no idea that Bob was feeling this way.*

Cultural issues, family values: How do the parents feel about smoking, in general?

The parents were emphatically against Bob's smoking. John had smoked earlier in his life and had decided to quit for health reasons. The family was very religious and had firm values about living a temperate life. This was an area where John had frequently lectured to Bob, and there had been many attempts to get Bob to stop smoking.

Family interaction and structure: How did the family handle other issues?

By this time, Bob was much more comfortable discussing his relationship with his parents directly. He complained about how his mother "nagged and interrogated" him about his school work when he came home. He would retreat and go to his room, or become distant by "veging in front of the TV."

Transforming assessment to intervention through reframing.

By the end of the third session, the therapist moved further into formal interventions by beginning to make implicit family process more explicit: "It seems that there are some things going on in the family that have been invisible until now. One is the fact that Bob was struggling and feeling overwhelmed by the coaches, but no one in the family knew. Another is that John has been depressed at work, but only Kristin knew, and she has become overwhelmed by his depression and the stress of her work. Even though Dad envies Bob's size and ability, I wonder if Bob is really more like Dad on the inside, sensitive and caring, which makes it harder to tolerate his competitive relationship with the coaches. At the risk of being called a quitter at school and disappointing Dad at home, maybe getting caught smoking was the best way for him to change the direction of his life. By the same token, it sounds like Kristin has needed more support than she has been able to get in the family, and she has dealt with her struggle by trying to get Bob to do things that would be more helpful to her. When we meet next time, I would like to get your reactions to these ideas and see if you're ready to develop a plan of action for meeting your goals."

The formal assessment for which the family had contracted concluded with the third session. As the process unfolded, it became an opportunity for the family to shift their focus from the immediate intensity of the presenting problem to a more reflective focus on their life together. In addition, the therapist was able to continue the joining process, to identify strengths, and to experiment with reframing in order to determine the clients' cognitive flexibility. The degree to which they were open to the reframing became information used in developing a treatment plan. Would direct or indirect interventions be more useful with this family? Would perceptual change, behavioral change, or both be needed for this family to achieve their goals?

In order to adopt a pragmatic approach, the beginning clinician must understand something about how different hypotheses relate to the change process. In the case of the Wilsons, the therapist made the following tentative hypotheses:

Gender-Related
1. Bob may have felt trapped into playing basketball by the expectations of the coaches and his father. His lack of self-esteem may be related to interactions with other males and resulting feelings of inadequacy.
2. Bob's mother may also have expectations of him that he perceives as overwhelming.
3. Since Kristin stated, "I wish someone would worry about me once in a while," she may be a catalyst for change in the area of gender patterns, if her feelings are a manifestation of disempowerment in her marriage.

Culture-Related
4. The Wilsons both come from rural, religious backgrounds. Conformity to parental authority is expected. Bob may be breaking with tradition and feeling the effects of parental disapproval; however, both parents seem firm about adherence to family traditions.
5. Both parents have jobs in the helping professions. They believe in the values of respect, empathy, and promoting self-esteem within their family. These values may become catalysts for change in their relationship with Bob.

Intergenerational

6. Bob's grandparents have not been resources for this family. Both parents report a lack of closeness with their families of origin. Lingering conflict over their own disengagement may make it difficult for them to be comfortable with Bob's individuation.

7. John's adolescent image of himself as a 98-pound weakling may prevent him from empathizing with his son, and may thus contribute to Bob's discouragement. The pain that John still experiences over his inadequacies as a youth may become a catalyst for resolving personal beliefs that complicate his relationship with Bob.

8. There are cross-generational similarities in the temperament of Kristin and Sue, John and Bob. Perhaps Bob's low self-esteem is related to John's style of coping.

Life-Cycle

9. The family successfully completed early stages of development but experienced overwhelming discomfort after 1980 as a result of job stress that precipitated a change in life-style and a significant sense of disengagement among all members. Bob's low self-esteem may be a consequence of parental stress which leaves them no energy to address the tasks of families with adolescents and prevents the family from grieving their losses since 1980.

Family Structure

10. There may be a complementarity in the marital and parental subsystem that leaves Kristin overfunctioning for John and Bob but underfunctioning for herself. Her sense of overresponsibility for Bob may be the force behind her "interrogations" of Bob that leave him feeling criticized and suffocated. John's underinvolvement may leave Bob feeling abandoned.

11. The interaction pattern that surrounds Bob's depression usually runs as follows: Bob comes home from school, Mother becomes involved by questioning Bob's homework, Bob retreats, Father becomes involved by lecturing, Bob retreats, Sue returns from school activities, and the family focuses on her accomplishments.

Individual Development

12. Bob is different from his father athletically, but similar to John in temperament. His aversion to the subculture of male competition could be looked upon as a strength and as a way in which he is loyal to his father's humanitarian values.

13. Bob's intent is to please his father. However, he feels abused by coaching strategies, embarrassed with his friends, and misunderstood within his family. Seen in this context, his actions (smoking and withdrawal) could be regarded as resources, in that they served to help him out of his dilemmas at school with the coaches and at home with his mother and father.

Since some of the hypotheses were related to resources for change and some were not, it is appropriate to ask which of these hypotheses will fit best with the family's goals. The presenting problem was Bob, who was caught smoking and suspended from the basketball team. The parents stated that they wished Bob would open up and discuss his problems. Because of the parents' background (that is, their expectation of conformity to parental authority) and disengagement from their family of origin, the therapist might hypothesize that they do not have a model for encouraging Bob to open up. This may be exacerbated by the pain that the father still carries from his adolescence. Acting on this hypothesis, the therapist might explore the parents' family of origin, to understand how the past gets played out in the present. What current belief systems and new frames of meaning from the culture and family of origin can the therapist find to assist the Wilsons in resolving the problem? On the other hand, the therapist may also hypothesize that unrealistic gender expectations are contributing to the problem. This might lead the therapist to emphasize Kristin's desire to get help as a strength or to explore alternative ways in which Bob can meet his masculine needs or his mother's expectations.

The therapist may also view Bob's problem as a metaphor for the parents' job stress and may wish to explore some alternative ways to cope with that stress; or the therapist may hypothesize that the problem is structural and that if Kristin curbed her impulse to be helpful, Bob could learn to be more responsible; or it may be that Mr. and Mrs. Wilson need to work together and help Bob become more responsible. The therapist must also consider individual strengths—such as Bob's loyalty to his father and internal resources—when choosing an intervention.

Knowing the parents' stated goals for therapy—wanting Bob to feel better about himself and wanting to improve communication and intimacy in the family—the therapist may review the list of hypotheses and see which ones might relate to their stated goal. Hypotheses 3, 5, 7, 12, and 13 all recognize potential resources and strengths that might lead to change. Since intimacy and communication are often blocked by problematic interactional sequences, the therapist used hypotheses 3, 5, and 6 to motivate the family to accept some tasks that would indirectly address hypotheses 10 and 11. By appealing to the parents' strengths and good intentions, the therapist made an assignment for Kristin to quit asking Bob about his homework at any time during a two-week experiment. In the meantime, Bob could decide in the next two weeks what he would initiate and talk about on his own regarding his progress in school. In addition, the parents were asked to find one night a week that was exclusively reserved for themselves and to set aside time in which Kristin was given a chance to vent her feelings and John would be willing to do more listening to her.

In addition, the therapist decided to address hypotheses 12 and 13 directly by reframing Bob's behavior, the reason for his smoking, the dilemma he had found himself in, and the strength that he had been exhibiting. After two weeks, the family reported Bob's depression was lifting and he and Kristin had had no conflicted encounters about homework. He had successfully initiated conversation on his own about school progress, and Kristin was relieved and satisfied with this. The family desired to continue with the current experiment and were also asked to add another dimension to their plan: John was asked to find some time to talk with Bob about how John felt as a young man when he began smoking himself. He was to share his memory of his feelings toward parents, peers, and others at the time he started smoking. Then he was to also share his feelings and thoughts during the time when, as an older man, he had decided to quit smoking on his own. The parents agreed to maintain their plan and asked if they could attend the next session alone. During this session (the sixth), they reported continuing improvement in their relationship with Bob and used the time to discuss their own relationship—the imbalance and disempowerment that Kristin had been feeling and ways that they as a couple could restructure their lives for improved satisfaction.

Sluzki (1992) has commented that all family therapy models share certain assessment procedures that make them effective in facilitating change. He suggests that all models gather certain information about the family in the form of stories that families relate to the therapist. Regardless of whether the therapist's theme is life-cycle, intergenerational relationships, or nuclear family structure, the therapist takes the family's story and begins to evolve an alternative story:

> In order for new stories . . . to consolidate themselves in the therapeutic conversation, they must evolve from and yet contain elements of the old, "familiar" stories. The transformed stories are usually a recombination of the components of the old story to which new elements—characters, plot, logic, moral order—have been introduced either by the therapist, by the patient, or by the family as a result of, for example, circular questioning, and they are consolidated by all the participants throughout the therapeutic conversation. (p. 220)

Thus, it is possible that any assessment from any model of family therapy is a plausible foundation for the remainder of the change process. In the case of the Wilsons, the next three sessions involved the development of the plan and its follow-up. The family reported success in accomplishing their goals; there were no further school problems with Bob. They terminated after six sessions. An analysis of how change actually occurred in this case must take into consideration the impact of the structured assessment process and the in-session interventions embedded in the questions and dialogue that took place during the genogram and through tracking their longitudinal sequences. Also included in the change process were the tasks and assignments that helped the family modify their behavior between sessions. The assessment was an opportunity for the family to tell their story and have an audience in the form of the therapist, who could reflect back their story with only slight modifications (through reframing, for example). The intervention stage was an opportunity for behavior change to start and, if successful, stabilize during the last weeks of the treatment period.

The process evolved through several stages, each with its own sense of mystery as to what the family would bring to it. With experience, the practitioner can develop a sense of timing and rhythm in being able to move comfortably from one stage to the next. The following chapter will address the macroprocess of treatment planning, which will help the beginning family therapist put the process of therapy in each particular case into a larger perspective.

Part Three

TREATMENT
SKILLS

Chapter Eight

Developing a Treatment Plan

Developing Goals
>Prioritizing Areas of Change
>Making Goals Concrete and Specific
>Developing Goals from Family Strengths
>Building on Existing Strengths

Involving Family Members
>Overcoming Initial Resistances
>Connecting with Family Members

Involving the Network
>Interview Strategies
>Developing a Collaboration Team
>Guidelines for the Collaboration Team Interview
>Obstacles to Collaboration

Choosing Interventions

T reatment plans should be based on assessment data for the family. Each treatment plan should be individualized and should fit the unique charac- teristics of the family and interactive culture. For example, in one family where there is parent-child conflict, the treatment plan might call for conflict management skills. In another family with a similar problem, but more hostility, the plan might call for separate sessions with the parent and child, to establish trust. Sometimes a treatment plan can be presented in the initial contract for service. In those cases, clients already have their problem defined in concrete, behavioral terms, and the process of problem resolution is straightforward. For example, if the family is seeking a consultation in order to decide on a strategy for the long-term care of an elderly parent, the goal may be to decide who will be responsible for which tasks, after some psychoeducational sessions regarding the impact of long-term care on families. This direction could be decided upon in the initial session and described to the family as part of the therapeutic contract. In another case, parents may be seeking help for the behavioral problems of their daughter. Their goal may be for her to stop fighting with other children on the playground at school. A common treatment plan for such a presenting problem would be to explore the relationships between the family and the school, between the daughter and the playground group, and between the individual family members. The family therapist, the family, and the school might form a collabo- rative team. Then the family therapist could facilitate cooperation among all parties in developing corrective strategies. This direction might also be formu- lated in the initial session and suggested to the family for their consideration during the contracting stage of that session.

Regardless of the complexity of the case, most treatment plans involve some combination of the elements illustrated in these examples. First, goals are developed from assessment data to fit each unique situation. Second, the family and larger network are considered as potential participants. Third, interventions that fit the family's developmental level and the clinician's skill level are chosen, either spontaneously or deliberately. This chapter will review each of these elements of treatment planning.

Developing Goals

In most cases, client goals begin as abstract desires (for example, "I want help dealing with my low self-esteem" or, "We want to communicate better"). The family therapist helps the family to clarify such desires until behavioral and perceptual elements of the problem are identified as specific goals ("I want to be able to go to a party and have something interesting to say" or, "When we discuss finances, we'll be able to resolve the conflict to our satisfaction"). The treatment plan may be described as including the assessment process, which clarifies the nature of the problem and a subsequent plan of action, or as consisting only of the sequence of interventions set in motion as a result of the assessment process. In either case, the treatment plan should address the family's goals and hypotheses generated during the assessment process. A good treatment plan requires the therapist to analyze hypotheses in order to (1) prioritize areas of change; (2) make goals concrete and specific; (3) build on existing strengths.

Prioritizing Areas of Change

One of the greatest dilemmas a therapist faces is knowing where to start treatment. Where the intervention begins is often determined by the therapist's own theoretical framework. The structural family therapist might intervene by developing an interactional relationship with the family. The therapist probes both to elicit information about the problem and to realign the organization of the family. The strategic family therapist, on the other hand, might intervene through messages or directives. Directives require the client to respond or behave in a specific way. Likewise, the intergenerational therapist attempts to maintain objectivity from the outset by (1) asking "thinking" questions rather than "feeling" questions and (2) avoiding triangulation by asking each family member to speak to the therapist rather than to each other. The experiential family therapist, on the other hand, focuses more on the personhood of the therapist and how to intervene with the use of self to accomplish the therapeutic goal. When developing a treatment plan, we suggest that beginning practitioners avoid interventions that are model-specific until after the family's goals have been prioritized and clarified.

If the family presents several problem areas, the beginning therapist must begin to set priorities for treatment. Four criteria are critical in making this determination. The **first criterion** is, Which problem is of most immediate importance to the family? The family must be asked to select the problem of greatest concern to them. For example, a couple may want to improve their marital relationship; a mother may want to get along better with her daughter; or two parents may need support in taking care of their infant. The therapist then must ask, "Which problem is most pressing to you?" or, "Which problem must you solve now?" Alternatively, the therapist might say, "So, the first issue we need to resolve is _____." Unless the therapist has reasons for choosing another area to change, the family is told that the one selected will be addressed initially.

In many cases, additional criteria must be considered in prioritizing areas of change. The **second criterion** is, Which problem has the greatest negative consequence if not handled immediately? While a family member may feel that a specific problem is of greatest concern to her (for example, loss of friends), another problem may have greater negative consequence (for example, loss of job or marriage breakup). A young adult may feel he needs to get along better with others but, unless he stops drinking, his health and safety are at risk. The therapist might ask the young adult what would happen if the drinking problem was not resolved. In this case, the consequences seem more severe for drinking than for lack of friends, thus warranting more immediate intervention.

By examining what has happened in the past with the same people under similar conditions, the therapist can better predict the consequences of the problem and weigh it accordingly. The therapist may ask, "What might happen if this problem is not resolved?" or, "What would likely happen to you if _____ occurred?" Once this is determined, the **third criterion** comes into play: Which problem can be corrected most easily, considering the resources and constraints? What forces (people, situations) stand in the way of problem resolution? What resources exist that could help solve the problem? For example, a mother who feels trapped by her children may list going to school to complete an advanced degree as a goal. If lack of money for a babysitter and her husband's resistance are obstacles, however, the therapist might ask, "What are some things that might prevent this problem from being solved?" and, "What are some things that will help you resolve the problem?"

Finally, the **fourth criterion** for prioritizing change is, Which problems require handling before other problems can be solved? For example, it makes little sense to work on improving the marriage if both spouses are abusing alcohol. Likewise, before parents can control their children, they must learn to work cooperatively. The therapist might ask what would happen if the problem were solved. Would the couple improve their marriage? Would they do a better job parenting their children?

In some cases, the therapist may wish to be more precise in determining the relative importance of each goal. Utilizing family goal recording, Fleuridas, Rosenthal, Leigh, and Leigh (1990) weigh each goal according to its relative importance to the family. They state:

> Often a family claims that the target complaint (for example, Mom's alcoholism or Dad's abuse) is the primary concern and far outweighs the other goal areas. When such a preference is acknowledged, the therapist proceeds by asking the family if the target area is twice or three times as important as the other goal areas (in that subsystem unit). Through this process of questioning, approximate weights of importance can be assigned to each subsystem unit (the sum of the subsystems' weights = 100%). (p. 394)

Family goal recording permits the therapist to evaluate change in the presenting concerns of couples and families (see Chapter Eleven).

Making Goals Concrete and Specific

In the problem definition stage, the therapist helps family members to decide what they want changed. For example, the therapist might begin by asking, "How would you like things to be different in this family?" or, "What is it that you would like your son to be doing instead?" The responses eventually become goal behaviors ("If your husband doesn't pay attention to you, how would you like him to show that he is paying attention?"). Later, when tracking the interactional sequence that is maintaining the problem, the therapist might say, "And then he yells at you. What would you like him to do instead of that?" or, "It sounds like when he talks to you that way you get angry and threaten him. How could he talk to you differently at that moment so you don't get angry with him?" Often, when tracking the interactional sequence, the therapist is asking family members to describe how they would like another family member to respond differently within the sequence of behavior preceding or following the identified problem. In earlier phases of the interview, the clinician is requesting only that family members give a general statement of what they want to be different. Later, in this portion of the interview, the therapist can help family members become more specific in formulating observable goals.

Goals should be stated clearly so that everyone can agree when the goal has been reached. For example, if parents report that they want their child "to pay attention," then the therapist must question the parent to determine what the child will be doing "to pay attention." Likewise, labels such as "unhappiness" and "anger" must be stated in such a way that they can be resolved.

The following suggestions represent several different ways to help family members describe changes (goals) in more observable terms:

1. *Ask each family member to describe how he or she would like things to be different.* The therapist might ask, "What changes would you like to see in this family?" or, "How would you like things to be different?"
2. *Ask family members to describe changes in positive rather than negative terms.* The therapist might comment, "I know you don't like the way your son said that. How would you like him to say it?"
3. *Ask family members to be specific about what they want changed.* The therapist might ask a question such as those that follow: "What do you mean by _____?" "What would your son be doing to show you that he can be trusted?" "How would you know that your mother cares about you?" "What would be one way he could help you?" "How would she show you that she has an improved self-concept?"

The therapist may often establish intermediate goals, each of which represents a step toward the final goal. This process helps make the family's problem more manageable. Consider a mother who cannot get her 15-year-old son to come home on time. The family lives in the grandmother's home. The grandmother complains that her daughter (the mother) doesn't know how to handle the son. The grandmother and mother argue over who should be in charge of the boy. The boy is out of control; however, the intermediate goal might be to have mother and grandmother agree on how the mother will manage her son's behavior. The grandmother also may need to become involved in some outside activities. Once these intermediate goals have been reached, the therapist could focus on the final goal—how the mother (and grandmother, if necessary) would get her son to come home at the designated time.

Once the therapist and family have agreed on the goal, the next step is to specify conditions under which the goal behavior will occur. The conditions of the desired behavior often will be interactionally based; that is, it may be that a mother needs to set limits with her son in the father's presence. The conditions under which the behavior is to occur indicate with whom and where the behavior is to take place. If family members are to plan an activity, the conditions state who will be present and where the activity will occur.

Once the goal has been specified in concrete terms, an acceptable level of performance must be established. This criterion specifies how well and how often the behavior is to be performed. For example, "to comply with parental requests" is not very useful as an indicator of successful performance. However, if the goal is restated as "complying with household parental requests 80% of the time and never breaking curfew," then the therapist, family, and others will know when the goal has been reached. This helps ensure that observers (probation officers, teachers, or others) will agree whether the goal has been met.

In determining how much change is needed, it is essential to specify how family members are currently behaving. This provides some standard by which to measure the family members' progress toward their individual goals and to determine the amount of learning needed by the family members to achieve the change they want. The amount of change agreed upon should be set low enough to ensure success; that is, the initial goals must be achievable. As a general rule, it is better to set the level of initial change too low rather than too high. If the criterion level is too high, the desired behavior often will not occur. Once an intermediate goal has been accomplished, it is possible to specify new changes that are now more achievable.

In defining the problem, family members are asked to describe changes that they would like to see in the family. These changes eventually are refined until they can be stated in the form of manageable and measurable goals. When therapists help family members specify measurable goals, they are making a therapeutic contract with the family to ensure a clear understanding of what everyone expects and how long it might take to reach the goals.

Developing Goals from Family Strengths

Goal setting should evolve out of family strengths rather than weaknesses. Focusing on the family's deficits without considering their strengths makes it difficult to establish a relationship where both the therapist and the family can be optimistic about change. Emphasizing strengths helps alter the family's self-image and gives family members hope that their goals can be attained.

In establishing goals based on strengths, the therapist and family work in partnership. Instead of selecting goals for the family, the therapist listens to what the family would like changed and encourages them to express what they would like to be different. Family members often feel hopeless; thus, it is important to put them in charge of deciding on changes (goals). In some cases, the family's goals may be different from those of the therapist. A parent may wish to take care of a legal problem or illness, whereas the therapist may be concerned about the parent's relationship with the children. Parents often feel overwhelmed because they have multiple problems. The therapist should respond to the family's concern around these basic needs before dealing with higher-order needs such as parent-child relationships.

The therapist must interpret the family's definition of the problem in a different way, to give it new meaning. This new interpretation helps the family get in touch with their own strengths. Sometimes this is referred to as reframing the problem. Such an intervention may have a paradoxical effect. When a mother says, "I can't get him to do anything. He won't pay any attention to me," the therapist helps the mother to understand that her "caring" sometimes makes it difficult for her to set firm limits. When she perceives herself not as "weak" but as caring, she has a new way of thinking about the problem, so that it can be resolved. Paradoxically, the therapist then can help her to expand her sense of caring to include additional behaviors.

Another approach to the same problem might be to help the mother break down "paying attention" into small goals that are attainable. The therapist might start by asking, "What is something your son does when he is paying attention?" Then the goal is to increase something that is already happening to a small extent (O'Hanlon & Weiner-Davis, 1989). When the therapist creates an environment based on strengths, family members are more likely to set goals that can be met successfully.

If therapists start treatment according to these assumptions, they will focus on those areas that are working. The therapist will want to start by looking for small positive changes before examining bigger changes. This can be done by focusing on those aspects of the family that seem most changeable. The therapist might ask, "What would be a small sign that things are changing?" or, "What might be one thing you could do to change _____?" or, "What are some things you could do now to handle _____?" When family members are able to make small positive changes, they are more hopeful about handling bigger changes (O'Hanlon & Weiner-Davis, 1989).

Building on Existing Strengths

Family members who are overwhelmed by difficulties often lose touch with their strengths. In that case, a good therapist helps them to identify problem-solving strengths. This approach allows the family members to be more hopeful, to alter their view of themselves, and to feel more optimistic about change.

The following interview strategies are helpful in identifying strengths:

- *Emphasize positive statements reported by family members* (for example, "My mother listens to me when I have a problem"). It is also important to observe behaviors that reflect sensitivity, appreciation, or cooperation between family members.
- *Encourage family members to share their story about themselves.* The therapist should pay particular attention to those aspects of their story that reveal how the family has coped successfully with problems.
- *Note family interactions that reflect strengths and competency* (for example, "I like the way you help your daughter to find her own answers to the problem"). Underscoring positive family interactions helps the therapist to identify other strengths and competencies.
- *Emphasize those times that family members enjoy together.* What are they doing? What makes it enjoyable? These questions offer opportunities to discuss strengths and capabilities.

- *Reframe problems or negative statements in a more positive way* (for example, "Your anger shows how much you care about him"). A therapist reframes the problem by changing the conceptual or emotional viewpoint, so as to change the meaning of the problem without changing the facts. The situation doesn't change, but the interpretation does.
- *Emphasize the things that families do well.* All families have areas of strengths (such as patience, skills, and coping behavior). By asking questions, the therapist can learn how families utilize these strengths to solve problems (for example, "What works best with your child? Tell me about the times you were able to get him to _____. What did you do? How were you able to get him to _____? What does that say about your ability to get him to do that in the future?").

Eliciting family strengths will help the clinician to understand how families cope with problems, as well as how they promote growth and development.

These principles of treatment planning lay a foundation such as to maximize the effectiveness of any family therapy model that the clinician might prefer. This foundation is built upon the following assumptions: (1) There are several potentially effective ways to begin treatment; (2) families have resources and strengths to resolve problems; (3) families often are aware of alternative ways to alter a problem; (4) families will be more likely to implement a solution to the problem if they suggest it. If further treatment planning indicates family or network involvement, the family therapist must be prepared to direct the process in a manner such as to maintain the foundation that is being built.

Involving Family Members

When a family member first calls a therapist, the call can be regarded as an individual request for help and an indicator of stress in the family. The clinician must attempt to gather information that reflects the effects of the problem on other family members and the family's view of the problem. If made aware of relational information about the problem during intake, the individual will be more likely to understand why all family members should be present during therapy. Therapists should request the family's help in solving the problem.

In presenting a rationale for involving all family members, Garfield (1981) makes the following suggestions:

> When a family member begins to describe his problem, the therapist should listen sympathetically. He should also pay attention to the interactional aspects of the problem. For example, if a husband says, "I'm not getting along with my wife," or "My wife and I are having a terrible problem with our teenage daughter," or even "I've been awfully depressed and haven't discussed this with anyone in my family," he is already introducing interpersonal elements of the problem. The therapist may take note of this issue and return to it later when he explains the importance of including the other family mem-

bers in the evaluation. If the person describes the problem in personal terms, e.g. "I've been suffering from severe headaches and my family doctor tells me it's my nerves," the therapist may inquire if anyone in the house is aware of this problem and how they have responded to it. This reframes the problem in interactional terms, and allows the therapist to find out who else lives in the house and how they may be involved in the problem. (p. 6)

Therapists and intake workers should listen closely to how the caller describes the problem. For example, a wife may say, "We just don't communicate" or, "We don't get along." In some cases a parent may describe the problem in triangular terms: "She won't listen to us" or, "He minds everyone but me." In such cases the therapist should clarify to whom the caller is referring, and their relationship to the problem (see Chapter Four). Whatever the request for help, all family members who are related to the problem should be asked to attend the initial session.

Overcoming Initial Resistances

Family members may often be resistant to attending therapy sessions, especially if they feel blame or responsibility for the problem. In particular, fathers and husbands characteristically have been reluctant to discuss matters that they regard as private with someone outside the family. These problems become more deep-seated when the wife protects her husband ("My husband would never talk to a therapist" or, "He doesn't believe in counseling").

The beginning therapist must understand the protective nature of these responses and deal with them in a supportive manner. The real issue here seems to be *who* is responsible for bringing reluctant family members to therapy and *how* this might be accomplished. Some therapists (Minuchin, 1984) refuse to see the family unless all members are present. This obviously puts pressure on the family member to get the entire family to therapy. However, this tactic may backfire: The family member may drop out of therapy. Moreover, providing therapy only if the entire family is in attendance may be inconsistent with the policies at many mental health centers or family-service agencies.

Family members' reluctance to attend therapy often reflects the systemic nature of the problem. In this case, the therapist might first challenge the caller's belief system by saying, "I think you may be underestimating your husband" or, "What makes you think he doesn't want to share his feelings?" Sometimes, the therapist can point out the benefits of therapy by saying, "It might be a relief for him to talk about this with someone else" or, "It might be helpful if he heard what is really bothering you" or, "I think your kids would learn to share their feelings if they were here."

Beginning family therapists or students should consult with their supervisors to assess the motivational level of family members who make initial contacts (Nichols & Everett, 1988). What is the role of these individuals in the family system? Do they in fact want other family members to be present? Important information can often be gained by discussing what would happen if the therapist were to take on the responsibility of persuading reluctant members to attend therapy. The practitioner must pay attention to the individual's feelings, and address each area of discomfort with a plan such that the proposed conjoint session could avoid the client's worst fears (for example, "I'm afraid you will side with my husband against me"). However, if therapists do decide to make contact with other family members, they are taking responsibility away from the family. The authors believe that this should be attempted only when all efforts by family members have failed.

At that point, a therapeutic strategy for communicating with the reluctant family member should be discussed. When the absent spouse is uncooperative, the therapist might attempt to focus therapeutic efforts on the cooperating spouse. This procedure is often adopted in cases of substance abuse. David Treadway (1989) elaborates for the case where the husband is the reluctant partner:

> The other way I elicit the husband's cooperation is by asking him if he cares about his wife's anxiety and distress and if he would like to be helpful to her. This defines my work as help to her rather than an attempt to change him. I want him to take the position of aiding her in getting help with her part of the problem. Many drinkers will go along with this idea, because at least for the moment it takes the heat off them. For once their wives are being challenged about their own behavior. Anticipating and blocking the drinker's reactivity are essential to effective intervention with the spouse. (p. 40)

The strategy helps the therapist gradually to involve the resistant family member in therapy.

In the final analysis, the therapist must decide what to do in the event that not all the members of the family make their scheduled appointments. Many family therapists will meet with whomever attends the sessions. These therapists believe that the family system can change by working with one member of the system (O'Hanlon & Weiner-Davis, 1989). However, when the entire family attends the initial session, the therapist can better anticipate the effect of individual changes on the whole system. Additionally, the therapist will want to consult with the family about treatment for individuals, in order to help other family members cope and anticipate any changes in a positive way.

Connecting with Family Members

If family therapists are to be effective in this context, they must connect with the family. Connecting is both an attitude and a skill. To connect with the family, the therapist must convey acceptance of family members and respect for their way of seeing and doing things. It is critical to validate each family member and acknowledge his or her experience and actions. The therapist must let family members know that they are understood and their views are important. Family members must be encouraged to express themselves and to believe that their feelings and views are normal.

The therapist can join with family members in the following ways:

1. *Greet each member of the family by name.*
2. *Make friendly contact with each member.* The therapist asks the individual members what they do and where they live; shares information about the children; and so on.
3. *Respect the family hierarchy.* The therapist must begin with the parents when asking each member about his or her view of the problem.
4. *Acknowledge each member's experience, position, and actions* (for example, "Ms. Jones, I know you have tried your best to help your son. It shows how much you care about him"). Reinforcing or validating a family member will often help other members to view the problem differently.

When Boszormenyi-Nagy (1966) developed the strategy of multidirected partiality, one of his goals was to address the challenge of connecting with each member of the family. In his work, he systematically interacted with each family member, in order to understand each position and to communicate that understanding for each member to ratify or clarify. As he did so, he was able to gain a clear picture as to what each member thought about the presenting problem and what issues might become obstacles to change. In working with entire family groups or networks from the larger community, the skill of connecting with each member of the system will become a trademark of the evolving family therapist.

Involving the Network

The purpose of this section is to assist the therapist in identifying sources of support and resources for the family. Sources of support vary along a continuum beginning with the family unit and moving outward to social organizations. Sources of support might include: (1) nuclear or immediate family (children, parents, household members); (2) relatives (blood and marriage); (3) informal network members (friends, neighbors, co-workers, and others); (4) social organizations (church, clubs, and so on); (5) educational organizations and agencies (family agencies, health organizations, schools, and day-care centers); (6) professional services (such as counseling and early intervention services); and (7) policy-making groups and individuals (agency directors, school boards, county and state governments, and so on) (Dunst, Trivette, & Deal, 1988).

People who can be supportive to the family have many characteristics: (1) they are good at understanding others' needs; (2) they provide unconditional support (that is, they don't demand something in return for their help); (3) they provide a variety of helping activities (emotional support, instrumental support such as getting groceries, repairs, and so on); and (4) their support is a reciprocal process that benefits both the helper and the family members.

Interview Strategies

Strategies that the therapist can employ to identify sources of support and resources in the family are as follows:

- *Ask the family what they have done to resolve the problem.* The following questions are useful in assessing the family's existing network: "Who else is concerned about this problem?" "How do you know they are concerned?" "With whom do you discuss this problem?" "What kind of help do you want from him/her?" "Is that helpful? How so?" "What do they expect from you?" "Is this a person that could be helpful to you here?"

- *Brainstorm a list of persons from human service that are in regular contact with the family.* The therapist might ask, "Are you involved with _____?" or, "Who are you in contact with at this agency?" It is important to identify all human service personnel who come in contact with the family.
- *Identify neighbors or friends who can meet needs that cannot be met by the family.* The therapist might ask, "Is there someone else in your neighborhood who can help you with _____?" or, "Is there anyone who can make sure your child gets to school on _____?"
- *Ask the family if there's anything that would stop them from asking a resource person for help.* A family may be able to identify people that could help them but may be reluctant to ask for their support. Perhaps a family member does not want to be indebted or dependent on others. In other cases, the family may desire to approach others but lack the prerequisite skills to do so. Identifying barriers to utilizing resources will assist the therapist in dealing with these obstacles.

It is usually advisable to draw on informal or natural supports before utilizing professional support and resources. Natural supports are people who are resourceful and empathetic to the family. Professional support personnel should not replace natural supports; rather, they should strengthen these relationships. The natural supports offer opportunities for reciprocal aid, a critical element in empowering families. When family members can repay the support person, it strengthens their sense that they have to give as well as take.

In spite of the benefits of informal supports, the practitioner should also be aware that there are several legitimate barriers to their use:

- Family members may not have the skills to develop relationships with others.
- Family members may be reluctant to ask for help when there are racial or ethnic differences.
- Family members may be unwilling to approach others that they don't know.
- Family members may prefer to rely on themselves and not depend on others.
- Family members may be closed and reluctant to let others know their business.

In such cases, the family must use the therapist for support. When the family can use the therapist as a source of support, they will be more likely to acquire the competencies to obtain other support and resources. As the clinician works toward this end, collaboration with other professionals may also be helpful.

Developing a Collaboration Team

There are several ways to start a collaboration team, as follows.

1. The therapist must develop good relationships with larger systems such as schools, hospitals, and social service agencies. A beginning therapist might call to make an appointment in order to learn more about the organization. In

some cases, it might be helpful for the therapist to offer a free workshop or consultation on special cases.

2. Therapists should provide feedback to referral sources (school counselors, social workers, and so on) about current cases, when clients have given their permission.
3. Therapists should ask other professionals (collaborators) for their suggestions and ideas about cases. Would they be willing to provide assistance if asked?
4. Therapists should seek out professionals to form an interagency team that can deal with problems that come to the attention of various organizations.

In many settings (schools, hospitals, social service and mental health agencies), the family is assigned to a case manager or team. While the therapist may treat the family, the case manager or team determines the nature of treatment. In these settings, the therapist may not have access to all family members nor have control over welfare of the child. For example, in a school setting, the therapist does not have control over the educational plan for the child. The important issue here is how the therapist works with the team or network to empower the family.

A critical consideration is how the therapist can establish a collaborative relationship with team members to protect the boundaries of individual roles. Collaborative relationships are predicated largely on the problem-solving process. Team members (teachers, social workers, ministers, friends, and others) are encouraged to identify specific problems and generate solutions. The therapist facilitates full participation from all team members. Working with team members as mutual partners within their prescribed roles, the therapist establishes mutual trust with the collaboration team. Finally, positive changes in the family are more likely to be maintained when team members are involved fully.

Guidelines for the Collaboration Team Interview

The collaboration team interview has evolved from the ecostructural model of Harry Aponte (1976a) and has been described more recently by O'Callaghan (1988) and Boyd-Franklin (1989a). Brown and Vaccaro (1991) have developed a set of guidelines for the collaboration team based on these models (Box 8.1). The collaboration team interview is implemented currently with at-risk children and their families at public schools, social service agencies, and mental health centers.

The most essential consideration for the therapist in conducting the collaboration team interview is to remain neutral. Whether the therapist is inside or outside the system (school, social service agency, hospital, and so on), it is important not to be identified too closely with any particular part of the team. For example, if a therapist is too close to the staff in a school, the therapist may have difficulty in remaining neutral rather than siding with the school against the family. The position of neutrality allows the therapist the greatest latitude for effecting change.

The family therapist can do several other things to maintain a collaborative relationship with team members:

> ### *Box 8.1*   *Guidelines for Conducting a Family-School*
> ### *Collaboration Meeting*
>
> 1. Establish a positive climate for change.
> 2. Report the purpose of the meeting.
> 3. Have each participant tell how he or she sees the problem.
> 4. Discuss the strengths of the child.
> 5. Let participants tell what results they hope to see.
> 6. Decide how this can be accomplished. Who will do what? When?
> 7. Decide if other people need to be involved in the intervention.
> 8. Discuss obstacles to the intervention (for example, lack of transportation, schedule conflicts).
> 9. Decide how the participants will know if the intervention has been successful.
> 10. Decide if a follow-up meeting needs to be scheduled. If so, when?

- *Try to understand the family problem and how the team member perceives it.* Inherent in this understanding is some discussion of the extent to which the problem is affecting the team member, as well as the team member's expectations for the family. In this context, the therapist can clarify the team member's biases and unrealistic expectations.
- *Make frequent use of the word "we" in developing collaborative relationships with team members.* The word "we" helps to build a sense of cooperation and support among team members. The therapist should avoid criticizing fellow team members.
- *Examine attempted solutions on the part of team members.* Team members may want to refer the family to the family therapist without doing anything about the problem. For example, a school counselor may refer a child to a family therapist without attempting to address the problem itself. Unless the counselor has tried to solve the problem, the therapist may be unaware of its severity and uncertain of the school's commitment to do something about it. Moreover, if the counselor has intervened, the therapist needs to know the results of the attempted solution.
- *Work with individuals within their prescribed roles.* For example, classroom problems should be handled by the classroom teacher, conduct problems at home by the parents, and so on. Friends should be asked to provide support without usurping the executive role of parents. Respecting roles will help to establish a collaborative relationship with team members and avoid triangles and coalitions that interrupt the treatment plan.

Occasionally, the therapist may choose to shift to the role of advocate for a family if the family is having difficulty obtaining services or needs the weight of an expert to effect a change in the system. The second author has acted as an advocate for families, primarily around issues of educational placement, when appropriate procedures were not being followed or testing data were not being interpreted accurately to parents. But it is preferable to move back to a more neutral stance as quickly as possible. To step in and act as an advocate for parents reduces their own sense of power and competence and creates a coalition with the parents that restricts the range of therapy and limits the therapist's role with the school personnel.

In summary, the increased emphasis on family preservation and home-based services has led to therapeutic practices characterized by collaboration between families and community organizations (schools, churches, and other agencies). Thus, the therapist must assist families to become aware of resources and support. Moreover, the therapist must move beyond simply making families aware of services and programs to helping them become effective and successful in accessing them. It is critical that the family be empowered to take action on their own behalf; the therapist cannot simply act for the family.

Obstacles to Collaboration

In preparing for collaboration, the beginning practitioner is well advised to anticipate as many potential problems as possible (Amatea & Sherrard, 1989). Amatea and Sherrard (1991, p. 6) list the following obstacles to collaboration in school settings. Their original words appear in italics.

1. *Educators and therapists are engaged in different systems and traditions, which often makes communication and team work problematic.* For example, educators often handle the needs of the school and community, which requires them to develop rules and expectations for that group. By contrast, therapists deal with the specific beliefs and patterns depicted by the family members before them.

2. *Therapists can often become triangulated in the pattern of blaming and counterblaming between adults at home and school.* The school can often blame the therapist because they perceive (s)he is allied with the family. This may serve as an obstacle to working cooperatively with school personnel.

3. *Many therapists are unfamiliar with school contexts and learning/schooling issues.* Unless they are willing to become active learners about the realities of school life and educational practice from educators, they will not be able to collaborate effectively.

4. *The engagement of school personnel in addition to family members in the resolution of a child's problem requires a redefinition of traditional notions of family confidentiality and parameters as to what information is to be shared and with whom.*

5. *Insurance reimbursement is not organized to fund collaborative team efforts between family therapists and school personnel.* Collaborative team efforts often require additional time which does not get reimbursed by insurance carrier.

When these obstacles are overcome, the collaboration process may become an intervention that effects change on its own. At other times, the collaboration sets the stage for other interventions that relate to specific hypotheses formulated by the family therapist through ongoing assessment. The next section reviews guidelines for choosing interventions.

Choosing Interventions

After the therapeutic goal has been established, a therapeutic intervention must be chosen; that is, after one or more problem behaviors have been selected, therapists must decide what they are going to do with the family to bring about the stated goals. More importantly, they must determine a logical rationale for using a particular intervention. The critical question about choosing an intervention is, "What intervention, by whom, is most effective for the family, with what specific problem, and under which set of circumstances?" (Paul, 1967).

Given any specific family intervention, a therapist can build a rationale for working with almost any problem within a specific theoretical model. For instance, the structural therapist can readily give and support a rationale for dealing with most problems consistently using a structural approach. On the other hand, the behavioral family therapist, the strategic therapist, and the intergenerational therapist can do likewise. However, the therapeutic experience must meet the family's goal and not simply reflect the therapist's own theoretical biases. For instance, some approaches are differentially effective, depending on the presenting problem. Psychosomatic problems have been treated most effectively through the structural approach (Aponte & Van Deusen, 1981), and there is little or no evidence of symptom substitution. On the other hand, couples who are in conflict often respond better to a communication and problem-solving approach (Jacobson, 1984).

In providing guidelines for determining an appropriate intervention, we do not intend to imply that only one particular approach can work with a particular type of problem. This is not the case, although certain interventions have proven more effective than others in ameliorating certain types of problems. In fact, there is some overlap between interventions that are effective in changing behavior problems. Although each strategy is discussed separately in Chapter Nine, more than one intervention will likely be used with any particular family in actual practice. For example, a couple lacking the skills to interact appropriately with each other may need a problem-solving and communication skills program. After learning how to communicate with each other, they may be given the in-session task of working out a curfew with their adolescent daughter without interruptions from the younger siblings.

While the major family therapy models offer a wide range of interventions, little has been written to guide the practitioner in deciding which model might be most effective with a given family. Wright and Leahey (1984) characterize common interventions in the field of family therapy along a continuum of *direct* and *indirect*. Direct interventions are compliance-based—straightforward attempts at change with cooperative clients. Direct interventions include psychoeducation, task assignments, and directives. Indirect interventions are not based on compliance; they are less threatening attempts at change with clients who are less comfortable with the direction that the therapist has chosen. Indirect interventions include questions, strategic tasks, positive connotations, and paradoxes. Thus, the family therapist should explore the consequences of change with a given family in order to determine whether direct or indirect interventions are appropriate (for example, "Can you think of anything negative that might occur when you solve this problem?").

Research studies on the family therapy of adolescent drug abusers have noted a developing trend regarding the choice of interventions (Selekman & Todd, 1991). Two studies reported that, when the family was more disorganized, a direct approach was more effective; when the family was more rigid, an indirect approach was more effective. Anderson, Reiss, and Hogarty (1986) have had success with a psychoeducational family approach to managing schizophrenic behavior in which education is combined with the development of a cooperative relationship with the family in order to provide ongoing care to a family member. Such approaches are pragmatic, rather than model-specific; they develop hypotheses about how change will occur, rather than about what the problem is and what is needed to correct it.

A minimum requirement in deciding on the intervention is that the therapist must make a thorough analysis of the context in which the problem occurs; that is, the therapist must have asked, and got answers to, the following questions before determining an appropriate intervention:

1. What is the problem and how often does it occur, or how intense is it?
2. What are the consequences of the problem behavior to the family and to others in the environment (for example, teachers, friends, and neighbors)?
3. What resources to promote change does the family have in their environment?
4. What effects would a change in the problem behavior have on the family and others?

In summary, the therapist must formulate hypotheses regarding the problem to determine an appropriate intervention plan. The therapist must examine nonverbal clues such as tone of voice, facial expressions, or eye contact with other family members. Why does the family believe this problem occurs? What do they feel would help to resolve the problem? Who speaks for whom in deciding these issues? How do other family members view the problem? Using these data, the therapist formulates hypotheses and appropriate interventions. The therapist should be ready to alter the treatment plan if the family presents new information or rejects the initial proposal.

Chapter Nine

Facilitating Change

Managing In-Session Process
>   Focusing
>   Increasing Intensity
>   Boundary Marking
>   Unbalancing
>   Making the Covert Overt

Reconstructing Belief Systems
>   Identifying Current Belief Systems
>   Reframing the Meaning of Symptoms
>   Stressing Complementarity
>   Emphasizing Strengths
>   Using Metaphors

Exploring New Behaviors
>   Generating Alternative Solutions
>   Resolving Conflict
>   Coaching Communication
>   Assigning Tasks
>   Developing Rituals

Addressing Client Resistance

F' ..mily therapists must be facilitators of change. Such a process can take many forms since, most often, the clinician chooses, adapts, and combines interventions from various schools of thought. The result, however, should be a strategy for a specific family in a specific culture at a specific stage in their life-cycle. While there are a variety of strategies available, the following are the major categories of therapist behaviors and processes, which represent interventions that target behavioral change, perceptual change, or both: (1) managing in-session process; (2) reconstructing belief systems; (3) exploring new solutions; and (4) addressing client resistance.

Managing In-Session Process

All families evolve interactional patterns that vary in their degree of flexibility and permeability. Some family patterns may be too rigid (inflexible) and therefore make it difficult for family members to adjust to new situations. The permeability of a family pattern or subsystem pattern refers to the amount of access that family members have across boundary lines (for example, children's access to parents). Some families' patterns are too permeable and allow too much access (or interference by other family members or society). In that case, the therapist must block such patterns, to permit new more functional patterns to evolve.

As the therapist begins to accommodate to the family system, she or he observes behavioral or transactional clues to areas of possible dysfunction. The therapist may then want to focus on these areas and formulate hypotheses for testing. For example, to explore parental interactions, the therapist might focus on the behavior of one of the children, who is interrupting the parents' conversation. Accordingly, the therapist suggests that the parents "get the child to behave," so that the discussion can continue. If the child continues to interrupt the parental interaction, the therapist intervenes with a variety of techniques (Minuchin & Fishman, 1981). The therapist may wish to focus on a particular topic; build intensity by lengthening the time of interaction; or limit participation to specific members as a way of boundary marking. Other conditions might require the therapist to unbalance the system or to make the covert overt to alter family interactional patterns. Each of these options will be considered in turn.

Focusing

Focus refers to the therapist's selection of an area to explore from the vast quantity of information presented by the family. Initially, the therapist focuses on the content of family communication—what the family is saying—but soon the focus shifts to the process—how the family members interact with each other. For example, parents may report that their child is "out of control." Without disregarding this content, the therapist is concerned primarily with observing how family members interact with each other: Do family members speak for each other? When the child begins to speak, does Mom or Dad interrupt him or her? Do parents argue about how to solve the problem? Focusing on the process helps the family to function better as a system. The following techniques are helpful in focusing:

1. *Look for areas of content that might illustrate how family members typically interact with each other.* Some problems are too small or too large; that is, some problems are of such little concern or so severe that family members are unwilling to discuss them. It is sometimes important to look for recurring themes such as, "Mom doesn't trust me" or, "Dad has to make the decision." These areas often say the most about the family's interaction pattern.
2. *Avoid jumping from one area of content to the other.* Beginning therapists often make the mistake of searching for *the* area that resolves the family's problem. Consequently, they move from area to area and never focus on what the family gives them to understand the family's process.
3. *Ask permission before focusing on a specific area.* By asking the family's permission, the therapist ensures that the family has control over the content and gains useful clues to the family's interaction pattern.

As an illustration of focusing, consider the case of a family who comes to therapy because their daughter is so "disagreeable." The mother and father present themselves as perfectly happy and compatible, except for their daughter's behavior. Early in the session, the therapist begins to notice that each parent's description of how he or she responds to their daughter's unpleasantness appears to displease the other parent. Their expression of disagreement is a detail that does not fit with the content level of their report. The therapist slowly expands the conversation about how they disagree. As the session unfolds, the therapist develops a hypothesis: "This family doesn't know how to express disagreement." By focusing the therapy on this theme, the therapist could work to change the family structure by reframing their beliefs about disagreements—that is, by persuading them that family disagreements are normal and even beneficial.

Increasing Intensity

Intensity is a term used to describe the degree to which an emotion is being felt in the session. Family systems have coping styles that evolve to reduce anxiety by absorbing or deflecting outside intrusions. These protective mechanisms become dysfunctional only when the system's boundaries are so impenetrable that information necessary for change is deflected or when the family's boundaries are so permeable that individual boundaries must compensate for the lack of system security. Either way, some families have a low threshold for experiencing anxiety and will attempt to modify the therapist's message by making it fit into their preestablished response patterns.

It is important to emphasize that transmission of a message to the family by the therapist does not mean that the family is ready to act on the message. They may have heard the message and responded to it in a positive manner but failed to make any changes. Therapists, therefore, should cultivate a personal style that accommodates intensity by widening their range of potential responses beyond those that are deemed appropriate by cultural norms. Drama, timing, and intensity are not part of daily discourse, and a family therapist must be comfortable with the tension such behaviors can create.

Techniques for building intensity include the following (Minuchin & Fishman, 1981):

1. *Use a simple repetition of the message.* Simple repetition creates intensity because the therapist focuses on one theme, resisting the family's attempts to avoid the message. The therapist may continue to repeat the question or highlight the same message in a variety of ways until she or he gets the desired response. The therapist may also create intensity by repeating messages that appear to be different yet focus on a single direction for change.

2. *Encourage continuation of the interaction beyond the family's comfort limit.* This pushes the family past the regulatory threshold that usually warns members they are entering an area of discomfort. In some cases, the extension elicits the necessary conflict or yields access to normally unavailable family resources (such as warmth and tenderness). In either case, the family breaks out of its predictable path and experiences new patterns of relating.

3. *Avoid accepting the family's expectation of how the therapist should relate to them.* The therapist, for example, may insist that all family members attend the session even though some family members insist they cannot come; or, in some cases, the therapist may appear confused when the family requests an expert opinion.

4. *Manipulate the physical space of the therapy session.* By moving closer to a family member, or moving two members closer to each other, the therapist is able to take advantage of the emotional response inherent in a change in personal boundaries. Because family members grow up learning the comfortable distance to maintain with other members, closer proximity creates momentary tension. If the tension is similar to the therapeutic message, the therapist is able to increase intensity.

To illustrate how a therapist might utilize these techniques, consider a parent with a teenager who doesn't get to school on time. The therapist might repeat the message by (1) letting the child wake himself and (2) letting him walk to school if he misses the bus. These messages are different, but both send the message that the parent needs to encourage the teenager's responsibility. The therapist might encourage the mother and child to move closer together when they discuss the issue, thereby violating the normal comfort zone. The therapist continues to keep the parent and teenager on the problem despite their attempts to avoid the issue.

Boundary Marking

Boundary marking comprises a series of operations that have the common goal of changing the family's structural boundaries. As the therapist begins to accommodate to the family system, he or she observes behavioral and transactional clues that aid in identifying the existing boundary structure of the family. Interruptions by family members are blocked so that transactions can be completed. In some cases, individuals or subsystems (parents or children) might participate in a separate session with the therapist to strengthen this behavior. For example, a therapist may meet with an adolescent boy to help him understand his mother's concerns and discuss some ways he can respond to these concerns. Likewise, he may meet with the mother to help her to recognize his needs for autonomy. Once individual sessions are completed, a conjoint session could be held to discuss these issues.

The therapist can mark boundaries in the following ways:

1. *Rearrange the seating arrangement.* The therapist can rearrange the seating to allow family members to carry out their functions. If a child is sitting between her parents, the therapist might move her further away, so that the parents can discuss their issues without interruption.
2. *Reframe the problem.* When therapists reframe or reinterpret a family's view, they are reconstructing reality. Families often get locked into problems because they see the problem from only one perspective. A discussion of how to reframe the problem is included in the next section.
3. *Block interaction patterns.* The therapist can block inappropriate interactions by (1) moving closer to the family member, (2) raising a hand to stop the interaction, and (3) giving a directive. Staying in close proximity to family members permits the family therapist to disrupt an interaction by physical contact (a touch of the hand).

For example, a family consisting of a single mother, 20-year-old twin daughters, and a 15-year-old daughter who had been truant from school was referred to a family service agency. In the initial session, the therapist turned to the 15-year-old and inquired whether she had trouble waking up in the morning. At this point, the twins began to complain how difficult it was to wake her up and how they had to use extreme measures to pull her out of bed. Assuming a weak parental and sibling subsystem, the therapist changed the seating arrangement by putting the mother and the 15-year-old next to each other, with one twin next to the 15-year-old and the other next to the therapist. He suggested that the twins were taking over the mother's job and neglecting their responsibilities. When the therapist focused on the mother's expectations for her 15-year-old daughter, she was interrupted by the twin. At that point, the therapist raised his hand to block the twin and reframed the interruption—as a need to avoid her own responsibilities by helping the mother.

Unbalancing

In family therapy, unbalancing comprises those operations by which the therapist attempts to tip the balance of power within a subsystem or between subsystems. Specifically, the therapist uses unbalancing techniques purposefully to align or affiliate with a particular family member who is in a position of low power. By asking for help, the family grants power (or influence) to the therapist, who then uses that power therapeutically. The only time that this power may not exist is when the family is externally commanded to therapy, as by a court referral.

The family members often grant power under the assumption that the power will be exercised equally or that they personally will not feel its weight—that is, that only the "sick" member will be asked to change. On the contrary, in therapy, the therapist's power is often used to support one family member at the expense of the others in an attempt to alter the family structure, thus creating new alternatives that will allow for greater complexity and flexibility in the family system. The therapist can unbalance the family system in the following ways:

1. *Align with a family member who has less power.* The therapist aligns with a family member not because he or she necessarily agrees with that member's position but because he or she wants to lend power to a family member to modify the structure. The therapist might say, "I can see why you would feel that way" or, "She needs to be convinced of your position."

2. *Refuse to recognize a family member.* This technique is extremely powerful because it challenges the excluded family member's need to belong. A disengaged, oppositional, or controlling member of the family may begin to fight the therapist for a way back into the family. Because therapists control the interaction, they can influence how a family member comes back in; that is, the price of admission may be participation or tolerance or whatever would facilitate an improved system.

An example of unbalancing can be found in the case of the single mother, twin daughters, and 15-year-old "troublemaker." The therapist used his power to unbalance the inappropriate parental subsystem. He empowered the mother to fire the twins from their parental role, even though the action and resulting loss of role placed temporary stress on the twins. He also did not let up on the pressure when the twins tried to re-involve themselves. The family therapist is able to maneuver in this manner because the treatment plan focuses on the whole family system or organism and not on its individual members.

In the case where the therapist sides with a family member—saying, in effect, "I agree with you. They need to be convinced of your position"—it is important to note that the content of the interaction matters less than the structural issues; that is, the therapist aligns with a family member simply as a means of modifying the family structure. For instance, the therapist may align with a depressed wife in her complaints about her husband's work habits, not because the therapist also objects to the work habits, but because the therapist hopes to unbalance the marital subsystem.

Making the Covert Overt

Dysfunctional families are often characterized by vague communication and unclear role expectations. When a problem arises, the family often adheres to the same old rules and customs. Satir (1972) describes these families as "closed systems where family members are cautious about what they say." In these families, honest self-expression is discouraged and considered deviant by the family. Such families often reach an impasse during a life-cycle transition.

When passing through this transition, interactions become more rigidified and symptomatic behavior may develop.

If therapists are to be effective with these families, they must make the covert messages overt. Satir (1972) suggests several ways to encourage honest and open communication.

1. *Ask family members to speak in the first person and take the "I-position."* When a family member uses referents such as "we" or "they" (for example, "We don't like to go to Father's house"), the therapist should ask the family member to speak for himself or herself ("Tell me what you want to do"). "I" statements are a good indication of whether family members are taking responsibility for themselves. The therapist can often encourage the family member to take an "I-position" by first saying "I feel . . ." and then allowing the family member to complete the sentence with his or her own feelings (for example, "I feel unhappy"). Family members who are able to state their own feelings are taking responsibility for themselves.

2. *Ask family members to level with each other.* When family members level with each other, their tone of voice matches their words and bodily expression. The therapist can get family members to level with each other by asking them to be specific ("Be specific, and tell him what you want him to do").

3. *Help family members to sculpt the structure of the family.* Family sculpture may be used throughout the therapeutic process to increase family members' awareness of perception and thereby alter family relationships. To implement this technique, the therapist positions each family member in a composite living sculpture as other members see him or her. Satir (1972) also asks family members to express feelings through exaggerated facial expressions such as extreme smiling or frowning at each other. Family members may also be encouraged to express the way things are or the way they would like them to be. In some cases, family members may be asked to role-play their feelings.

These techniques help the therapist raise the family's self-awareness to a new level. When clients are helped to address issues that they normally observe but do not discuss, they begin to "metacommunicate" (Watzlawick, Beavin, & Jackson, 1967)—to communicate about their own interpersonal process. As this occurs, individual family members begin to accept the reality that each family problem involves more than their own singular points of view.

As practitioners attend to in-session process through directive structural interventions, families are helped to develop more order in their interactions and clearer understanding in their communication. They begin to develop more self-control (to refrain from interrupting others, for example), and parents begin to see effective leadership modeled by the therapist. These interventions address the microprocess of the family on a behavioral level; the therapist may also assess the need for the microprocess to be addressed on a perceptual level. This entails addressing the language and beliefs that the family incorporates into their understanding of the problem.

Reconstructing Belief Systems

The influence of social constructionists on traditional structural-strategic models of family therapy has prompted an increased interest in how beliefs, values, myths, and perceptions restrain family members from choosing alternative behaviors and solutions (Bateson, 1972; Selvini Palazzoli et al., 1978; White, 1986). Selekman and Todd (1991) noted the limitations of their structural-strategic approach with a certain subgroup of adolescent substance abusers. Generally, when there had been multigenerational drug abuse or past treatment failures, they found indirect interventions to be more effective. Interventions that address perceptions and beliefs are generally more indirect than structural interventions. In this section, we review a few basic interventions that will help the beginning practitioner address problematic aspects of the family's belief system and language patterns. The strategic use of language affords a new understanding of family problems.

Identifying Current Belief Systems

Several family therapy models have emphasized the importance of belief systems in contributing to the problems that families bring to therapy (Brown & Christensen, 1986). Indeed, self-defeating thoughts typically lead to feelings of self-pity, anger, and blame. None of these reactions are constructive. Rather, they lead a person to feel that things should not be as they are because he or she doesn't like them that way, or else they make the person feel inadequate or incapable. In either case, the anxiety, depression, or feelings of inadequacy prevent family members from behaving in a constructive fashion to change the situation. Different family members process cognitions or beliefs in different ways. For example, suppose that a person walks across the room and trips over someone's foot, falling to the floor. One person's first reaction may be extreme anger. Another person may feel little or no anger. The different reactions are due to different belief systems. The first person probably said something like, "That rude, inconsiderate clod! He has the nerve to trip me! I know he did that purposely." On the other hand, the second person may have said something like, "Oops, I'd better start watching where I'm going. He didn't mean to trip me. It was an accident." The therapist should be sensitive to these differences and respond accordingly.

The family members' belief systems are often at the core of the problem. Snider (1992) discusses this issue as follows:

> Some clients present themselves with a symptom such as depression or anxiety. After evaluation, it becomes clear that their agenda is to change someone else's behavior to get them into therapy. I saw one woman who presented symptoms of depression. After reviewing her situation, it became clear that she thought her husband should be in therapy. Her presumption was that if he changed then she would not have any problems . . . Sometimes people seek therapy because they

are alone and lonely. I saw an elderly widow whose children lived in other parts of the country. She had had a successful experience in therapy many years earlier. She presented symptoms around a difficulty in relationship with her children. After discussion, she acknowledged that there was nothing wrong with her relationship to them except the distance between them. She needed to talk and felt that this would be an appropriate entree. Her fantasy was that I would help her find a way to get her children to move back to the same city. (p. 145)

Understanding the family members' belief systems helps the therapist to understand the underlying problems and formulate goals for change.

In identifying current belief systems, the therapist should explore the presence of constructive and nonconstructive beliefs related to the problem. The therapist can identify current belief systems in the following ways:

1. *Identify beliefs that contribute to the problem.* Helpful questions include: "What do you think when _____ is going on?" "What makes it better?" "What makes it worse?" "What goes through your mind during this time?"
2. *Ask family members to complete incomplete sentences.* Such sentences might begin: "I think . . ."; "I believe . . ."; "I should . . ."; "My husband thinks I want . . ."; "When my wife comes in the door I think . . .."
3. *Identify family members' self-talk.* Everyone engages in some kind of internal dialogue. This dialogue or self-talk expresses the family members' belief system. The therapist can identify self-talk through the following questions: "What do you say to yourself at this time?" "When she uses that tone of voice what do you tell yourself?" "What are you telling yourself before this happens?"

By identifying current beliefs and thoughts that contribute to the problem, the therapist can identify thought patterns that must change before constructive action can be taken to correct the problem.

Reframing the Meaning of Symptoms

Reframing—sometimes known as relabeling—refers to a change or modification in the family members' thoughts or view of the problem. When therapists reframe a family's view, they are suggesting a change in the family's definition of the problem. Reframing often shifts the focus off the identified patient or scapegoat and onto the family system in which each family member is an interdependent part (Watzlawick et al., 1974). Thus, reframing alters the way the family thinks about the problem.

In reframing, the therapist must first alter the family's view of reality. By the technique of focusing, the therapist must take bits and pieces of what the family supplies and provide information that forms a new perspective. The therapist attempts to create a therapeutic reality from a family reality. For example, a family may describe their son as "defiant" or "hard to control," whereas the therapist may view the son as "independent" or "discriminative." By voicing these alternative descriptions, the therapist helps the family to see their son in another way. Such a reconstruction can only be possible, however, if the family has a worldview that includes such a possibility. For example, the therapist may reframe a child's tantrums or uncontrollable behavior as a signal that the parents have taught their child how to express independence, but this may be ineffective if it is too far from family or societal norms.

The therapist can also accomplish reframing by taking the symptom and giving it universal qualities. For example, a child who is having difficulty following rules may be redefined as "having difficulty growing up." If a therapist is working with a family whose religious culture emphasizes a dominant patriarchal order, the therapist might challenge the image of a distant, emotionally controlled father by saying, "Surely you realize that it is only the courageous patriarch who is able to show tenderness to his family." By drawing on universal symbols, the therapist is able to pair a dysfunctional family belief with a universal belief that offers a new frame or view of the problem.

In addition to these strategies, the therapist can also reframe the meaning of the symptom in the following ways:

1. *Relabel problem behaviors to give them more positive meanings.* Giving new labels often provides family members with a new way of thinking about the problem, so that it can be resolved. For example, therapists can relabel "jealousy" as "caring." "Anger" can be relabeled as "desiring attention."

2. *Relabel deficits as strengths.* All behavior can be viewed positively and negatively, depending on the person's perspective. For example, a child who has trouble getting things done may be viewed as a "thinker" or a "perfectionist," depending on the circumstances. Family members are more likely to accept a reframe if their strengths are emphasized.

3. *Reframe the context of the problem.* Reframing the context of the problem permits the family to "explore and decide when, where, and with whom a given problem behavior is useful or appropriate" (Cormier & Cormier, 1991). Every behavior has costs and benefits. Thus, when a wife complains that her husband leaves during their arguments, the therapist might help the couple to identify those situations (contexts) where leaving is useful (for example, when there is a threat of violence).

4. *Give homework to reinforce new beliefs.* Cormier and Cormier (1991) believe that homework helps family members to practice aspects of the problem that go undetected. For example, a husband and wife might be required to observe those times when the husband attempts to walk away from a situation. What was going on? What was each thinking at the time? What happened afterwards? The therapist can then discuss this information to help the family discover new beliefs and perceptions of the problem.

Reframing helps family members to get unstuck from rigid thought patterns that contribute to the problem. A new view or perspective will help the family to look for alternative solutions to their dilemma.

Stressing Complementarity

The therapist often finds it useful to help family members understand that they are interconnected in ways that make one member's actions complementary to another's. For example, a therapist might underline a couple's complementarity by congratulating the wife for the husband's change in behavior. The therapist in this case is teaching the couple that they do affect each other and that they have the potential to do so constructively. This intervention also allows the husband to reconnect with his wife, by encouraging him to praise her for helping him express his feelings. Complementarity also helps the family understand their relationship over time. During an assessment, if family members begin to describe each other as opposites in some way, the therapist should note these as potential examples of complementarity. Some common examples occurring in most families are shy versus outgoing, dominant versus submissive, stable versus unstable, and emotional versus rational. While these labels may need to be reframed for the family, the dynamic of complementarity can still be addressed.

Jorge Colapinto (1991) describes the process of complementarity as follows:

> Family rules develop primarily through a process of correlated differentiation: The behaviors of any two family members mutually accommodate in such a way that one develops selective aspects of himself or herself, while the other develops a complementary trait. Typical examples are the harsh and soft parents, the active and passive spouse, the left brain and the right brain siblings. When all the members of the family are considered, the resulting image is like a jigsaw puzzle, where the irregular borders of the various pieces fit—complement— each other. Carrying the metaphor further, the salient borders of each piece represent the traits expected from each member (harshness, passivity, left brain) while the concave sections represent traits not expected. In well-functioning families, complementarity takes the form of effective teamwork. (pp. 422–423)

Complementary relationships become a problem when they fail to provide flexibility for individual members. Traditional, fixed male and female roles often have costs that lead to problems. A father who insists on making all the decisions may take away the mother's executive role when she is home with the children. At the same time, the father may feel overly responsible, which doesn't permit him to enjoy or play with the children. When these patterns become fixed, families experience problems in moving through developmental transitions.

The therapist can emphasize complementary roles in the following ways:

1. *Ask a family member to relate his or her behavior to what another family member is doing.* For example, a husband who describes himself as "jealous" may be asked what he is noticing about his wife when he begins to feel jealous ("What things do you see or hear her doing when you begin to feel jealous?").
2. *Congratulate a family member for another member's accomplishments.* For example, a wife may be congratulated for helping her husband to express his

feelings. Here it is important to look for small changes in a family member's behavior that contribute to another family member's behavior (for example, a smile that another family member notices and reacts to).

Complementarity broadens the family's perceptual framework by emphasizing the interpersonal nature of the problem. Thus, rather than focusing on a problem residing within the individual (such as jealousy), the therapist focuses on current interactions that contribute to the problem (such as the husband's behavior). Moreover, the therapist can emphasize complementarity to punctuate interactions that alleviate the symptomatic behavior (e.g., therapist congratulates the husband for the wife's change in behavior). The therapist is thus teaching them that they do affect each other, and they have the potential to do so constructively.

Emphasizing Strengths

The exploration of strength in the family is not limited to any one therapeutic maneuver. This core technique of family therapy is based on the assumption that, under the right conditions, the family has within itself the necessary ingredients for development. Such optimistic assumptions form part of a strategy to create a therapeutic reality. Whether finding and emphasizing competence in the identified patient or creating intensity by implying that a couple can work their conflict out if they just continue arguing, the therapist communicates an optimism based on the family's own unique strengths.

The therapist can emphasize strengths in several ways:

1. *Emphasize those things that families do well.* Family members rarely identify their strengths. Instead, they "demonstrate and describe strengths and capabilities by way of example" (as in, "When my wife has to be at the hospital with Johnny, we all pitch in to do whatever needs to get done around the house") (Dunst et al., 1988, p. 73). The therapist should underscore these behaviors ("You obviously know how to pull together to help each other") and their implications for resolving their problem. White (1986) believes that, if the therapist focuses on exceptions to the problem, clients are able to see aspects of themselves that reflect a new view or story of themselves.
2. *Ask family members to talk about ways they coped successfully with the problem.* Learning how family members have coped successfully with other problems will help them to be more aware of their strengths when confronting current problems (for example, "How did you handle this in the past?" or, "How were you able to overcome this problem?").
3. *Ask family members to describe their daily schedule.* Asking family members to talk about a typical day (as in, "Tell me what happens when you all are home for dinner") will help the therapist learn how the family deals with difficult tasks. Moreover, describing daily routines often provides information about resources (such as enjoyment) and how the family handles their daily needs (Dunst et al., 1988).

The ability to identify strengths can be a major asset in empowering families to resolve their problems. O'Hanlon and Weiner-Davis (1989) believe that therapeutic approaches based on strengths and possibilities "create self-fulfilling prophecies"; that is, when therapists and families are optimistic, positive changes are likely to occur.

Using Metaphors

A metaphor is a word or phrase that characterizes family relationships; or a condition, such as a symptom, that represents another condition by analogy. In using metaphorical tasks, the therapist chooses an activity (such as writing bad checks) that resembles the problem (say, a daughter's overinvolvement with her mother). The activity must be one that family members can discuss and in which they can produce change. The therapist will typically assign tasks—such as having a heated discussion and obtaining separate checking accounts—that will produce a change in the desired area—for instance, increasing autonomy (Haley, 1976b). If the mother and daughter are able to accomplish the task—that is, get separate checking accounts and pay their own bills—they will be more likely to accomplish separation around the more difficult issues later on.

There are six steps to the design of appropriate metaphors (Cormier & Cormier, 1991):

1. *Examine the nature of the family member's problem.* The symptom may often be a metaphorical label for conceptualizing the problem. A metaphorical message usually contains an explicit element (for example, "I have a headache") as well as an implicit element (for example, "I want more attention" or, "I am unhappy"). The therapist must identify the problem or theme and develop a metaphor that is parallel to the theme or problem.
2. *Choose a representative "character" for the metaphor (such as an animal, personal symptom, or inanimate object).* It is helpful to have a character that the therapist can use in developing the metaphor ("So, when you come in the door, you are like a bull in a china shop").
3. *Select words in the metaphor that match the family member's visual, auditory, and kinesthetic frame of reference.* For example, the second author recently suggested to an electrician and his wife that their marriage needed to be "rewired." Similar metaphors could be used with a mechanic ("Your marriage needs a tune-up") or doctor ("You need a new prescription").
4. *Develop an interactional process in the metaphor to match the interactional process in the problem.* The cycle of interaction in the metaphor should parallel the pattern of interaction around the problem. For example, the family's interactions about the child's problem will be similar to their pattern regarding the mother's problem when one is a metaphor for the other.
5. *Expand or embellish the character to promote behavioral change.* For example, a therapist may knock on the table as if it was a door, as a metaphor for a new marriage.

6. *Develop a story that includes an element of mystery.* For example, the therapist may tell a story of a person who miraculously overcame a disease and went through a transformation that brought a new meaning to her life.

In some cases, the therapist will give a directive metaphorically, without making explicit what he or she wants the family to do. Family members are oftentimes more willing to follow this kind of directive, because they aren't really aware that they have received one. When therapists give a metaphorical directive, they are encouraging family members to behave in a way that resembles the way they want them to behave in the symptom areas, such as assigning a couple to have a gourmet meal as a metaphor for a better sex life (Haley, 1976b).

Exploring New Behaviors

Generating Alternative Solutions

Generating alternative solutions is central to the problem-solving process; the goal is to identify as many potential solutions as possible. This process is based on the following three assumptions: (1) There are a number of potentially effective ways to handle a problem; (2) families are often aware of some alternative ways to alter a problem; and (3) generating solutions increases the likelihood of selecting a manageable solution to the problem. Families will be more likely to implement a solution if they suggest it. When the family generates alternative solutions, it helps the family to take greater ownership of the solution and work collaboratively with the therapist.

In generating alternative solutions, the therapist uses a brainstorming procedure. There are three basic rules for good brainstorming: (1) If the therapist or family member suggests an alternative solution (for example, "Maybe I need to set a time aside for homework"), each party refrains from critiquing the other; (2) the therapist and family can take an idea and improve on it; (3) both parties should attempt to generate as many solutions as possible. The more solutions generated, the more likely it is that an effective solution will be found.

The therapist can generate alternative solutions in the following ways:

1. *Explore possible solutions to the problem.* The therapist might say, "Let's think of some ways you could handle this situation" or, "What are some things you could do now to handle this problem?"
2. *Encourage family members to improve on another member's idea.* The therapist might say, "What do you think about John's suggestion? Do you have anything you want to add to it?"
3. *Ask family members how two or more ideas can be combined into a better idea.* In some cases, two suggestions can readily be combined into a better idea ("So, Mary, you want to wait to talk about the problem after dinner and, John, you want to be relaxed. What might be a good time and place to talk this issue over?").

Resolving Conflict

Skills in conflict resolution and problem solving comprise a set of well-developed strategies for dealing with disagreements when they arise (Stuart, 1980). Problem solving and conflict resolution have proven effective in treating marital conflict (Jacobson & Margolin, 1979). The process has two distinct phases: problem definition and problem resolution. In the problem definition phase, the critical issue or problem—for example, "You don't care about me"—is defined in operational terms. An operational definition of the problem is much more likely to lead to an effective response.

The problem resolution phase emphasizes behavior change rather than insight. It is best to choose a solution that can be implemented by the family with a minimum of help. Solutions should be kept simple, since complex plans often fail because the costs (in time and energy) outweigh the benefits (say, parenting skills).

There are several things a therapist can do to help families choose the best solution.

1. *Choose a solution that is acceptable to family members.* Once the family has generated alternative solutions, the therapist can help the family to select one of them. Family members have the option of striking out any that are unacceptable. The remaining solutions can be subjected to a cost-benefit analysis for all family members. The best solution is then selected from the most promising alternatives. Note that the best solution will produce an outcome that requires some accommodation from all family members.

2. *Decide how the solution will be implemented.* How will the solution be put into practice, and who will work with the family to carry it out? Because specificity and consistency are essential to success here, it is often helpful to prepare a written plan or contract listing procedures, where the plan is to be implemented, conditions, resources (both personal and material), and the amount of time that it will be in effect. The plan ensures that the family and therapist follow the agreed-upon steps and do not change their practices midway through the program. It also reminds the family of the resources they will need. The following questions can be used to develop a written plan:

What is the chosen solution?
What are the steps to carry out the solution?
Who will work with the family to help them carry out the plan?
When will the plan begin and end?
Who else should be involved in this plan?
When do we meet again?

3. *Evaluate the proposed solution.* How will each family member carry out their agreed-upon responsibilities? Are responsibilities or tasks being carried out according to the specifications in the contract? These questions can best be answered through data—self-reports, collateral reports from social workers or

teachers, and so on. Once information is collected, the therapist should hold a meeting with the family to discuss progress toward the goals adopted.

4. *Renegotiate the contract, if necessary.* The evaluation may suggest that the contract should be renegotiated. Do the results meet the desired level of satisfaction for the family? If not, are more cost-effective solutions available to reach the goals? What has the family learned from the attempted solution that would help them find a better way to resolve their problem? What adjustments (changes in behavior) must be made to reach the desired goals? In some cases, the family's level of satisfaction may not increase as the goals are attained. Here the therapist should help family members decide whether negotiated agreements—what they will talk to each other about and under what conditions—will be more satisfying over time or whether the family should set new goals.

Coaching Communication

Regardless of the therapist's orientation, coaching communication is a core component of therapeutic change strategies. Coaching communication is effective for couples (Rappaport, 1976), parents and adolescents (Crando & Ginsberg, 1976), and divorced parents (for example, Brown, Brown, & Portes, 1991). Related programs often last from 3 to 15 weeks and contain the following core components.

Modeling The first step in helping a couple to communicate more effectively is to demonstrate, or model, the appropriate communication skill; that is, the behavior therapist shows each spouse what the response looks like or how it sounds. Therapists themselves model behavior throughout the treatment process. Modeling has been effective in teaching information-seeking behavior (Krumboltz, Varenhorst, & Thoresen, 1967), reducing feelings of alienation (Warner & Hansen, 1970), and improving attitudes toward drug abuse (Warner, Swisher, & Horan, 1973).

Another common practice is to provide live or symbolic models—on audiotapes or videotapes, for example—who show, in sequential steps, the specific behaviors necessary to solve the problem (Hosford & de Visser, 1974). Taped or filmed models have been successfully used (Hansen, Pound, & Warner, 1976). The models only demonstrate the desired behaviors; there is no opportunity for interaction between the models and the spouses. However, the taped models may help to stimulate discussion, which is important in order to prevent rote imitation by the spouses. If new behaviors are to be effective, spouses need to learn a variety of responses for a particular problem situation.

The therapist may also wish to develop models for each of several sessions. For example, the therapist could develop tapes that teach each spouse to (1) listen, (2) express a compliment, (3) express appreciation, (4) ask for help, (5) give feedback, and (6) express affection (Goldstein, 1973). Each skill could be modeled and practiced during a session, if the spouses' skill level allows. Each modeling sequence could thus represent a closer approximation of the final behavior.

Effective modeling includes the following procedures:

1. *Model a clear delineation of the desired behavior.* The behavior must be identified clearly, so that family members know precisely what the therapist is actually modeling. If the modeling sequence is too vague, there is little likelihood that any learning will take place. For example, rather than trying to model "awareness" to a family member, the therapist should operationalize this by identifying and labeling emotions. To teach relationship skills, the therapist might break the relationship down into "expressing" and "responding." These areas might be broken down further into subskills—responding to anger, affection, and so on. It is always beneficial to operationalize the skill that is to be learned; that is, the skill should be such that it can be seen and heard. After operationalizing the skill, the therapist explains what the model (in this case, the therapist) will be saying or doing and tells family members what they should look for. For example, if a family member is having difficulty "asking for help," the therapist might say, "John, I need you to _____ when I'm feeling down."

2. *Model behaviors that will hold the family members' attention.* Familiar and relevant experiences are more likely to hold attention and facilitate learning. Also, models are generally most effective when they are the same sex as a family member and similar in appearance, age, and so on. Because of this, the therapist may want the family to identify personal resources (friends) who could serve as models. If the family member is having difficulty entering a social situation, a friend who is accepted in that situation and who is similar to the family member might be asked to model or demonstrate how to get involved. The therapist might say, "I would like you to show Mary what to do when she wants to have a conversation with others." A model who verbalizes his or her own uncertainty (as in, "I'm not sure, but here is one way to try it") and offers subsequent problem-solving or coping strategies can be helpful in eliciting the family members' attention. Another useful technique is to emphasize those behaviors to be modeled: The therapist might ask the model to speak more loudly during the relevant responses or to repeat a key passage ("Would you repeat that, please"). Tone of voice and mannerisms can also be used to gain the family members' attention.

3. *Ask family members to discuss what they have observed.* Unless family members are able to understand and retain the essential characteristics of the model's behavior, the intervention will be of no avail. In cases where the modeled behavior is particularly abstract, retention may be facilitated if either the model or therapist discusses the important features of the model's performance. For example, a model demonstrating how to express affection to a family member could discuss different ways to show affection. The therapist could evaluate the family members' understanding by asking them to summarize the main features or general rules of the model's performance.

4. *Reinforce the modeled behavior.* The therapist must provide incentives so as to encourage family members to perform the modeled behavior. When modeled behavior is not reinforced, initiation will not occur; the likelihood that imitative behavior will occur increases with the probability of receiving reinforcement. To reinforce the modeled behavior, the therapist might respond to the model's statements with positive comments ("That's an interesting point" or,

"That's a thoughtful idea"). By observing that the model is reinforced for expressing an opinion or solving a problem, the family members learn the most effective response in that situation.

Instruction   Once the family has attended to and understood the model's behavior, the therapist should provide instructions before the family begins practicing the new behavior. The therapist can focus attention on the relevant and essential aspects of the model's performance. The instructions may be spoken or written by the therapist, or else provided in the form of an audiotape or videotape. The therapist might say, "Watch how I show appreciation to your husband," and then model the appropriate behavior, adding, "Now I want you to show appreciation for something your husband has done recently." Instructions can be provided in the following ways:

1. *Prompt specific behaviors for members to try out.* The therapist is now essentially serving as coach who prompts specific behavior for the family to try out. Instructions generally may be positive—do this—or negative—don't do that. The therapist gives numerous specific examples. Instructing a wife to give feedback to her husband, the therapist might say: "Look directly at your husband and tell him how it makes you feel when he doesn't call to say he won't be home. Don't just accuse him of being inconsiderate."

2. *Help family members decide when to give feedback to each other.* The therapist might discuss when to give feedback—for example, "when you have time to sit down" or "when you are not so angry"—since family members may know what to say but not when to say it. By going over the demonstration, the therapist can pinpoint behaviors by the model (therapist, friend) and discuss why such behaviors can serve as a cue to a family member to perform a specific behavior.

Practice   Having received instructions on what to say and do, the family is ready to practice the behavior; practice is an essential part of the learning process, since people learn by doing. Family members role-play new relationships or problem-solving behaviors. If either spouse shows resistance to this idea, the therapist can provide examples of the usefulness of practice. The crucial point is that each family member must feel that he or she is not just learning a role that is artificial and unusable. Consequently, the role-playing situations should be as realistic as possible and should include verbal responses with which each family member feels comfortable. The following are important guidelines:

1. *Prepare the family member for practice.* The family must accept the idea that practice would be an appropriate way to develop new coping or problem-solving behaviors. If the family shows some resistance to this idea, the therapist can provide examples where practice has proven useful. Experience, drill, rehearsal, recitation, homework, and exercises all involve practice. The therapist might say, "Maybe we could practice expressing appreciation to your son. I'll role-play your son, and we'll see how it goes. If you have trouble thinking of something to say, I'll help you."

2. *Start with a situation that the family can perform with little difficulty.* Practice is more successful when the initial situation is familiar to the family. For example, in a parent-adolescent conflict, the therapist might ask both parties to start by "talking about something that happened at school today." If they are unable to do this, the therapist might ask them to engage in less threatening activities such as sitting next to each other. Regardless of the activity, the therapist should begin with a nonthreatening situation.

3. *Break the behavior down into small steps.* These steps should range in complexity from simple (such as giving a compliment) to the complete new behavior (such as asking for help). In this case, the social interaction varies according to the level of difficulty.

4. *Prompt family members when they can't think of what to say or do.* The therapist can provide a sentence that fits within the context of the interaction (for example, "It's important to me to know how you feel"). It is essential that the prompt occur only when the family member pauses or hesitates (generally for about five seconds). In addition, the therapist can use hand signals to raise or lower the family member's voice or to motion for him to come closer. Prompts should be faded as family members become able to practice the behavior unaided. At this point the therapist should praise the family members for expressing the desired behavior in their own words.

Feedback   When family members have practiced the skills, each must receive feedback on their performance. Such feedback provides an incentive for improvement. Information received about poor performance can be potentially as helpful as knowledge regarding positive performance. The following guidelines are important in providing feedback:

1. *Solicit the family's ideas about feedback prior to practice.* The therapist might say, " I'll observe you and try to give you some helpful hints." When a family member denies or disagrees with feedback from the therapist ("That's not the way it sounded to me") or attempts to justify his response ("The reason I said that was . . ."), then feedback was probably not solicited or agreed upon prior to practice.

2. *Describe rather than evaluate the family members' behaviors.* For example, the therapist might replay a videotape of what a family member said and comment, "Here you say 'My mother thinks I should . . . .' Do you remember we agreed you would say, 'I think I should . . . .'?" The therapist's feedback statements should avoid blame. Statements such as, "That just doesn't sound right" or "I don't know why you can't do that" fail to provide helpful information to the family.

3. *Reinforce a family member's response and at the same time prompt similar responses.* For example, the therapist might say, "That's a good question to get him to talk to you. Sometimes, however, your husband may not want to talk about his job. Can you think of some other questions you could ask him?" By prompting additional questions, the therapist not only helps to reinforce the spouse's use of questions in a practice session but also facilitates its generalization to other situations and people.

The therapist should provide opportunities for the family to practice their skills at home, and should supply guidelines or worksheets to facilitate such practice. Therapy is more effective when family members are able to practice skills successfully in everyday interactions.

Assigning Tasks

Tasks attempt to change the sequence of interaction in the family. They may help a family to become more organized, establish operational boundaries, set rules, or establish family goals (Madanes, 1981). Tasks might include (1) advice, (2) explanations or suggestions, or (3) directives to change the interactional sequence in the family (Papp, 1980). For example, in the case of a family with a mother and daughter who are overinvolved and a father who is peripheral, the therapist might give the following explanation to the mother: "Your daughter needs to treat you with respect. She will be able to do that when you have your husband's support. Right now he gets called on as the bad guy when you aren't able to deal with her. This is a critical time when your daughter needs to spend more time with her father." Unfortunately, advice may not be successful because family members often know what to do but don't know how to do it.

In many cases, the therapist must convince the family to follow the directive or task. This may be difficult, unless each family member sees some payoff. Persuading a family to perform a task will depend on the type of task, the family, and the kind of relationship the therapist has with the family (Haley, 1976). For example, there may not be a payoff for adolescents to talk in a session if they aren't certain that their parents care about them or if they can get their way without talking. In a case like this, the therapist's directive must provide some benefits (for example, more privileges or parental concern) for the adolescent, as well as for other members of the family.

Haley (1976b) offers several suggestions to therapists for getting families to follow their tasks or directives:

1. *Discuss everything the family has done to try to solve the problem.* By this device the therapist can avoid making suggestions that have already been tried. The therapist should lead the family to the final conclusion that everything has been tried and nothing has worked. At this point, the therapist is in a position to offer the family something different.

2. *Ask family members to discuss the negative consequences if their problem is not handled now (that is "What is going to happen if this problem is not resolved?").* Aversive consequences will probably be different for different members of the family. Nevertheless, examining the negative consequences of the problem for each family member emphasizes the intensity of the problem. A mother and her adolescent daughter, for instance, get into conflicts; both cry and are unhappy, and neither gets her way. The mother doesn't get the kind of respect she deserves and the daughter doesn't get any privileges. It is important for the therapist to emphasize those consequences and to project what might happen if the problem is not resolved.

3. *Assign a task that is reasonable and easily accomplished.* In order to ensure that the family can complete the task at home, it is often necessary to get the family to complete the task in the session. For example, the therapist may want an adolescent daughter to have a conversation with her mother without interruptions by her father. Therefore, the therapist may ask the daughter to talk with her mother in session while the father reads a magazine. The therapist might suggest an activity that both of them might enjoy doing together. If the father interrupts before the mother and daughter complete the task, the therapist may wish to devise something else for the father to do, such as running an errand, so as to improve the chances that he will not interrupt when mother and daughter attempt to complete a conversation at home. The therapist can also ensure that the task will be accomplished by providing adequate instructions. In this instance, the therapist focuses attention on the relevant and essential aspects of each family member's performance. Before the family begins the task, the therapist might instruct the father that it will be difficult for him to stay out of it and that he needs to find something else to do instead.

4. *Assign a task to fit the ability and performance level of the family members.* In the film *Family with a Little Fire* (Minuchin, 1974), the task is focused on the scapegoated child's fire setting. The therapist, Braulio Montalvo, asks the mother to spend five minutes each day teaching her daughter how to light matches correctly. He also instructs the parental child who stands between mother and child to watch the other children while the mother is teaching the child. This task is suited to each family member's level of ability.

5. *Use authority to get the family to follow the directive or task.* Sometimes the therapist must use his or her knowledge and expertise to get the family to comply. It is important for the therapist to accept the role of expert, rather than asking the family what they think they should do. The therapist might say, for example, "From my experience, I'd say that this is a critical time for your son, and he needs time with his father." The therapist is really saying, "On the basis of my expertise, I believe that it is important for you to do this." Sometimes the therapist may ask whether the family or family member trusts him or her. If the family or family member says yes, the therapist might say, "Good, then I want you to do this because it is important. Trust me." Here the therapist uses trust to gain control of the interview.

6. *Give clear instructions to each member of the family.* Everyone should know what his or her responsibilities or role should be. If a therapist asks a father and daughter to do something together, then specific dates and times should be specified. By deciding in advance on a time, the father and daughter make a commitment to perform the task. Establishing a time also decreases the likelihood of interference by something else, such as work or TV. The therapist and the family should also decide who will take care of the other children and what the mother will be doing during that time. The therapist might ask family members to describe what they will be doing so that they are all clear about their roles. Family members should be encouraged to discuss anything that might interfere with the completion of the task.

Developing Rituals

Rituals can address a number of therapeutic goals related to rigid family rules and omitted developmental tasks in the life-cycle. The Milan team (Selvini Palazzoli et al., 1978) designed specific strategic instructions in the form of family rituals. Their ritualized prescriptions were designed for "breaking up those behaviors through which each parent disqualifies and sabotages the initiatives and directions of the other parent in his relation with the children" (Selvini Palazzoli et al., 1978, p. 3). Such prescriptions can be repeated with the same format for any type of family. Rituals are used instead of interpretation, which is often ineffective in altering the rules of the system. At the end of an assessment period, the therapist helps the family develop a ritual. The following is a common Milan-style prescription:

> On even days of the week—Tuesdays, Thursdays, and Saturdays— beginning from tomorrow onwards until the date of the next session and fixing the time between X o'clock and Y o'clock (making sure that the whole family will be at home during this time), whatever Z does (name of patient, followed by a list of his symptomatic behaviors), father will decide alone, at his absolute discretion, what to do with Z. Mother will have to behave as if she were not there. On odd days of the week—Mondays, Wednesdays, and Fridays—at the same time, whatever Z may do, mother will have full power to decide what course of action to follow regarding Z. Father will have to behave as if he were not there. On Sundays, everyone must behave spontaneously. Each parent, on the days assigned to him or her, must record in a diary any infringement by the partner of the prescription according to which he is expected to behave as if he were not there. (In some cases the job of recording the possible mistakes of one of the parents has been entrusted to a child acting as a recorder or to the patient himself if he is fit for the task.) (Selvini Palazzoli et al., 1978, p. 5)

Selvini Palazzoli et al. (1978) note that the ritualized prescription operates at several levels. First, the rules of the game are changed to prevent interferences from occurring. Second, parents are blocked from competing for the therapist's approval, since their efforts only serve to deflect attention from the problem (relationship). Finally, the therapist gains information, regardless of whether the family follows the prescription. This information can be used to design subsequent interventions.

The following guidelines are helpful in designing rituals:

1. *Prescribe one or more aspects of the problem. Those problematic thoughts and behaviors then form the content of the ritual.* For example, a boy who threw frequent "out-of-control" temper tantrums was asked to continue having his tantrums but to have them in a special place at home and only after school, when he could really have time to throw one.
2. *Provide a rationale for the ritual, so as to increase the likelihood of compliance.* For example, the therapist might suggest to the family that structuring the temper tantrums in this way will help family members to gain control of the problem or help the therapist to better understand the problem.

Another type of ritual, suggested by Imber-Black, Roberts, and Whiting (1988), helps families address unresolved developmental issues by grieving traumatic losses, completing developmental milestones, or celebrating and stabilizing progress. Such rituals form a part of many religious and societal traditions, but may have been overlooked as a family's problem was developing. For example, if families have suffered a traumatic death or loss, the therapist may develop special grieving rituals for the family, in order to facilitate the further healing necessary to break a dysfunctional pattern. These rituals are most effective when the influence of the loss on the presenting problem has been recognized and the family becomes the author of the ceremony, determining the participants and the desired meaning of the ritual.

Sometimes, families will skip important developmental milestones that later become metaphors for the presenting problem. For example, when couples elope or forgo a honeymoon, family therapists may use this as a metaphor for skipping some important developmental task, such as creating a strong marital attachment. As the couple identifies elements of the marriage that were skipped and need to be developed, the planning of a honeymoon or special anniversary celebration can symbolize the completion of relationship tasks facilitated during the course of therapy.

Other rituals celebrate the completion of therapy as a rite of passage (Epston & White, 1992); for example, a triangulated child may be helped to disengage from the position of "marital therapist" and given a new position as "liberated sixth-grader," free to explore how children grow up when they don't have to worry about their parents' marriage. A concluding ritual then allows the family to celebrate such achievements in the company of significant others. Thus, the culmination of therapy is not seen as a private termination or as implying loss of the therapeutic relationship. Rather, such rituals help families to stay focused on the changes they have made. They also normalize therapy by incorporating societal traditions into the process.

Addressing Client Resistance

The term "resistance" has become a cliche in the field of psychotherapy. Most often, it connotes the client's lack of cooperation with the practitioner. However, in family therapy, there is a strong bias toward the notion that resistance is an interactional event characterized by the professional's lack of understanding about what is important to the family. For example, battered women are often considered resistant when they fail to follow professional advice that places physical safety above psychological safety. While there is widespread agreement about the importance of physical safety as a human right, professionals are frequently guilty of blaming the innocent when they label clients as resistant or stubborn without understanding the history that has influenced their beliefs about self, others, and the world around them. It is our observation that in many difficult cases involving elder abuse, domestic violence, and child sexual abuse, distinct perceptual patterns have a significant influence over the behavioral patterns that develop in family life. Thus, it is incumbent upon family therapists to understand the unique thought processes of clients, rather than to label them resistant or stubborn. As therapist skill develops in this area, client resistance will diminish.

When family therapists reach a therapeutic impasse, one way to address client thought processes is to search for a positive connotation to some element of the problem. For example, Selvini Palazzoli et al. (1978) describe a 10-year-old boy who exhibited psychotic symptoms following the death of his grandfather. At the end of the first session, the therapist told the boy that he was "doing a good thing" (p. 81). The therapist further noted that the grandfather was a "central pillar of the family" and kept the family together. The boy was told that he had assumed his grandfather's role to maintain balance in the family and that he should continue this role until the next session. Here the therapist used "positive connotation" to maintain homeostasis in the family, rather than to challenge it. The boy had taken the grandfather's place to maintain a heterosexual balance in a family that, following the grandfather's death, had been dominated by women. The use of positive connotation allows the therapist to join with the family at a time of crisis and to understand the problem in the light of complicated systemic dynamics.

If families fail to follow a prescription, the Milan team might write paradoxical letters that admit defeat or helplessness (for example, "Your family has special power" or, "I feel a sense of helplessness"). When therapists acknowledge their powerlessness, some families will continue in therapy and discuss their influence on the therapist when they are united (Weeks & Abate, 1982). Furthermore, paradoxical letters allow the therapist to stop arguing for something that the family does not want. The family, in turn, often rebounds to begin changing on their own terms. Thus, the Milan team uses the family's resistance to produce change in the system. The paradoxical letters "allow the therapist or team to stay in a position from which maximum change can be achieved" (Hoffman, 1981, p. 303).

When symptoms have become chronic, although numerous people are trying to help the family or individual to change, it is often wise to take a cautious position about the timing and amount of change: Restrain the family when it begins to show improvement. Restraining interventions are used to help the therapist move at a pace that is optimal for the family. In essence, the therapist is saying, "I'm not sure this change would be beneficial. I realize the problem has certain disadvantages, but there may be benefits to this situation that need to be identified first, so that improvement in one part of your life won't lead to unforeseen consequences somewhere else. Can you think of any conditions that might get worse if this problem were to be resolved?" As families are encouraged and allowed to identify certain dilemmas that may have been covert, the therapist offers genuineness and warmth to the family in addressing these unforeseen consequences before change begins in earnest.

These examples are commonly referred to as "paradoxical interventions." However, we offer them not as strategic manipulations that may satisfy a practitioner's need for compliance, but as suggestions for understanding human nature at a deeper level, the level of personal and relational dilemmas that often makes change a complicated process for families. If beginning practitioners address resistance as an issue of therapist inexperience, rather than as a personal attribute of the client, therapeutic impasses will become signals that this deeper level of understanding is needed in order to break the impasse. Then, it is possible to return to the models of assessment reviewed in Chapter Six and choose another area of emphasis until the understanding is achieved.

In summary, the family will be most able to resolve its problems when the therapist takes a directive approach to managing in-session process, mobilizes perceptual and behavioral change, and remains nonjudgmental toward unique client characteristics that may be at the heart of a treatment impasse. As beginning practitioners learn to integrate these areas of expertise, they will also be able to recognize how each model of family therapy addresses these elements in some way. Then, they are able to develop their own innovations by combining various models so as to address the issues in a way that is most comfortable or useful for the family.

Chapter Ten

Integrating Treatment Through Case Reviews

The Burns Family

Jean and Dan

A s the beginning practitioner starts to implement assessment and treatment skills, confusion and anxiety inevitably attend the learning process. However, as in-session experience accumulates, practitioners will be able to review their own therapeutic behavior, assessing what parts of the process may need attention. Because therapeutic process is so complex and fast-paced, it is sometimes only in retrospect that the practitioner can make sense of it. Though the elements discussed thus far have often been thought of as separate skills, they are rarely that distinct in practice. Thus, professional growth and development often depends upon therapists' willingness to reflect on the therapeutic process, which cannot be expected to conform to a step-by-step recipe; instead, beginning practitioners must endeavor to identify missing elements or possible options for improving the experience.

In this chapter, two cases are reviewed to help clinicians understand how the practice of family therapy can evolve in many different ways. The clients were seen long before this book was written; therefore, the cases vary according to the style of the practitioner. However, they are used to contrast ways in which basic skills can be implemented. The first case is an example of a short, strategic intervention; the second illustrates a more lengthy assessment process before treatment of the presenting problem begins. In addition, different models are used to conceptualize the problem and different family types influence the choice of interventions.

The Burns Family

Mrs. Burns, a single parent, and her 10-year-old son, Keith, were referred by the school counselor because of Keith's fighting and poor grades. In the initial intake interview, Mrs. Burns reported that since her divorce she had had to work nights and hadn't been able to spend enough time with Keith. Mrs. Burns attended the first session alone because Keith was ill.

Therapist: I'm glad you could get off from work, and I'm sorry Keith is ill today.

Mrs. Burns: Well, I've been looking forward to talking with you. Keith has been very difficult for me to handle for a while but he seems to be getting even worse recently. He's just about too much for me to handle.

Therapist: Tell me what you mean.

Mrs. Burns: You know, he just won't mind or do his schoolwork. I

In this sequence, the therapist joins with the client by asking questions to attain greater specificity and by clarifying her thoughts and feelings regarding the problem she has identified.

just don't know what to do with him.

Therapist: Sounds like you're really frustrated with him.

Mrs. Burns: That's for sure. I'm glad for days he has activities after school because he keeps me stressed out. Then I feel guilty about not wanting him there.

Therapist: Your feelings are mixed then. Although you know the house is more pleasant when he's not there, you think you should want him to be there.

Mrs. Burns: Yes. It doesn't make much sense, does it?

Therapist: What contact have you had with the school?

Mrs. Burns: Not much. I've talked with Mrs. Brown about his schoolwork. I've never talked with her alone, though. Do you think you could do that? I think you might get something out of her. She won't tell me why he does the things he does.

Therapist: Well, Mrs. Burns, I might call her just to get more information about Keith, but I'd prefer that you and I meet with her and his teacher to figure out how to get him to behave better.

Mrs. Burns: I've really tried everything I know. I can't imagine doing anything else with him.

Therapist: Are you willing to try some different things?

Mrs. Burns: Yes, but I can't think what.

Therapist: Well, I'm sure we'll think of some things. But first, I'd like to better understand

During this sequence, the client gives some clues as to her expectation about the role of the therapist as advocate, go-between, and so on. The therapist helps to clarify the process by which he can fulfill such a role.

As the therapeutic relationship evolves, the therapist creates the expectation for change and asks for client cooperation in the process. "Trying some different things" becomes an informal description of the direction of therapy. Then, the therapist pursues a more specific definition of the problem.

what Keith does that you don't like.

Mrs. Burns: OK, I told you he won't mind and he does poorly at school.

Therapist: What do you mean when you say he doesn't mind?

The therapist asks more questions to help define the problem in terms of interactional sequences on the assumption that behavioral patterns consist of circular repeating cycles.

Mrs. Burns: Just that. If I tell him to pick up his clothes or be home on time, he just doesn't do it. When I tell him to do his homework, he just ignores me.

Therapist: Does he tell you he's not going to do what you tell him or does he just act as though he will and then not follow through?

The problem is operationalized by means of questions that put the cycles in behavioral terms, with specific reports of what was actually done or said.

Mrs. Burns: Keith says things like, "OK, later," and then just doesn't do it.

Therapist: When does this usually happen?

Mrs. Burns: Mostly right after school when he wants to watch TV.

Therapist: What happens when he doesn't do it?

Mrs. Burns: Sometimes I get mad and yell at him, but there's not much I can do.

Therapist: So you want Keith to do what you tell him. And you mentioned his poor school-work. Tell me more about that.

The therapist helps the client to identify all problem areas before beginning to prioritize.

Mrs. Burns: Last grading period he got three D's and he's always done well in school before. His teacher says he doesn't turn in his assignments and that he disrupts the class by talking out loud and talking to other students when they're supposed to be working. I've spoken to him about this and told him not to do it, but he denies that he talks to other students.

Therapist: You'd like to see him talk less, then, turn in more assignments, and get better grades.

Mrs. Burns: Right! That would certainly make life easier for all of us.

Therapist: We now have him minding you, completing assignments, and improving grades. Are there other things you're concerned about?

Mrs. Burns: Yes. Really, I'm bothered that Keith has so few friends. Well, really, he doesn't have any close friends. I think Keith just doesn't know how to act around other kids.

Therapist: How does he act?

Mrs. Burns: He's silly.

Therapist: What does he do that's silly?

Continued clarification to obtain behavioral descriptions of what family members report.

Mrs. Burns: He hits people to get attention, or he will interrupt and talk very loudly. I don't know how he is at school.

Therapist: We could probably have a talk with his teacher sometime to find out.

Mrs. Burns: That would help. As I said, I just don't know what to do now.

Therapist: OK, you've mentioned three problem areas— Keith's failure to mind, his poor grades, and his peer relationships. Are there others?

Mrs. Burns: No, those about cover everything.

Therapist: Which of these problems is of most immediate concern to you? Which would you want to change first?

After exploring the areas of greatest concern to the client, the therapist and client prioritize the problems and clarify the issues regarding the most pressing of them.

Mrs. Burns: Getting him to mind. If he did that, it would help me.

Therapist: All right. Let's work on that one first. You've said he minds least right after school when he's watching TV. Is there a particular place where you have the biggest problem?

Mrs. Burns: Yes, usually in the TV room. For one thing, half the time he doesn't seem to hear me. When I tell him to do something, he may not respond at all.

Therapist: You mentioned before that he sometimes says, "OK, later."

Operationalizing the problem behavior.

Mrs. Burns: Yes, when I raise my voice, he makes a promise to do it later. If I talk in a tone of voice like I'm using with you now, he probably wouldn't even answer.

Therapist: How do you usually react when he doesn't answer?

Mrs. Burns: It depends on what I want him to do . . . or what kind of mood I'm in. Sometimes I just go on and do it myself. Other times I yell at him. Then he promises to do it later, and it usually turns into a yelling match, because he doesn't do it at all.

Determining who owns the problem.

Therapist: Does anyone else have difficulty getting him to mind?

Mrs. Burns: Primarily me. My boyfriend occasionally gets mad at him, but he actually asks Keith to do very few things. I think Keith does what he's told to do at school except for assigned work. Mrs. Brown says he isn't really a discipline problem, but that he just doesn't finish his work.

Therapist: You're the one who is mainly concerned about getting him to mind more then. What have you tried so far to get him to mind?

Mrs. Burns: Yelling. Threatening him.

Therapist: How has it worked?

Mrs. Burns: It hasn't. That's why I'm here.

Therapist: Let's work on it together. Now, are you satisfied with first working on getting Keith to mind and then attacking the other concerns?

Mrs. Burns: Fine.

Therapist: It would be important for Keith to be at our next session.

Mrs. Burns: Yes. He should be OK by then. So next week at this time?

Therapist: Yes, if that will work for you.

With a specific problem identified, the therapist develops a contract for change in which the structure (who will attend) and the order of the process is agreed upon.

In the second session Keith was present. In the early part of the session, the therapist joined with Keith. Later, the therapist worked with Mrs. Burns and Keith to find a solution to the problem.

Therapist: Tell me some things about yourself, Keith.

Keith: I like to play ball.

Therapist: What kind of ball?

Keith: Oh, . . . basketball and baseball.

Therapist: Do you play with your neighbors?

Keith: Yeah.

Therapist: Play at school too?

Keith: Yes. I play intermurals.

Therapist: Good! What else do you like to do?

Keith: Not much. I like to listen to music.

Therapist: What kind?

Keith: Peaches.

Therapist: I'm showing my age! What do they play?

Keith: Soft rock.

Therapist: OK. Do you listen to music with your friends?

Keith: Yeah.

Therapist: Good. Well, your mother and I had a chance to talk. Maybe she can share her concerns first, and then I would like to hear from you.

Mrs. Burns: Well, I would like you to mind. When I ask you to do something, I would like you to do it. I want you to quit promising to do things and start doing them.

Keith: Like what?

Mrs. Burns: Doing chores, coming in on time, doing your homework.

Keith: I do those things.

Mrs. Burns: Yes, sometimes, but only after I get after you.

Since Keith was absent from the first session, it is important to spend time joining with him before addressing the identified problem from the first session.

It is important to return to the process of defining the problem in order to develop a collaborative relationship with the person who was previously absent. In this case, the information that comes forth from Keith helps to highlight the relational nature of the problem. Since there are different points of view, the therapist can now change the original definition of the problem from "Keith won't mind" to "We have a disagreement."

Keith: I do my work.

Therapist: So there seems to be some disagreement. Keith, you seem to believe that you get your work done and, Mom, you say he gets it done once in a while but only after you hound him.

Mrs. Burns: Yes.

Keith: [Nods]

Therapist: I'm wondering if you could both keep a record of what is happening. Mrs. Burns, maybe you could write down each time you ask Keith to do something. Let's put this in the left-hand column. Next to it, write down how many times you ask him, and in the right-hand column write whether he does it. Would you be willing to keep a chart of these things?

Rather than trying to establish truth in the midst of the disagreement, the therapist takes advantage of the disagreement to develop a therapeutic task that will implicitly bring about behavioral change if the clients are able to carry it out, because they are being asked to change from trying to solve the problem to simply gathering information. At the same time, the nature of the task sets the stage for the cognitive changes that may come about from information gained in the task.

Mrs. Burns: Yeah, it might keep me really busy writing it all down.

Therapist: I know you care about him and want him to be responsible.

Mrs. Burns: I'll do it. Do I write down every time I ask him to do something?

Although the therapist is remaining neutral in prescribing the task, he continues to provide reassurance and support by noting the mother's good intentions (resources).

Therapist: Yes, . . . and, Keith, I would like you to record each time you do something when your mother requests it. [Shows Keith the chart] If you do this until next Tuesday, it will give us six days of information.

Mrs. Burns: OK. You want us back at the same time?

Therapist: Yes.

Mrs. Burns: Fine.

Therapist: Just remember you are just getting the information; you are not trying to change anything.

Mrs. Burns: Right.

Keith: [Nods]

In the third session, the therapist discussed the information with Mrs. Burns and Keith.

Therapist: Well, how did it go?

Mrs. Burns: I got everything written down here. What I found out was that he really does what I tell him to do sometimes and I guess I don't remember those times.

Therapist: Let's take a look at your chart.

During the remainder of the third session, the therapist noted that Mrs. Burns was making an average of ten requests per day of Keith. In addition, Keith reported that Mrs. Burns's boyfriend, Max, made an average of three requests per day. Sometimes, Mrs. Burns and Max were making requests simultaneously. Both Mrs. Burns and Keith reported that Keith's average level of compliance with his mother was 40%. In addition, Keith complied with all three of Max's requests. The therapist praised Mrs. Burns's and Keith's efforts and asked that Mrs. Burns bring Max to the next session.

In the fourth session, the therapist suggested that Mrs. Burns and Max come to an agreement about what Keith's daily responsibilities should be. With Keith, they could then decide how those duties should be carried out. Mrs. Burns should be the one to communicate with Keith about

In reviewing the information, the therapist can now follow the treatment contract by exploring the changes in thinking and behavior that have occurred during the past week.

A successful treatment program was established when Mrs. Burns and Max were able to agree on Keith's responsibilities and the consequences for compliant behavior. The self-recording procedure that Mrs. Burns and Keith carried out helped them to become aware of specific interactional sequences as they occurred.

his tasks. The therapist also suggested that no more than five requests be made of Keith per day. Max agreed to help monitor the program and to support Mrs. Burns and Keith. If Keith completed all his responsibilities on four out of five days, he would be permitted to go to the Rollerdome on Saturday. The therapist encouraged both of them to continue recording Mrs. Burns's requests and Keith's compliance rate.

Three weeks later, a followup session found Mrs. Burns pleased that Keith was complying with each request on four out of five days. Keith and Max also reported satisfaction with the program. The therapist encouraged the family to maintain the same procedures, so that they could be more aware of their requests and Keith's reaction to their requests. The family was encouraged to call if they had further difficulties.

By minimizing instructions, the therapist was able to empower the family to manage the problem. Moreover, Max was able to play a neutral but supportive role to each, an important structural consideration for a third party who becomes involved with a single-parent family.

This case illustrates how self-observation can help family members to be more aware of their behavior and how they interact with each other. In the follow-up session, the therapist assesses with the family whether the program is progressing satisfactorily. If there are problems in implementing the program, or if the program is not working, the therapist helps troubleshoot with the family. In this case, there were no particular problems after Mrs. Burns reduced the number of demands on her son. If problems were to arise in the future, the therapist would again go through the problem-solving process with the family and determine alternative procedures to be administered.

Jean and Dan

Jean and her husband, Dan, came to counseling at Jean's request, on account of her frustration and admitted lack of bonding with her 2-year-old son, Jason. She stated that she was often angry and disappointed with his responses to her attempted nurturing and was feeling increasingly violent toward him. She had been referred to the family therapist by a friend and by a local social service agency. When she called for an appointment, the therapist asked if she would be willing to invite her husband and if she thought her husband was willing to attend the first session. Jean responded positively to both suggestions and brought Dan to the first session. The initial discussion elicited observations from Dan and Jean about the problem.

As a baby, Jason was "not cuddly," "wanted to be up" most of the time, and was very active. Jean also described him as a "textbook boy." Jason skipped the crawling stage and was walking by his eighth month. Such accelerated development occurred in spite of seizures at seven months and repeated ear infections during infancy. Jean said she felt rejected by Jason and was lonely. Dan indicated that his wife's problems had left him feeling lonely as well. Jean stated that she wanted help with parenting and also with her depression, for which she was currently on medication. Dan indicated that Jean "had a history" of these problems.

The family therapist began to explore recent events and the specific process that brought them to the point of seeking counseling. That process included the following factors:

1. Shortly after Jason was born, Jean went back to work "too soon" as a labor and delivery nurse. She became emotionally and physically exhausted after six weeks and stopped working. At that time, she reported feeling guilty about leaving the baby and feeling rejected by Jason's behavior. As she became increasingly depressed, a psychiatrist prescribed an antidepressant and met with her periodically to monitor the medication; however, he provided no ongoing counseling.

2. During a difficult period with Jason, Jean heard an announcement on TV about a program that offered help to parents who were feeling abusive toward their children. She called the program and went for an initial screening. During this screening, Jean was given the oppor-

The therapist used the problem-definition stage to join with the couple. Jean was given the opportunity to describe her experience and perceptions without being challenged. Dan was asked for his point of view as well. The therapist gained an understanding of their experience by summarizing what was heard and by asking questions. An important aspect was the therapist's curiosity about how the problems affected each of them. *Such inquiry helped to identify areas of pain for both partners. Since Jean was the client of record, the therapist was looking for issues that could motivate Dan to participate for his own well-being. Both partners implied that the problem was Jean's "condition." Thus, at this stage, the therapist was alerted to the need to define the goals of counseling in a conjoint way.*

The referral process was explored for two reasons: (1) to understand Jean's level of motivation for counseling and to determine if she had felt pressured into calling by well-meaning social service personnel; (2) to understand the progression of recent events leading up to the referral, which might signal the level of desperation or danger experienced by family members.

These inquiries revealed Jean's personal motivation for counseling (internal rather than external) and a number of other sources of help that she had identified. While she was distraught, her lack of isolation helped neutralize the danger that she might become violent. However, the number of potential "authorities" involved was a signal for the therapist to clarify her role and determine how each of these helpers would impact each other. The ultimate question was, Who in this network can support therapeutic progress and who might unwittingly interfere in the process?

tunity to join a support group for parents at risk and to participate in an educational program. In addition, the worker suggested that Jean seek counseling, something that agency did not provide.

At this point, the therapist asked if the couple was considering any other sources of help and added counseling to the list, which now included:

1. Psychiatrist
2. Support group
3. Educational program (possibly)
4. Counseling (possibly)

The couple mentioned that a member of the clergy had been consulted but was not giving any ongoing help at that time.

After listing these sources of help for the couple to reflect upon, the family therapist expressed concern that they might be feeling overwhelmed because of the number of helpers involved with the problem and an overload of information for each of them. Agreeing with this assessment, Jean described how she had been "going in all directions" in her desperation to get help and be responsible. The therapist asked the couple to discuss which of the helpers were the most important to them and offered to help them organize a course of action with the other helpers before focusing attention on the presenting problem. The rationale provided was that Jean would probably not be able to benefit from the counseling if there were too many people offering diverse points of view. Thus, the initial goal became that of prioritizing her sources of help and coordinating the most important ones in order to develop a compatible

During this stage of the process, the therapist assumed the role of director, as the couple and therapist determined the best working relationship. The therapist provided leadership in developing priorities; however, the client provided the ranking of importance, so that the direction remained client-centered. The therapist was prepared to advise them to delay therapy if they had listed it last in their order of priorities. However, since Jean validated the therapist's hypothesis that information overload had become an additional problem, the organizational focus by the therapist became an intervention as well as a preliminary contract for service.

Sometimes beginning practitioners fail to see the benefit in taking extra time to clarify the politics of the larger system (client and helpers)and the smaller therapeutic system (therapist and client). However, a therapist in a practice with voluntary clients has no control, but only potential influence, over the larger system, which may play an important role in certain aspects of the therapeutic process. Thus, by focusing on how clients can organize the other influences, the therapist can proceed with appropriate support but with minimal interference from other agencies. In addition, this is an effective intervention for clients who already feel out of control in some part of their life. Their sense of empowerment further dissipates potential danger and creates a hopeful, collegial relationship with the therapist, before the presenting problem is addressed. Since the clients understand that the preliminary goal will help the therapeutic system become more effective, they are satisfied that their concerns are being addressed.

treatment plan. Since Jean stated that counseling was more important to her than the educational program, she was helped to take a more directive role in delaying her enrollment in this optional program. In addition, since her medication and the support group were very helpful to her, the family therapist discussed possible ways of coordinating counseling services with these other sources of help. Jean was asked whether she thought she might be in danger of hurting Jason between the first and second session. She replied, "No." The first session ended with an initial contract to develop a plan of coordination between all parties involved. When this was accomplished to everyone's satisfaction, the presenting problem would then be addressed in greater detail.

In the second session, Jean and her husband brought back information from the psychiatrist that clarified his role as simply monitoring and prescribing medication. He was open to discussing Jean's situation with the family therapist, but was not providing counseling services at that time. In addition, Jean was able to clarify what she hoped to accomplish in counseling that would be different from her experiences with her support group.

With these issues clarified, the therapeutic system could move ahead in developing goals and a contract for service that would specifically address Jean's original concern—her problems with her son. By this time, the family therapist had joined with the couple through empowering them to be more assertive with outside influences in their lives. In addition, Dan had expressed his own frustrations, thereby providing the therapist with an opportunity

If the potential for violence had been greater in this situation, the therapist would have helped the couple develop a plan for safety first (see Chapter Five), then addressed the larger system, and left the traditional therapeutic goals for last.

The assignment helped Jean to understand the expectations she had for the therapist and it also helped the therapist to understand what role could complement, and not conflict with, the influence of Jean's support group.

to engage him more personally in the therapeutic contract.

Therapist: Dan, it sounds like things haven't been too good for you lately. You mentioned last week how lonely your marriage had been since Jason was born.

Dan: That's true, things haven't been all that rosy.

Therapist: Well, I'm wondering if you would be interested in an agreement for counseling in which we state that we'll not only work to make things better for Jean, but we'll also take a look at how things could be better for you, too.

Dan: That would be OK.

Jean: I know I'm not being a very good wife right now . . . ..

Therapist: That may be how it seems right now, but that's not what I was referring to. Usually, when a couple first marries and has complications such as you have with a first child, it's very common for spouses to go through a period of stress and conflict. [To Dan:] Although Jean's problems were your motivation for coming, I feel a responsibility to help you with those problems in a way that will strengthen rather than threaten your marriage. The best way to do that is to involve Dan and include him in the problem-solving process.

Dan: I'd like that.

Therapist: Jean, would it be OK with you if we include Dan,

Although Dan had agreed to come to the first session and was willing to help Jean, there was no explicit understanding that he would address his own concerns except as they related to solving the problem of Jean's frustration and depression. Therefore, the therapist initiated a conversation with Dan, in order to understand whether he was comfortable with the idea of identifying and owning positive outcomes for himself.

If he had responded negatively, the therapist would have accepted Dan's response and acknowledged Dan's wisdom in recognizing his limits and in being firm about what is best for him. Then, the therapist could ask Dan to describe more fully what aspect of the therapy process seemed problematic for him. At that point, the therapist might be able to address those concerns. If not, Dan might be willing to act as an intermittent consultant, agreeing to attend occasional sessions, or he might be willing to make occasional check-ins with the therapist by telephone. These would be used to continue the joining process and to learn more about how the therapy process could be sensitive to his needs.

Since the therapist was able to engage Dan, the goal of therapy can be expanded to include a strengthening of the relationship. In this way, the marriage becomes a focus for change as well as a resource in solving the presenting problem. Such an orientation carries with it the assumption that presenting problems are influenced by the significant relationships of those who define the problem. By involving significant others in solving the presenting problem, the family therapist makes a choice to facilitate a solution that will impact the client's relational system in the best possible way.

rather than you coming by yourself?

Jean: Yes. I think it would help. We don't communicate very well.

Therapist: Dan, what do you think about Jean's observation?

Dan: She's right. We need some help. I'll come if it will help.

Therapist: So, if our agreement included the strengthening of your relationship, does that sound like it might make things better for you at home?

Dan: Yes, that sounds good.

Since the couple was in the early stages of the family life-cycle and the immediate problem (feelings of violence toward the child) was under control, the therapist chose a psycho-educational approach, with a longer assessment period, in order to help the couple reflect on the developmental context of the presenting problem. In addition, since their stated goal did not include specific behavioral objectives, the assessment process could be used to identify particular interactional sequences in their life that could be targeted for change.

At this point, noting that their observations and definition of the problem had already been discussed at length, the therapist suggested that they participate together in a thorough assessment process as a means of reviewing the many changes and adjustments that had taken place in their young married lives. Such an assessment could also provide them with a perspective that would be useful in developing strategies to solve the present problem and to meet other challenges that occur as a natural part of family life. The assessment process was described as a series of three to five sessions that would help the family therapist understand their unique experiences together and help them select the best strategy for finding a solution. The couple agreed to this contract; the husband characterized his involvement as a way to strengthen their relationship. The therapist asked Jean if her feelings of violence toward Jason were so strong that a five-week delay before the beginning of treatment might be dangerous. She indicated that knowing she was now getting help made her feel better, and said she could call members of her support group if she began to feel too desperate.

The third and fourth sessions were spent reviewing information that the couple identified as important for the therapist to know. Jean reported having suicidal thoughts and wanting to find a way to escape the stresses she was now feeling. She stated that she had no plan and did not want to die; however, she continued to feel overwhelmed and guilty about her relationship with Jason. In reviewing the history of these feelings, she revealed a suicide attempt during her high school years and described her pattern of coping during emotional difficulties. She found it hard to prioritize and often felt disorganized, not knowing where to begin. At the same time, she would become angry at Dan for his inability to be more helpful to her. Dan felt depressed and wished he had more confidence in himself. He said he had been feeling increasingly discouraged and was considering dropping out of electronics school. Both partners said they wanted to make changes in these areas and wanted to save face as well, since they were embarrassed about their problems and wanted to look more competent in the eyes of their families.

The fifth session was devoted to a developmental review of the couple's courtship, marriage, and early married life. Keeping in mind Jean's initial goal of feeling better about her son and eliminating all feelings of violence toward him, the family therapist used these sessions to discover and highlight information that might put Jean's feelings in a larger context, so as to allow the couple to redefine the problem in some way that would lead to its resolution. As the couple described the ups and downs of their lives, the therapist portrayed these events not as problems to be solved, but rather as life experiences from which they were learning new skills. The review process became a vehicle for increased intimacy between Jean and Dan, who took the opportunity to reflect on their life together and to develop a shared understanding about their strengths and weaknesses. In addition, the family therapist was able to identify how existing strengths in the couple could be used to develop additional problem-solving skills.

As Jean and Dan reviewed their early courtship, they recalled their attraction to each other: Dan perceived Jean as "sincere, cute, and together"; Jean perceived Dan to be "handsome and shy." Their early married life was characterized by financial struggles, followed by a pregnancy after the first year. Because of complications, Jean was ordered to bed by her doctor during the month in which she was scheduled to take her state nursing exam. It was during this period that the couple began to feel alienated from each other and Jean's depression began to surface.

The therapist used the telling of the couple's story to point out their accomplishments in spite of the hardships. Jean had graduated from college. Dan was being used at school as a tutor because of his competence. They had felt close and hopeful in spite of financial problems. As they began to experience increased distance and frustration, they remained committed to the marriage and continued to try to improve the situation. Their endurance was identified as a strength, and their patience under the onslaught of complications was emphasized.

The therapist noticed that the initial attraction of Jean and Dan included clues about what they might be expecting from each other. If Dan thought Jean was "together," he might be unprepared for a wife who would need his help and support. In addition, when Jean thought of Dan as "shy," she may have assumed that this would be a relationship where her sense of initiative and willingness to nurture could be valued. The therapist identified the complementarity of the couple (one as giver and one as receiver) as a possible locus of developmental crisis: Now that Jean had been stretched to her limit by life experience and unforeseen complications, she felt guilty that she could not fulfill her unspoken role in the marriage. Dan also felt disappointed that the previous relational patterns were not being maintained. In addition, Jean's anger at Dan could be seen as an indication that she was aware of the imbalance and was asking for a change.

Since the complementarity of the couple followed traditional gender stereotypes, the therapist was careful not to characterize Jean's anger at Dan as weak, since Jean perceived a lack of

During the sixth session, Jean reported that her suicidal thoughts had resumed, as she remembered her sexual permissiveness during her courtship with Dan. She felt guilty for violating the standards of her family of origin and remembered her role in her family as a "shining star." The therapist suggested that they spend more time understanding the patterns related to each spouse's family of origin; however, Jean asked for a session alone to discuss a problem with her employer that had reached a crisis. The therapist cooperated with Jean's request and the seventh and eighth sessions were spent developing strategies to help Jean be more assertive with her supervisor.

When Dan returned to the ninth session, Jean reported that she had begun to understand her feelings toward Jason as part of her personal need to be a perfect shining star. As she began to notice these feelings dominating her, she started to address her internal process, as a way of detaching from her negative feelings toward Jason. She began to realize that this need for perfection was an unrealistic goal, which had come from her role in her family of origin. The couple agreed that Jean's family was sometimes a help and sometimes a hindrance to their well-being. As family-of-origin issues were explored,

reciprocity in the marriage. At the same time, the therapist empathized with Dan's disappointment, treating it as an understandable by-product brought on by life events that rendered Jean unable to maintain her role unconditionally. In such discussions, the couple was invited to consider how their roles could be more flexible— how they could take turns in the supportive role, rather than polarizing to a rigid extreme. However, when Jean began to discuss her feelings of hopelessness, the therapist decided to delay more extensive marital intervention until Jean's depression improved.

Although the therapist wanted to help with the developmental task of negotiating boundaries with in-laws, it was more important to cooperate with what Jean felt was an impending crisis. By remaining flexible and democratic, the therapist was able to maintain a collegial relationship with Jean and to cooperate with her priorities. With the depression still pronounced, it was also necessary for the therapist to empower Jean by validating what was most relevant to her.

At this time, the client volunteered clues about how she was integrating information from the larger context (for example, life-cycle, marital dynamics, family of origin) with the presenting problem. However, if the client had not indicated that the therapeutic process was still relevant to the presenting problem, it would have been the therapist's responsibility to raise the question and review the sessions to date, with the intent of renegotiating a clearer understanding of what needed to be addressed (child management strategies, marital communication, or other issues). At the middle stage of therapy, if the initial issues are no longer the focus, it is the couple successfully executed a new plan in which Dan could support Jean when she was more assertive with her parents. She had feared their disapproval all her life. Rather than let them know when she was fearful or feeling inadequate, she had constantly tried to live up to her shining star image. She was able to understand her earlier suicide attempt as a time in her life when she was keeping negative feelings to herself and was driven by high expectations from self and family. As Jean and Dan both became more assertive with their families, they also began to feel a sense of equal status with their parents and a sense of increased competence. By the fifteenth session, both were enjoying Jason more and were feeling a sense of accomplishment in their progress.

Two months passed before the next group of sessions. Jean and Dan reported heavy work schedules, which they had no choice but to endure. Upon returning, both were feeling distant and out of control. They expressed a need to have time for each other. Marital and health issues were addressed during the remaining 15 sessions. The therapist used reports of conflict to reframe arguments as opportunities for increased communication. Couple interaction patterns were reported: Jean would become upset and "blow up" but then recant her complaint and back down. Dan would try to pacify Jean and "jump around," as he tried to guess what she really wanted.

In addition, they began to identify a pattern of overresponsibility in Jean and underresponsibility in Dan. She was consistently the initiator

important to clarify who initiated the change of focus. When clinicians initiate the change (for example, from feelings toward son to feelings toward family of origin), they should also initiate a discussion about how this change affects the client. Does the change seem relevant to the client? Does the therapist's rationale satisfy a client's questions? Is there a direction that would seem more relevant to the client?

In this case, the process had influenced the couple to view the problem developmentally, as they reviewed their marital development—and now Jean's personal development—through many life transitions. Jean was taking the initiative to move in the direction of her family issues, and Dan was willing to explore his own family-of-origin relationships as a result.

At this point in the process, the couple felt no further need to address Jean's original concerns regarding Jason. Instead, they brought a definition of the problem that had clear relational components and was explicitly marital in nature. This gave the therapist the opportunity to address earlier hypotheses regarding the complementarity in the marriage.

In earlier stages of therapy, the therapist had remained indirect, addressing only the most immediate aspects that related to the original presenting problem. However, the small pragmatic changes that had been made months before were not enough to challenge the couple's original "private marital contract" and its complementarity, which spread to other aspects of their relationship. Dan had become more involved with child care and home management; however, these were in the marriage; most decisions were her idea. Dan would comply, rather than negotiate with Jean around his preferences or differing point of view. When the couple began to use their arguments as opportunities to negotiate differences, Dan became more involved in decisions and Jean felt more support with household responsibilities. They began to experience improved marital communication, largely on account of becoming more assertive with each other, rather than avoiding conflict through distance. Ultimately, they decided to terminate therapy so that they could begin saving their money instead to buy a home. The therapist complimented them on their ability to prioritize and take control of their lives in such an assertive manner. They were left with the option of returning for support, if needed. Two years later, they successfully purchased their first home and, in approximately two more years, they had a second child with no complications and reported that they were doing fine.

seen as necessary to help Jean, not as a rewriting of significant marital expectations.

Now that Jean's depression had lifted and the couple was asking for marital counseling, the therapist could resurrect previous hypotheses about the relationship and address them directly. Drawing upon literature about gender relationships and birth-order roles, the therapist took a psychoeducational approach by raising the issue of over- and underresponsibility.

After tracking interactional sequences, the therapist would ask them to describe the outcomes they would have preferred and what each person's options were for bringing about more satisfying interactions. In response to the therapist's coaching and reassurance, the couple learned to tolerate each other's anger and to understand the thoughts and intentions that were influencing their behaviors. As communication brought a deeper level of intimacy and more concrete requests for behavioral changes, their marital roles became broader and more flexible. Emotional support became more reciprocal: Dan realized that he had strength to offer Jean, and Jean realized that she had the right to ask Dan to make some sacrifices for the relationship.

This case illustrates the convergence of culture, gender, life-cycle, family structure, family of origin, and personal constructs in the formation of the presenting problem. When a couple has a child, the three automatically form a triangle (family structure influenced by life-cycle changes). Jean became close to Jason and developed depression when he did not respond according to her expectations (personal constructs). Her expectations of self and Jason came from her role as a shining star (culture and family of origin influencing personal constructs). The couple's pattern of over- and underresponsibility was addressed at the parenting level and, later, at the level of marital roles and communication (gender issues influencing family structure). The therapist first intervened with the family and larger system by helping them to challenge cultural assumptions about seeking help. Next, Dan was engaged as an important player in the therapeutic process. This intervention created a context for change in gender balances and family structure. Problem solving around Jean's work issues validated her ability to take charge of her life and became a positive prelude to addressing her issues with her family of origin in a more assertive way. As the couple worked together on these earlier issues, they developed the trust and intimacy needed to become more assertive and negotiable with each other. And what about Jason? The presenting problem was redefined in light of all these factors, and positive changes occurred as each systemic issue became an area of growth for both parents.

To sum up, we have attempted to integrate treatment concepts through two case reviews. In the Burns family, the therapist was able to get the family to agree on the problem and a self-observation procedure to assess the interactional patterns around the problem. By reducing Mrs. Burns's frequency of requests and getting her boyfriend to support Mrs. Burns and Keith in their new behavior, the therapist was able to empower the family to manage the problem. In the case of Jean and Dan, the therapist provided an integration of treatment models to create a context for change in gender roles and family structure.

The treatment offered to both of these families is not presented as a model to be replicated and therefore is deliberately not recorded in specific detail. Instead, both case reviews serve only as a guide for integrating treatment concepts and methods. Therapists are obligated to use their own sensitive, creative, and flexible ideas in integrating treatment with their client families. As such integrations develop, evaluative feedback from clients can help the family therapist maintain a relevant and individualized direction.

Chapter Eleven

Conducting Evaluations, Terminations, and Follow-Ups

I n the course of family therapy, evaluations take place in many different ways. Chapter Three discussed evaluations as a final stage in the therapeutic process and as an ongoing review that happens as family therapists assess their effectiveness. In addition, evaluations of family process may occur during initial assessments if therapists employ formal evaluation measures such as objective questionnaires or research instruments. These forms of evaluation are used in treatment planning and in developing an understanding of family members' experience. Later in the process, evaluations may take the form of noting treatment outcomes that provide the impetus for a new treatment plan, termination, supervision, or research. If these forms are placed in an order corresponding to therapeutic process, the beginning practitioner could conceptualize the various forms of evaluation in the following manner:

1. Objective evaluations can be administered during the assessment stage of therapy to aid in understanding family process and in formulating treatment plans.
2. Ongoing microevaluations can take place session by session as a conversational feedback loop that informs the clinician as to how family members are reacting to the therapeutic process.
3. Outcome evaluations can gather qualitative (verbal) or quantitative (behavioral or numerical) information that helps the family therapist document the completion of goals or the need to revise treatment goals or plans.
4. Evaluations in training and research can document therapist skill levels and general therapeutic patterns.

This chapter will focus on these forms of evaluation and how they can be used at different points along the therapeutic process.

Evaluating Family Process

Evaluations that relate specifically to client variables occur in a variety of situations. Clients may evaluate themselves with an expectation of improvement in some aspect of their well-being. Traditionally, therapists have adopted the role of expert and evaluated their clients. This may happen during the initial assessment phase in treatment and is sometimes formally accomplished by administering objective instruments. In addition, third parties, such as schools and social services, may desire some type of evaluation related to client behavior if they initiate referral. Because of this, even if family therapists hope to maintain a focus on the family's strengths, it is virtually impossible to escape situations where the goals of the client or others dictate that therapists provide an evaluation in their role as expert.

Family process measures are often designed as paper-and-pencil questionnaires that provide family therapists with a family member's self-report of his or her own behaviors or perceptions. Of the various instruments commonly in use, we will discuss the Family Adaptability and Cohesion Evaluation Scale (FACES), the Locke-Wallace Marital Status Inventory (L-W), the Dyadic Adjustment Scale (DAS), the Marital Precounseling Inventory (MPI), and the Divorce Adjustment Inventories (DAI).

The Family Adaptability and Cohesion Evaluation Scale, third edition (FACES III), is based on the Olson Circumplex Model (Olson, Porter, & Ravee, 1985). This inventory measures family members' perceptions of family process and provides a score upon the two dimensions of adaptability and cohesion. Adaptability refers to flexibility of roles, rules, and relationships during times of stress. Cohesion refers to the sense of emotional bonding experienced by family members. FACES III is the most recent version of the inventory and is widely used to discriminate between control groups and families with varying degrees of dysfunction. Family therapists often use FACES III in research and in obtaining a baseline of family functioning prior to treatment.

The Locke-Wallace Marital Status Inventory contains a set of true/false items that are used to assess steps toward dissolution of the marriage. According to Weiss and Perry (1979), the test was designed to provide "an intensity scale (for example, Guttman scale) such that any given step would necessarily include all preceding steps. Thus, before one sought legal aid for a divorce it would be reasonable to assume that one had thoughts about divorce and engaged in behaviors preparatory to that of seeking legal advice" (p. 17). Because this inventory describes intensity, it is possible for the clinician to use the information in deciding whether crisis intervention is needed or whether a less dramatic treatment plan is warranted.

Spanier (1976) included many items from the Locke-Wallace inventory (Locke & Wallace, 1959) in his assessment scale. Weiss and Perry (1979) altered the items omitted by Spanier so that both measures are incorporated into one questionnaire, called the Dyadic Adjustment Scale. The DAS is somewhat more modern in its wording than the Locke-Wallace inventory and provides four factor scales: Dyadic Consensus (for example, problem solving), Dyadic Satisfaction (for example, "good feelings" and "sentiment" in the relationship), Dyadic Cohesion (for example, outside interests, exchange of ideas, cooperation), and Affectional Expression (for example, sexual and emotional expression). The DAS instrument is easy to score and may be very useful to the behavioral family therapist because it conceptualizes the marital relationship as a set of specific behaviors that may be targeted for increase or decrease.

The Marital Precounseling Inventory (Stuart & Stuart, 1972) is administered prior to treatment so as to aid treatment planning. The inventory is 11 pages long and provides assessment information in the following areas: daily activities of both spouses; general goals and resources for change; spouse satisfaction and targets for change in 12 areas of marital and family functioning; rationales for decision making; and level of commitment to the marriage (Stuart, 1976). MPI serves several purposes. It provides the therapist with data for planning a treatment program, and it also helps to orient the couple to treatment. Each spouse can often anticipate those issues that will be discussed. At the end of treatment, the inventory can be completed to evaluate therapy.

The DAI (Brown, Eichenberger, Portes, & Christensen, 1991) provides both child and parent ratings of divorce adjustment. The DAI for parents consists of 31 Likert scale items that offer a numerical range of responses related to family functioning, children's coping skills, and social support systems before and after divorce. The DAI for children consists of 25 Likert scale items that assess the child's adjustment to divorce. Clinicians are able to help parents facilitate the adjustment of their children through the use and discussion of the results.

These instruments serve a variety of assessment functions. First, they provide objective measures of overt and covert behavior important to the satisfaction of the relationship. Second, instruments often reveal information that family members might be reluctant to provide in an interview; for example, a spouse may find it embarrassing to discuss sexual issues in the interview. The therapist can often use this information to help family members focus on critical issues that might otherwise be avoided. Finally, instruments often provide an ongoing measure of subjective satisfaction that cannot be obtained through direct observation.

When using self-report scales and inventories, there are several considerations:

1. *Select instruments that measure specific areas of family functioning.* This is of critical importance. For example, the DAI (Brown, Eichenberger, Portes, & Christensen, 1991) contains subscales that measure parental interaction and parent-child interaction, both critical variables in divorce adjustment.
2. *Select instruments that have been validated on similar populations.* If the instrument of choice is normed on a population similar (in terms of socioeconomic status, race, ethnic group, and so on) to the client family, the client-family scores can be compared with the norm group. If norms are not available for the client family's group, interpretations are likely to be unfair and negatively biased.
3. *Use the scales or checklists in conjunction with other evaluation data.* By using scales and inventories to corroborate other evaluation data—observations, goal attainment scales, and self-reports—the therapist can be more confident that change has actually occurred.

The biggest limitation in using scales or inventories is that they are global and often fail to pinpoint specific concerns of the family; that is, marital adjustment or satisfaction scales may provide an index of marital quality but may not be an adequate measure of the problem the family brings to therapy. Furthermore, scales and inventories may not be appropriate for minority families (if the appropriate cultural norms are not available), some family members who have little education, or families who are hesitant to disclose certain information before developing comfort with the therapist. If a family has already suffered some degree of prejudice from a comparison to cultural norms, such instruments should be used with caution and with a neutral explanation of how results will be interpreted. For example, inventories that primarily describe internal family process can provide families with descriptive information about their relationships, rather than a diagnostic score that indicates health or dysfunction.

Evaluating Therapeutic Process

The therapeutic relationship is central to the facilitation of change and should be monitored on many levels as family therapy progresses. This evaluation should include the perceptions of the practitioner and of the family. Without feedback from each side of the interaction, it is difficult for clinicians, supervisors, or researchers to account for strengths and weaknesses in the interpersonal process between therapist and family. What is the relationship like? Is it accomplishing the desired goals? Is it authoritarian, cooperative, or collegial? This assessment may focus on each person's role and expectations in the relationship, as well as how these are manifest in therapeutic interactions. What type of communication patterns can be described in therapy sessions? Are therapist and family able to "communicate about their communication" with each other? This type of evaluation is subjective in nature and should be used regularly to avoid misunderstandings, to troubleshoot when the clinician feels a lack of therapeutic progress, and in situations where the clinician anticipates a potential problem from a subsequent part of the treatment plan.

Family Perceptions

Family members may be privately evaluating the therapist with respect to trustworthiness, empathy, safety, helpfulness, and so on. This level of evaluation is based on subjective criteria chosen by each person and is often related to first impressions of interpersonal comfort. At this level of evaluation, discussion must be initiated by therapists, because the topic can be intimate and threatening for family and therapist. To ask families about how they are experiencing the process elicits information that may imply how therapists are doing their job. Nevertheless, beginning family therapists can minimize their sense of threat in such an interaction by regarding the clients' perceptions as information about what is most comfortable for them. Therapist competency is then related to a willingness to ask the questions, and not to the content of the answers. Family therapists can conduct this type of evaluation in a spirit of reflection, communicating self-confidence and concern about the well-being of the client. Is the family feeling comfortable with the process? Does the process seem beneficial and hopeful? Is it too structured? Too unstructured? Too authoritarian? Relevant? Not relevant?

An interesting research project that addressed client perceptions of family therapists was conducted by Newfield, Kuehl, Joanning, and Quinn (1991) with families who had participated in family therapy as part of a study of adolescent substance abuse. In this qualitative study, independent interviewers asked participants to describe their experience of the family therapy process, their perceptions of the therapist, and their views of the outcome. The purpose of the project was to obtain qualitative information about therapy from a lay point of view. The investigators characterized professional clinicians as members of a culture (with a distinctive language and expectations) that is different from the culture of those who seek their services. In this qualitative research, the main questions focused on what occurred in the process and the implications of these occurrences. The results of this research suggested that clients were most satisfied with treatment when therapy matched their conceptualizations of the problem. Consequently, an anthropological view of the therapeutic experience uses the language and expectations of clients to understand the process, rather than technical theories that are rooted in the culture of the profession.

Often, beginning practitioners are most threatened by openly expressed anger, criticism, or despair from family members. However, we find it useful to help trainees anticipate their most feared stumbling blocks and develop a repertoire of questions and responses that encourage open discussion of client experience. For example, some clinicians give clients permission to express disagreement or discontent ("It's normal for family members to become upset over some aspects of the therapy process. Can you think of anything so far that has been upsetting or confusing for you?"). Family members may be uncomfortable with some part of the process (for example, questions or responses from the therapist that inadvertently offend someone). When this is discovered, the therapist can legitimize their experience ("I'm sorry for the misunderstanding; you did the right thing to let me know about it") or put their feelings into a larger perspective ("I can understand how you would come to feel this way. You're not the only one who has had this type of experience, and sometimes we professionals need help in knowing how you're feeling about our work together"). Very often, anger can be reframed as pain, thereby alerting the practitioner to some aspect of the process that has become threatening for a family member. Dominance can be reframed as fear, which alerts the therapist to a covert sense of vulnerability. When clients express despair ("This isn't doing any good"), the therapist can inquire about expectations and priorities of the client that may need to be addressed more directly. Despair may also prompt the therapist to explain the process more fully and to shift the target of change—for example, from behavioral to cognitive or from cognitive to behavioral. Family members who are more literal or concrete (results-oriented) often want behavioral change to be manifest first. Family members who are more intuitive (process-oriented) often want cognitive change that impacts their internal experience.

It is recommended that practitioners ask for client perceptions of therapeutic process before and after various stages of assessment and treatment. For example, if a family has agreed to cooperate with the construction of a genogram in an initial interview, the practitioner may still want to ask the family in the beginning of the second session if they feel comfortable proceeding in that direction—for example, "On a scale from 1 to 10, how comfortable are you with our plan for today?" By acknowledging that some families are uncomfortable with the process or do not think it is a relevant exercise for their particular problem, the family therapist provides the family with an opportunity to discuss their thoughts, second thoughts, or questions about the process. It also gives the therapist an opportunity to search for a rationale that makes sense to the family or to search for a different approach.

Careful observation of nonverbal messages is another important vehicle for gauging client perceptions. Many family members are too threatened to make direct disclosures about their experience. In that case, the observation of behavioral patterns and sequences over time provides useful information on how the process fits the clients. For example, family therapists may discover that clients respond to some direction, advice, or task with a "yes, but" pattern. This pattern can be interpreted as a nonverbal message that the direction or task does not fit. In addition, such a pattern should be thought of as a courteous power struggle between therapist and family member, which should be avoided through therapist flexibility. When the therapist can take a one-down position and state a desire to change the process so that the family feels more comfortable, the family is encouraged to trust more and to be more direct with the therapist.

One way of learning from nonverbal messages involves noting how families respond to homework and out-of-session tasks. De Shazer (1985) lists five possible responses that clients may make to a given task assignment and five suggested responses from the therapist. Even when a family does something opposite to the task or fails to fulfill the assignment at all, therapists are encouraged to view the family's response as a message that the family is instinctively doing what is best for them. By such nonverbal observation, the therapist learns to understand messages that are sent through behavior instead of words.

As family therapists become skilled at eliciting microevaluations from family perceptions, they will discover that such evaluations become interventions. These turning points of change in the therapeutic relationship become models for change in family relationships. In addition, the effectiveness of the therapeutic relationship is influenced by perceptions, beliefs, and attitudes that develop within the therapist. These will now be examined.

Therapist Perceptions

The therapist may be evaluating clients with respect to level of cooperation, severity of the problem, and so on. In addition to focusing on the family's perception of the process, clinicians must also pay attention to their own perceptions and misperceptions of the process. If a therapist is feeling stuck but finds that the client is satisfied with the process, what does that say about the theory that the practitioner is using as a lens? By the same token, if both therapist and client are feeling dissatisfied with the process, blame can be centered on the process and not on either party. Then, both parties can work together to cooperatively resolve their dissatisfaction. Besides modeling problem-solving skills, the family therapist also demonstrates a willingness to admit mistakes and to explore misunderstandings. When the client is feeling dissatisfied, but the practitioner believes that all is well, it is important for clinicians to distinguish assumption from fact or, in constructivist terms, to distinguish their personal reality from the reality of the client.

When reviewing their own perceptions, family therapists should remember that their behavior is often an extension of their beliefs and intentions. Using the Awareness Wheel from the Couple Communication Program (Miller et al., 1988), it is possible for the clinician to identify what thoughts and intentions may have been operating during problematic interactions. A therapist who has chosen a specific model of family therapy to practice may also compare his or her own perceptions with the assumptions adopted by the model. For example, suppose that a therapist's goal is to conduct a session from an intergenerational point of view. The fundamental assumptions of that model include an acknowledgment that past relationships and interactions affect present relationships and interactions and the assertion that thoughts and intentions are often taught by one generation to another. Thus, if the therapist inquires about family and cultural values, significant intergenerational relationships, and the evolution of the client's experience in the family of origin, these behaviors would reflect an intergenerational point of view. However, if the therapist becomes concerned with a client's weight problem without directing therapeutic conversation toward how the weight is related to intergenerational dynamics, the therapist's conduct might indicate a lack of self-confidence in executing the model, a conflicting belief (for example, "If I try to relate the problem to a larger issue, the client may disagree"), or a belief that eliminates the model altogether (for example, "Weight is not related to intergenerational dynamics; it is related to present behavior and life-style").

Therapists should also take the opportunity to evaluate their own perceptions when they leave a session feeling angry, defeated, or confused. At these times, reflecting on expectations for self, client, and the process itself is in order. Is the therapist expecting too much from the family? Is the therapist becoming dependent on client behavior for a feeling of success? Has the therapist remembered to utilize strengths and idiosyncrasies of the family in the proposed solution to the problem? Has the therapist found a way to value the unique and sometimes contrary style of a family? By means of these questions, which constitute a form of self-supervision, clinicians are able to develop learning and process goals that can further their own cognitive and behavioral development. In addition, the traditional supervisory process can shed light on therapists' perceptions of the process. Objective evaluations can also provide an external review of therapeutic process.

Periodic Evaluations of the Process

In many instances, periodic evaluations of the process will prevent impasses from occurring. Coleman (1985) suggests that treatment failures are often related to a variety of factors, including theoretical issues, process issues, motivation and consumerism, goal setting, the therapeutic alliance, personal issues of the therapist, and relationships with larger systems. If an impasse has occurred, an evaluation of these factors might provide a constructive resolution. For many beginning family therapists struggling to put their nascent skills to work, it is a challenge to initiate an evaluation. Since negative evaluations make learning difficult, it is human nature to avoid the possibility of criticism until more confidence is gained. However, such evaluations can be as simple as reviewing the history of therapy to date. Beginning practitioners can also use the outline from Chapter Five to analyze the beginning stages of therapy. Was any important topic skipped? Was the information about previous treatment history detailed? Was the discussion about goals and expectations candid? What might the client still be hesitant to disclose? What would the family need for the therapeutic relationship to become more comfortable? As clinicians begin to experiment with periodic evaluations of their own process through the eyes of the family, they will discover the importance of such information in facilitating therapeutic progress.

While discussions about the therapeutic relationship may often be informal and impromptu, it is also possible to evaluate therapeutic interaction in a formal way for supervision or research. Supervisors may observe therapeutic exchanges first-hand in order to understand the nature of the therapeutic relationship. In some training programs, sessions are recorded on audiotape to enable beginning practitioners to review their communication patterns and to monitor their grasp of various skills. For example, a formal evaluation might consist of the practitioner reviewing a tape of a family therapy session and counting how many circular questions were asked of the family. If there was a part of the session when the therapist felt stuck, the evaluation could also include a review of circular questions to see which ones could have been asked during the period of difficulty.

In addition, therapeutic process can be formally evaluated through models of interactional analysis that are used for research. The Couple Communication Program can be used for this purpose, since communication may readily be broken down into each category of the Awareness Wheel and then quantified, by noting the frequencies in each category. The Relational Coding Scheme is another model that analyzes communication into categories such as questions, support, assertions, talkovers, and so on (Ericson & Rogers [1973]). An analysis of therapeutic interaction with this method would categorize each message from each person and quantify how many of each type of statements were made. In additional analyses, this coding scheme produces data that describe the sequence and patterns of each exchange over time. For example, if the client made frequent assertions that were often followed by the therapist asking frequent questions, this recurring pattern could be noted by the formal analysis.

Thus, it is possible to conduct formal and informal evaluations of each person's experience in the therapeutic process and of the nature of specific micro-interactions within the relationship and also to assess the ongoing relationship and its effectiveness. In focusing on therapeutic process in these ways, the beginning practitioner begins to see that the process of family therapy is, indeed, a complex set of interactions that accommodate multiple points of view and are experienced on multiple levels. These interactions become the means used by the clinician to bring about change. Such change is measured at another level of clinical evaluation, which usually focuses on treatment outcomes.

Evaluating Outcomes of Family Therapy

There are several formal methods for determining whether goals have been met in therapy: measuring behavioral changes, goal attainment scales, self-reports, and behavioral checklists. These methods may be used separately, or in combination, to determine whether goal behaviors have been successfully reached.

Measuring Behavioral Changes

Of the various evaluation designs the therapist may utilize, the most useful for tracking specific behavioral changes are time-series designs, where data are collected over different points in time. Some of these have been developed for experimental purposes and, therefore, may not be practical for the therapist, who, in many cases, must change the family's behavior in the shortest possible time. Only those designs that are of practical use in family therapy will be discussed here.

The AB design   The simplest time-series approach is the AB design. Here the therapist or family first record baseline rates of target behaviors (positive interactions, arguments, and so on). Having plotted the baseline level of behavior, the therapist and family set an objective. It is helpful to specify the number of consecutive days on which the criterion must be achieved, so as to provide an objective determination of when the goal has been reached. The therapist or family gathers a second set of data during the implementation phase of the program. Data may be collected continuously throughout the program or at specific times. For example, during baseline, a couple averaged only 5 minutes of positive interaction per day for one week. On the basis of this information, the therapist and family decided the couple should set a goal of at least 15 minutes each day for positive (problem-free) interaction. Figure 11.1 illustrates that the goal was reached.

The AB design in this instance provides an easy means of evaluating one behavior of one family in one setting. The therapist may only need to collect baseline data for several days (until there is some consistency in the rate), then set a reasonable objective, and continue collecting data to measure changes. By graphing data, therapist and family can set realistic goals and monitor those goals on a daily basis.

The therapist should be mindful that other events might also be influencing the behavior of the family. For example, while the couple set aside time for positive interaction, both spouses may have been getting encouragement from friends and family to do more things with each other. However, even though this

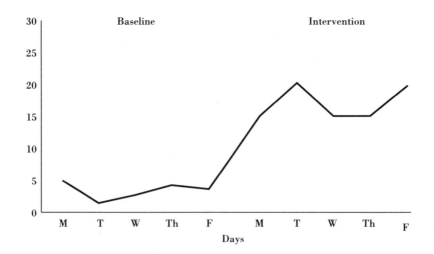

Figure 11.1

design does not control for error resulting from competing events, it is an acceptable means for determining whether an objective has been met.

The multiple baseline   In some instances, therapists may be interested in more than one target behavior for a particular family, or they may want to measure changes on a specific behavior for more than one family or situation. In that case, a multiple baseline is used. For example, a second target behavior for the couple just discussed was the amount of time spent arguing with their son. When they reached the first goal (15 minutes per day of positive interaction), the family, under the therapist's guidance, set a second goal: to reduce the amount of negative interaction with their son from 25 to 5 minutes daily.

Figure 11.2 illustrates an increase in the couple's positive interaction time when exposed to the first intervention (that is, structured time for positive interaction), while the amount of negative interaction time with the son (which is not being treated) shows little change. The latter quantity only decreases when the second intervention is introduced. By exposing each target behavior—positive couple interaction and negative interaction time with the son—to the intervention, the therapist can determine if the intervention is actually responsible for meeting the goal; that is, each family behavior should change only as it is exposed to the intervention and not before. It should be noted that the behaviors studied in the multiple baseline are not necessarily isolated: For example, positive interactions probably impact on negative interactions and vice versa.

There are many instances where the target behavior will occur in more than one situation (home, school, work, neighborhood, and so on). In this case, the therapist can use the multiple baseline to evaluate the target behaviors of the family in different situations. For example, negative requests (complaints or

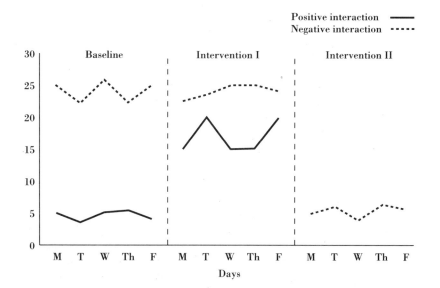

Figure 11.2

demands) by a child can be monitored both at home and at school. If parents are able to successfully reduce the child's negative requests at home, while the level of negative requests remains the same at school, then a similar intervention can be implemented at school with the assistance of the therapist and the family. The multiple baseline is useful here in determining the success of an intervention when the problem occurs in more than one setting.

Comparative data from taped interviews   Although the graphing procedures described earlier were applied primarily to discrete behaviors that can be easily observed and recorded, the same principle can be applied to data that is more difficult to observe and quantify. For instance, the therapeutic goal may be to improve marital satisfaction, as measured by the number of positive statements each spouse makes about the other. Marital satisfaction can obviously be measured in other ways; the important thing is that all goals be operationalized so that there is some way of measuring progress. For instance, if the goal is stated only as improvement in the relationship, this may mean different things to different people, and it is difficult to measure success. Assuming that the number of positive statements that each spouse makes about the other is a reasonable measure of marital satisfaction, the therapist can tape interviews and record the number of positive versus negative statements. Using the first session or two as a baseline, the therapist can then chart this behavior as intervention is implemented.

Even when objectives are operationalized, there are varying ranges of objectivity. For example, the therapist must often depend on clients' self-reports of behaviors such as anxiety, marital discord, and drug use, and there may be no way to verify the accuracy of such reports. Still, if the evaluation data are to be obtained by self-recording of client behavior, there is some evidence that the very act of self-recording is itself effective in promoting the desired behavior.

The therapist must follow several guidelines when using behavioral observation:

1. *Use repeated observations to evaluate behavior change.* Repeated measures provide a more accurate evaluation of therapeutic goals. Infrequent observations often reflect random changes in behavior and fail to provide an accurate representation of behavior before and after treatment.
2. *Ask family members to practice self-observation.* For example, a family member might be taught to observe and record the number of angry thoughts he or she has about another family member.
3. *Record behavioral observations on a prepared form.* The form should include the date, session number, family member's name, observer, operational definition of the problem, times of observation, length of interval, and setting or activity.
4. *Provide a graphic summary of the behavior.* The therapist should enter the time of recording (minutes, days, and so on) on the horizontal axis, from far left to far right, and the number of target behaviors on the vertical axis.
5. *Determine whether further observations are necessary.* If baseline or pretreatment data are characterized by extreme variation or a gradual increase or decrease, further observations should be collected until some stability is

noted. Of course, these considerations must be weighed against the need for prompt treatment; if the problem behavior is severely disturbing (as in the case of violence), treatment should supersede behavioral observation. Too much time spent in collecting baseline data may reduce the time available for treatment, which is of greater importance.

There are several limitations to self-observation as a means of recording behavior change. First, family members may change their behavior during the period of observation to please the therapist. This is particularly true for family members who have a need to please others. Second, some family members may not follow through monitoring behavior change because of the time or effort required to keep accurate records. This is often the case when the therapist has not chosen a focus that is meaningful to family members. Finally, since self-observation can often produce a behavior change, the data may not accurately reflect the situation in the absence of observation (Barlow, Hayes, & Nelson, 1984).

Goal Attainment Scales

A second method for evaluating goals specifies the level or amount of change—how much families must do in order to reach the desired goal. In this case, the level of attainment determines whether the goals have been successfully reached. Cormier and Cormier (1991) offer an example:

> Suppose a client wants to increase the number of assertive opinions she expresses orally with her husband. If she now withholds all her opinions, her level of change might be stated at a lower level than that defined for another client who already expresses some opinions. And if the client's husband is accustomed to her refraining from giving opinions, this might affect the degree of change made, at least initially. The counselor's and client's primary concern is to establish a level that is manageable, and that the client can attain with some success. (p. 233)

Achievable goals should be determined by the current level of problem behavior, the desired level of goal behavior, available support and resources, and the desire to change. One way to establish achievable and measurable goals is through the use of goal attainment scaling. This procedure (Kiresuk & Sherman, 1979) involves three basic steps and ends with a written product mutually agreeable to the therapist and the family.

Box 11.1 is an adaptation of goal attainment scaling, which is titled "Goal Attainment Review." This shows a completed goal attainment review for a family. Note that the goals are stated in performance terms and specify the criteria for success. Consequently, measurement is relatively simple, and evaluation of goal attainment is straightforward. There are several procedures to follow in using the goal attainment scale:

1. *State the goal in measurable terms.* Goals should be stated clearly and should be decided mutually by the therapist and family. It is important to select goals that can be changed.

Box 11.1

CASE NAME <u>Mary Goddard</u> DATE <u>3/28/93</u>
CASE NUMBER <u>MA-03285</u> PHONE NUMBER <u>477-8240</u>

GOAL ATTAINMENT REVIEW*
(Client Constructed Outcome Goals)

		Contract Goal 1	Contract Goal 2	Contract Goal 3	Contract Goal 4
Weight of Goal (1-3)		Weight = 3	Weight = 3	Weight = 2	Weight =
G U I D E T O G O A L S	MUCH LESS THAN EXPECTED RESULTS = 0	Robbie will not complete his homework every night.	Robbie will complete his assigned work at school 2 or fewer days per week.	Robbie will argue with his mother more than 1x per day.	
	EXPECTED OR MOST LIKELY RESULTS = 1	Robbie will complete his homework every night.	Robbie will complete his assigned work in school 3 out of every 5 days.	Robbie will argue with his mother no more than 1x per day.	
	MUCH MORE THAN EXPECTED RESULTS = 2		Robbie will complete his assigned work in school 4–5 days per week.	Robbie will argue with his mother fewer than 1x per day.	
P R O G R E S S	3 MONTH REVIEW Treatment ____ Terminated _x_ Discontinued ____	Case terminated 6/16/93 Progress ____ Follow-up _1_ Date _6/22/93_	Progress ____ Follow-up _1_ Date _6/22/93_	Progress ____ Follow-up 2 Date _6/22/93_	Progress ____ Follow-up __ Date _____
F O L L O W U P	6 MONTH REVIEW Treatment ____ Terminated ____ Discontinued ____	Progress ____ Follow-up____ Date _____	Progress ____ Follow-up____ Date _____	Progress ____ Follow-up____ Date _____	Progress ____ Follow-up ___ Date _____

    2. *Assign a weight to each goal.* Some goals are more important than others and should be weighted to show their comparative value. These weights are relative and may be ranked on the scale 1 to 5, where 1 is the *least important* and 5 is the *most important*. It should be noted that it is the relative rather than absolute weight that is imperative (some goals may be assigned the same weight).

    3. *Determine the expected level of attainment.* The central question that must be asked here is, What is the current amount or duration of behavior? What is a reasonable or expected level of goal attainment? To answer these questions the family must have some knowledge of their current level of behavior (baseline). This information should be entered in the column "expected level of attainment."

		Contract Goal 1	Contract Goal 2	Contract Goal 3	Contract Goal 4
Box 11.1	*(continued)*				
Weight of Goal (1-3)		Weight =	Weight =	Weight =	Weight =
P R O G R E S S / F O L L O W U P	**9 MONTH REVIEW**				
	Treatment ____	Progress ____	Progress ____	Progress ____	Progress ____
	Terminated ____	Follow-up ____	Follow-up ____	Follow-up ____	Follow-up ____
	Discontinued ____	Date ____	Date ____	Date ____	Date ____
	12 MONTH REVIEW				
	Treatment ____	Progress ____	Progress ____	Progress ____	Progress ____
	Terminated ____	Follow-up ____	Follow-up ____	Follow-up ____	Follow-up ____
	Discontinued ____	Date ____	Date ____	Date ____	Date ____
	15 MONTH REVIEW				
	Treatment ____	Progress ____	Progress ____	Progress ____	Progress ____
	Terminated ____	Follow-up ____	Follow-up ____	Follow-up ____	Follow-up ____
	Discontinued ____	Date ____	Date ____	Date ____	Date ____

*The Goal Attainment Review is a derivative of the GAS.

4. *Determine other levels of attainment.* Once the "expected level of attainment" has been determined, the next step is to determine levels that are "more than expected" and "most favorable outcome." Likewise, the therapist and family must specify a "less than expected" and "most unfavorable outcome." In some cases, the appropriate levels may only be 1 or 2, as in the case of alcohol consumption, violence, or curfew. These levels should be entered in the left-hand column.

Goal attainment reviews have several limitations: (1) families often have difficulty in knowing what to expect from therapy; stating goals in objective terms or measurable terms may be very difficult; (2) family members often have difficulty presenting problems and specifying what is an "expected" or an acceptable level of attainment; moreover, they may have even more difficulties specifying "less than expected" levels of attainment; (3) the therapist and family may have difficulty completing a goal attainment review during the initial intake session. Adequate time must be allotted to complete a goal attainment review. In some cases a second session may be necessary.

Self-Reports

Self-reports are simply what family members say about their condition in the interview; that is, in this method, improvement is determined by what family members report to the therapist. This approach assumes that, if the family is improving, family members will report the improvement ("Everyone seems to be getting along better"). Likewise, little improvement would be characterized by statements such as, "Things are about the same" or, "I can't see any change." Self-reports represent the easiest way for the therapist to evaluate changes in the family, with the following considerations:

1. *Develop some specific questions to evaluate the family's progress.* Questions such as "How are things different than they were before?" or, "Tell me how things used to be and how they are now" will help to determine the effectiveness of therapy.
2. *Ask family members to scale their improvement.* The therapist can ask the family to describe their ability to handle the problem on a scale from 1—not able to handle the problem—to 10—able to handle the problem. These questions can be asked prior to, during, and following treatment.
3. *Ask family members how satisfied they are with therapy.* The therapist might ask, "Was therapy helpful? How so? What was most helpful to you?"
4. *Ask family members to describe what still needs to change.* When asking the family to identify anything that still needs to be done, the therapist may need to remind them of some issues that were raised but not worked on during sessions.

Although self-reports are the most common type of outcome evaluation, family therapists should be aware of their limitations: First, self-reports are open to bias, since family members may report what they believe will please the therapist. Thus, self-reports are quite subjective and may not be an accurate representation of the family's progress in treatment. Second, family members may be able to report how they feel today, but may not be able to reliably describe their behavior between sessions. Day-to-day behavioral changes are often difficult to recall without some written record. Finally, self-reports are nonstandardized and are often determined by therapeutic leads (nonverbal cues) that seek to elicit a certain description of behavior change. Different leads at different points in therapy may result in different descriptions of progress.

Evaluations for Termination and Follow-Up

Two criteria should be used in determining whether to continue therapy. First, family goals should be met. In some cases, the family or others (teachers, social workers, friends, or relatives) may feel the problem no longer exists. However, if family data fail to support this, therapy should continue until family goals have been met. Second, the goal may have been met, but the family or others in the environment may not be satisfied with the change produced. If the family or others are no longer satisfied with the change produced, then a new goal should be established. In other cases, the family may wish to pursue another related goal. If goals have been reached and no new goals have been set, the therapist and family can focus on the maintenance of behavior change.

In some cases, families terminate by not returning. This may occur for several reasons. The family may feel that therapy is not working, or they may become upset with the therapist. Occasionally, the family may be unwilling to change some of their behavior. Unless the therapist works through these concerns early in therapy, termination may be premature. There are several guidelines the therapist should follow when terminating with the family:

1. *Plan for termination in advance.* The therapist should be careful not to withdraw therapy abruptly, because in such cases the problem behavior generally returns to the pretreatment level. Families should be given an approximate estimate for the length of therapy. The use of a contract specifying a fixed number of sessions ensures a periodic review of therapy (Barker, 1981). Setting a specific time for termination helps the family and therapist plan for change. The therapist should be flexible about the frequency of sessions, which will depend upon the nature of the problem. The frequency of sessions should decrease when initial goals have been met (Wright & Leahey, 1984).

2. *Plan to gradually withdraw therapy.* If families have been heavily dependent upon therapy (as sometimes happens in cases of severe crisis), they are less likely to resist termination if therapy is withdrawn gradually. One method of gradual withdrawal is to increase the amount of time between sessions (perhaps to between three and five weeks). This step should be taken if families are unsure that they can maintain the desired changes. Todd (1986) discusses this withdrawal process as follows:

> As therapy begins to be successful in achieving the agreed-upon goals, the sessions are usually spaced at wider time intervals, such as moving to alternate weeks and progressing to once a month. This allows the spouses to do more of the work themselves and helps ensure that they can maintain the changes without the therapist. (p. 81)

Wright and Leahey (1984) suggest that families are more likely to believe they have the resources to deal with this problem when the therapist gives them credit for change. If families believe they were responsible for alleviating the presenting problem, they are likely to be more confident that they can handle future problems. Statements such as, "You handled this; you'll be able to handle a similar problem if it comes up" help the family to believe in their abilities outside of therapy.

3. *Summarize the major themes.* In terminating, the therapist should summarize the major themes of therapy (such as growing up) and observe closely to see whether the family agrees or disagrees with the summary statement. If the family disagrees, the therapist should note this and give them the opportunity to discuss their views. On some occasions, the therapist may ask the family to summarize the therapy.

4. *Ask the family to decide what would need to happen for them to return to therapy.* It is important for the therapist to help the family decide when they no longer can manage the problem and need to return to therapy. The therapist might say, "What would be the first sign that you no longer can handle this problem?" Tomm and Wright (1979) ask, "What would each of you have to do to bring the problem back?" Such questions should help family members to understand the specific changes that they have made in therapy. The therapist should help the family understand that returning to therapy does not mean that the family has failed. Instead, a follow-up session can be framed as a booster shot to help the family maintain desired changes. Then, if further services are sought, the therapist can reiterate that this is not an indicator of failure; instead,

additional therapy sessions are likely to be brief, since the family has demonstrated an ability to solve their problems (Todd, 1986).

5. *Reassure the family that they have the strengths and resources to deal with future problems.* In some cases, a family will present a new problem at the time of termination. If the problem is not serious, the therapist must reassure the family that they have the skills to deal with this problem on their own—without therapeutic intervention. If therapists have difficulty letting go of the family (for example, the therapist may get special nurturance and support from the family or may need the family to work out some unresolved issue), they should discuss such matters in supervision, in order to minimize client dependency as well as their own.

Conducting Follow-Up Evaluations

Once termination has been discussed, follow-up allows the therapist to find out how the family is progressing and to discuss new problems, if any have developed. Follow-up can be short-term (two to four weeks) or long-term (three to six months) after termination of treatment. In getting a date for follow-up, the therapist should assess the amount of time the family will need to maintain goal behaviors without therapeutic intervention.

There are several reasons for follow-up contact with the family. First, many families, particularly those who require intensive services, need a booster shot following termination. For example, family preservation programs that offer intensive, in-home, family crisis intervention often provide weekly or biweekly follow-up visits in the home. The purpose of these visits is to support desired behavior changes or troubleshoot any problems that the family may have in implementing the program (Kinney, Haopala, & Booth, 1991). Second, follow-up helps to assess the effectiveness of the intervention program, particularly the long-term effects of therapy. Third, planned follow-up encourages the family to monitor their own change program and thus benefit from contact with the therapist.

There are several ways the therapist can conduct follow-up:

1. *Conduct a follow-up interview in the home or office.* Follow-up interviews provide an opportunity for the family to discuss what is working and what still needs to change. Interviews are useful for reinforcing desired changes and problem solving, if necessary.
2. *Make a telephone call.* Telephone calls can be useful in assessing the effectiveness of the intervention, and also provide a cost-effective way of determining whether a follow-up interview is warranted.
3. *Mail a questionnaire to the family.* This is a quick way to assess the effectiveness of the program. Unfortunately, families may only report what they think will please the therapist; this method may lack objectivity.

Evaluations in Training

Formal evaluations of therapists are often model-specific; that is, they evaluate the trainee's mastery of the therapeutic process specified by a certain school of family therapy. For example, those learning structural family therapy might be evaluated according to their ability to mark boundaries or to set up enactments in a session. Those learning intergenerational family therapy might be evaluated according to how well they construct genograms and how effectively they facilitate intergenerational dialogue. Other models might emphasize the therapist's use of self or the therapist's ability to design specific directives and tasks.

Piercy, Laird, and Mohammed (1983) have developed a therapist rating scale that integrates several models of family therapy into a supervisory rating of the student or trainee. In this rating scale, each major school is represented as a cluster of behaviors that each family therapist can be challenged to master as part of their education and training. The rating scale provides a guide for the supervisor and therapist in setting training goals.

In addition to these formal methods of evaluating trainees, it is important for family therapists to monitor their own progress and development in personal ways. Clinicians can do this by being responsible for their own well-being as professionals and by becoming aware of those times when their physical or mental health may have a negative impact on their ability to provide effective service. While this type of evaluation is often underemphasized as part of formal training, it can help practitioners focus on personal factors that make them vulnerable to job stress and burnout. In addition, when family therapists evaluate their own patterns of fatigue and stagnation, their own creativity and growth can be maximized.

Evaluations As Clinical Research

As a group, clinicians are rarely apt to call themselves researchers or scientists. Very often, they are so immersed in the implicit subtleties of therapeutic experience that they dismiss scientific inquiry as irrelevant to clinical work. Particularly with beginning therapists, their energy is often directed exclusively toward skill mastery in specific sessions, as they discover what works with their clients. In addition, those learning family therapy often hold the belief that scientific rigor fails to acknowledge the human aspects of therapeutic experience.

In the traditional use of the term, research connotes an interest in the explicit, observable, and quantifiable parts of human experience. However, if research is defined as systematic inquiry, family therapists are more likely to see that clinical research can have great relevance to their work; one example is the growing trend toward qualitative research. Ethnographic studies on client perceptions can provide therapists with a mirror of their professional role (Newfield et al., 1991). In addition, Selekman and Todd (1991) argue in favor of "empirically-based clinical practice." From recent studies on family therapy effectiveness, they conclude that family-based research is beginning to show which type of intervention is most effective with which type of family. In their review, chronic, discouraged families did not respond well to "zealous optimism and pushy methods" (p. 321).

Thus, clinicians can participate in systematic inquiry for formal and informal research. Any time family therapists ask the same question in each case, they are engaging in systematic inquiry. When therapists notice similarities between families, presenting problems, and eventual solutions, this is a form of research. As clinicians begin to observe and understand these patterns, their work can be influenced by the new information. For example, they can begin to routinely ask families at the end of successful treatment what they remember as the least important topic discussed during sessions. Even though the answers may be diverse, family therapists can use the information as a mirror from which to view themselves in therapy. They may decide to emphasize or minimize aspects of the process on the basis of such client feedback.

An example of formal inquiry in clinical practice might be the categorization of completed cases according to presenting problems, type of family, number of sessions, type of intervention, and outcomes. Over time, the practitioner can begin to determine whether certain characteristics emerge as similarities or patterns that can be anticipated at the beginning of treatment in order to improve treatment effectiveness. For example, studies in adolescent drug abuse found that a structural-strategic model worked well with a variety of intact and single-parent families as long as they did not have parental or multiple drug abuse, unresolved losses, or financial or community problems. However, when these problems were present, an indirect approach such as that used by the Milan team was more successful (Selekman & Todd, 1991). Family therapists are currently learning more about the relevance of quantitative and qualitative research. As this continues, they will be able to identify parts of their clinical experience that are naturally occurring methods of research.

Summary

Evaluation is often omitted by beginning family therapists as an important part of the treatment process. However, the process of therapy is often stalemated without a mechanism to provide ongoing feedback and reflection about families and their therapy. While objective assessment instruments often provide quantitative information about family variables and therapy outcomes, informal feedback loops can provide qualitative information about the effectiveness of the therapeutic relationship and the fit between family, intervention, and clinician.

When evaluation is integrated into the practice of family therapy, beginning practitioners become flexible and responsive to the individual needs of families and family members. In addition, treatment planning becomes more systematic and effective. Family therapists develop a shared reality with their families, rather than a reality created in isolation from those who are expected to receive its benefits. Although considered here as a skill to be learned by the beginner, evaluation is also a threshold into intermediate and advanced practice; learning from experience and refinement on the basis of feedback are fundamental to advanced practice.

References

Amatea, E., & Sherrard, P. (1989). Reversing the school's response: A new approach to resolving persistent problems. *American Journal of Family Therapy, 17,* 15–26.

Amatea, E., & Sherrard, P. (1991, October). Systematic practice in schools provides a new frontier. *Family Therapy News,* pp. 5–6.

Anderson, C., Reiss, D., & Hogarty, G. (1986). *Schizophrenia and the family: A practitioner's guide to psycho-education and management.* New York: Guilford Press.

Anderson, S., & Bagarozzi, D. (Eds.) (1989). *Family myths: Psychotherapy implications.* New York: Haworth Press.

Aponte, H. (1976a). The family-school interview. *Family Process, 15,* 464–477.

Aponte, H. (1976b). Underorganization in the poor family. In P. J. Guern, Jr. (Ed.), *Family therapy: Theory and practice* (pp. 432–448). New York: Guilford Press.

Aponte, H., & Van Deusen, J. (1981). Structural family therapy. In A. S. P. Gurman & D. Kniskern (Eds.), *Handbook of family therapy* (pp. 310–360). New York: Brunner/Mazel.

Barker, P. (1981). *Basic family therapy.* Baltimore: University Park Press.

Barlow, P. H., Hayes, S. C., & Nelson, R. O. (1984). *The scientist practitioner: Research and accountability in clerical and educational settings.* New York: Pergamon Press.

Bateson, G. (1972). *Steps to an ecology of mind.* New York: Dutton.

Bateson, G. (1979). *Mind in nature: A necessary unity.* New York: Dutton.

Bateson, G., Jackson, D., Haley, J., & Weakland, J. (1956). Toward a theory of schizophrenia. *Behavioral Science, 1*(4), 251–264.

Bernal, G., & Flores-Ortiz, Y. (1991). Contextual family therapy with adolescent drug abusers. In T. Todd & M. Selekman (Eds.), *Family therapy approaches with adolescent substance abusers* (pp. 70–92). Needham Heights, MA: Allyn & Bacon.

Bodin, A. (1981). The interactional view: Family therapy approaches of the mental health institute. In A. S. Gurman & D. P. Kniskern (Eds.), *Handbook of family therapy* (pp. 267–309). New York: Brunner/Mazel.

Boscolo, L., Cecchin, G., Hoffman, L., & Penn, P. (1987). *Milan systemic family therapy: Conversations in theory and practice.* New York: Basic Books.

Boszormenyi-Nagy, I. (1966). From family therapy to a psychology of relationships: Fictions of the individual and fictions of the family. *Comprehensive Psychiatry, 7*, 408–423.

Boszormenyi-Nagy, I. (Ed.). (1987). *Foundations of contextual therapy: Collected papers.* New York: Brunner/Mazel.

Boszormenyi-Nagy, I., & Framo, J. (Eds.). (1965). *Intensive family therapy.* New York: Harper & Row.

Boszormenyi-Nagy, I., & Krasner, B. (1986). *Between give and take: A clinical guide to contextual therapy.* New York: Brunner/Mazel.

Boszormenyi-Nagy, I., & Spark, G. M. (1973). *Invisible loyalties: Reciprocity in intergenerational family therapy.* New York: Harper & Row.

Bowen, M. (1978). *Family therapy in clinical practice.* New York: Jason Aronson.

Boyd-Franklin, N. (1989). *Black families in therapy: A multi-system approach.* New York: Guilford Press.

Breunlin, D. (1985). Expanding the concept of stages in family therapy. In D. Breunlin (Ed.), *Stages: Patterns of change over time* (pp. 95–120). Rockville, MD: Aspen Systems.

Brock, G., & Barnard, C. (1988). *Procedures in family therapy.* Needham Heights, MA: Allyn & Bacon.

Broderick, C. B., & Schrader, S. S. (1991). The history of professional marriage and family therapy. In A. S. Gurman & D. P. Kniskern (Eds.), *Handbook of family therapy* (pp. 3–40). New York: Brunner/Mazel.

Brown, J., Brown, C., & Portes, P. (1991). *The families in transition program.* Louisville, KY: University of Louisville.

Brown, J., & Christensen, D. (1986). *Family therapy: Theory and practice.* Pacific Grove, CA: Brooks/Cole.

Brown, J. H., Eichenberger, S. A., Portes, P., & Christensen, D. N. (1991). Family functioning factors associated with the adjustment level of children of divorce. *Journal of Divorce and Remarriage, 17*, 81–95.

Brown, J. H., & Vaccaro, A. (1991). *A manual for resource and youth services coordinators.* Louisville, KY: University of Louisville & Cities in Schools.

Campbell, D., Draper, R., & Crutchley, E. (1991). The Milan systemic approach to family therapy. In A. S. Gurman & D. P. Kniskern (Eds.), *Handbook of family therapy* (Vol. 2, pp. 324–362). New York: Brunner/Mazel.

Carter, B., & McGoldrick, M. (Eds.). (1989a). *The changing family life cycle: Framework for family therapy* (2nd ed.). Needham Heights, MA: Allyn & Bacon.

Carter, B., & McGoldrick, M. (1989b). Forming a remarried family. In B. Carter & M. McGoldrick (Eds.), *The changing family life cycle: Framework for family therapy* (2nd ed., pp. 399–432). Needham Heights, MA: Allyn & Bacon.

Colapinto, J. (1982). Structural family therapy. In A. M. Horne & M. M. Ohlsen (Eds.), *Family counseling and therapy* (pp. 112–140). Itasca, IL: Peacock.

Colapinto, J. (1991). Structural family therapy. In A. S. Gurman & D. P. Kniskern (Eds.), *Handbook of family therapy* (Vol.2, pp. 417–443). New York: Brunner/Mazel.

Coleman, S. (Ed.). (1985). *Failures in family therapy.* New York: Guilford Press.

Cormier, W. H., & Cormier, L. S. (1991). *Interviewing strategies for helpers: Fundamental skills and cognitive behavioral interventions* (3rd ed.). Pacific Grove, CA: Brooks/Cole.

Crando, R., & Ginsberg, B. G. (1976). Communication in the father-son relationship: The parent adolescent relationship development program. *The Family Coordinator, 4*, 465–473.

De Shazer, S. (1985). *Keys to solution in brief therapy.* New York: Norton.

Duncan, B., & Parks, M. B. (1988). Integrating individual and systems approaches: Strategic-behavioral therapy. *Journal of Marital and Family Therapy, 14*, 151–161.

Dunst, C., Trivette, C., & Deal, A. (1988). *Enabling and empowering families: Principles and guidelines for practice.* Cambridge, MA: Brookline Books.

Durrant, M. (1988). Gwynne: A new recipe for life. *Case studies special edition.* Epping, NSW Australia: Eastwood Family Therapy Centre.

Duvall, E. (1977). *Marriage and family development* (5th ed.). Philadelphia: Lippincott.

Efran, J., Lukens, M., & Lukens, R. (1990). *Language, structure and change.* New York: Norton.

Epston, D., & White, M. (1992). *Experience, contradiction, narrative and imagination: Selected papers of David Epston and Michael White 1989-1991.* Adelaide, South Australia: Dulwich Centre Publications.

Erickson, M., & Rossi, E. (1979). *Hypnotherapy: An exploratory casework.* New York: Irvington.

Ericson, P., & Rogers, L. E. (1973). New procedures for analyzing relational communication. *Family Process, 12*(3), 245–268.

Falicov, C. (1988). *Family transitions: Continuity and change over the lifecycle.* New York: Guilford Press.

Falloon, I. R. (1991). Behavioral family therapy. In A. S. Gurman & D. P. Kniskern (Eds.), *Handbook of family therapy* (Vol. 2, pp. 65–95). New York: Brunner/Mazel.

Ferreira, A. (1963). Family myth and homeostasis. *Archives of General Psychiatry, 9*, 457–463.

Figley, C., & Nelson, T. (1989). Basic family therapy skills. I: Conceptualization and findings. *Journal of Marital and Family Therapy, 4*(14), 349–366.

Fleuridas, C., Nelson, T., & Rosenthal, D. M. (1986). The evolution of circular questions: Training family therapists. *Journal of Marital and Family Therapy, 12*(27), 113–128.

Fleuridas, C., Rosenthal, D. M., Leigh, G. K., & Leigh, T. E. (1990). Family goal recording: An adaptation of goal attainment scaling for enhancing family therapy assessment. *Journal of Marital and Family Therapy, 16*, 389–406.

Framo, J. (1976). Family of origin as a therapeutic resource for adults in marital and family therapy: You can and should go home again. *Family Process, 15*, 193–210.

Framo, J. (1981). The integration of marital therapy with sessions with family of origin. In A. S. Gurman & D. P. Kniskern (Eds.), *Handbook of family therapy* (pp. 133–158). New York: Brunner/Mazel.

Gambino, R. (1974). *Blood of my blood: The dilemma of Italian-Americans.* New York: Doubleday.

Garcia-Preto, N. (1982). Family therapy with Puerto Rican families. In M. McGoldrick, J. K. Pearce, & J. Giordano (Eds.), *Ethnicity and family therapy* (pp. 164–186). New York: Guilford Press.

Garfield, R. (1981). Mourning and its resolution for spouses in marital separation. In J. C. Hansen & L. Messinger (Eds.), *Therapy with remarriage and families* (pp. 1–15). Rockville, MD: Aspen Systems.

Garfield, S., & Bergin, A. (1978). *Handbook of psychotherapy and behavior change* (2nd ed.). New York: Wiley.

Goldner, V. (1988). Generation and gender: Normative and covert hierarchies. *Family Process, 27*, 17–31.

Goldstein, A. (1973). *Structured learning therapy.* New York: Academic Press.

Gurman, A. S., & Kniskern, D. P. (Eds.). (1981). *Handbook of family therapy.* New York: Brunner/Mazel.

Gurman, A. S., & Kniskern, D. P. (Eds.). (1991). *Handbook of family therapy* (Vol. 2). New York: Brunner/Mazel.

Haley, J. (1967). Toward a theory of pathological systems. In G. H. Zuk & I. Boszormenyi-Nagy (Eds.), *Family theory and disturbed families* (pp. 11–27). Palo Alto, CA: Science & Behavior Books.

Haley, J. (Ed.). (1976). *Problem-solving therapy.* San Francisco: Jossey-Bass.

Haley, J. (1980). *Leaving home: The therapy of disturbed young people.* New York: McGraw-Hill.

Hansen, J., Pound, R., & Warner, R. (1976). Use of modeling procedures. *Personnel and Guidance Journal, 54,* 242–245.

Hare-Mustin, R. (1978). A feminist approach to family therapy. *Family Process, 17,* 181–194.

Hargrave, T., & Anderson, W. (1992). *Finishing well: Aging and reparation in the intergenerational family.* New York: Brunner/Mazel.

Hiebert, W. (1980). Personal communication.

Hiebert, W., Gillespie, J., & Stahmann, R. (1993). *Dynamic assessment in couples therapy.* New York: Lexington Books.

Hoffman, L. (1981). *Foundations of family therapy.* New York: Basic Books.

Hoffman, L. (1983). A co-evolutionary framework for systemic family therapy. In J. Hansen & B. Keeney (Eds.), *Diagnosis and assessment in family therapy* (pp. 35–62). Rockville, MD: Aspen Systems.

Hosford, R., & de Visser, C. (1974). *Behavioral counseling: An introduction.* Washington, DC: American Personnel & Guidance Press.

Howard, J. (1978). *Families.* New York: Simon & Schuster.

Imber-Black, E. (Ed.). (1993). *Secrets in families and family therapy.* New York: Norton.

Imber-Black, E., Roberts, J., & Whiting, R. (1988). *Rituals in families and family therapy.* New York: Norton.

Jacobson, N. S. (1984). A component analysis of behavioral marital therapy: The relative effectiveness of behavior exchange and problem solving training. *Journal of Consulting and Clinical Psychology, 52,* 295–305.

Jacobson, N. S., Holtzworth-Monroe, A., & Schmaling, K. B. (1989). Marital therapy and spouse involvement in the treatment of depression, agoraphobia, and alcoholism. *Journal of Consulting and Clinical Psychology, 57,* 5–10.

Jacobson, N. S., & Margolin, B. (1979). *Marital therapy: Strategies based on social learning and behavior exchange principles.* New York: Brunner/Mazel.

Jenkins, A. (1991). *Invitations to responsibility.* Adelaide, South Australia: Dulwich Centre Publications.

Karpel, M. (1986). Questions, obstacles, and contributions. In M. A. Karpel (Ed.), *Family resources: The hidden partner in family therapy* (pp. 3–64). New York: Guilford Press.

Keith, D., & Whitaker, C. (1985). Failure: Our bold companion. In S. Coleman (Ed.), *Failures in family therapy* (pp. 8–26). New York: Guilford Press.

Kerr, M. (1981). Family systems theory and therapy. In A. S. Gurman & D. P. Kniskern (Eds.), *Handbook of family therapy* (pp. 226–266). New York: Brunner/Mazel.

Kinney, J., Haopala, P., & Booth, C. (1991). *Keeping families together: The homebuilders model.* New York: Aldine De Guiyter.

Kiresuk, T. J., & Sherman, R. E. (1979). Goal attainment scaling: A general method for evaluating community mental health programs. *Community Mental Health, 4,* 443–453.

Kramer, J. (1985). *Family interfaces: Transgenerational patterns.* New York: Brunner/Mazel.

Krumboltz, J., Varenhorst, B., & Thoresen, C. (1967). Nonverbal factors in effectiveness of models in counseling. *Journal of Counseling Psychology, 14,* 412–418.

Landau-Stanton, J., & Stanton, M. D. (1985). Treating suicidal adolescents and their families. In M. Pravder Mirkin & S. Koman (Eds.), *Handbook of adolescents and family therapy* (pp. 309–328). New York: Gardner Press.

Lankton, S. (1988). *Ericksonian hypnosis application, preparation and research* (Ericksonian Monograph No. 5). New York: Brunner/Mazel.

Lankton, S., & Lankton, C. (1983). *The answer within: A clinical framework of Ericksonian hypnotherapy.* New York: Brunner/Mazel.

Lankton, S., Lankton, C., & Matthews, W. (1991). Ericksonian family therapy. In A. S. Gurman & D. P. Kniskern (Eds.), *Handbook of family therapy* (Vol. 2, pp. 239–283). New York: Brunner/Mazel.

Lebow, J. L. (1987). Training psychologists in family therapy in Family Institute setting. *Journal of Family Psychology, 1,* 219–231.

Lewis, R., Piercy, F., Sprenkle, D., & Trepper, T. (1991). Family based interventions for helping drug abusing adolescents. *Journal of Adolescent Research, 5,* 82–95.

Locke, H., & Wallace, K. (1959). Short marital-adjustment and prediction tests: The reliability and validity. *Marriage and Family Living, 21,* 251–255.

Madanes, C. (1981). *Strategic family therapy.* San Francisco: Jossey-Bass.

Mahoney, M. J. (1991). *Human change processes.* New York: Basic Books.

McGoldrick, M. (1982). Ethnicity and family therapy: An overview. In M. McGoldrick, J. K. Pearce, & J. Giordano (Eds.), *Ethnicity and family therapy* (pp. 3–30). New York: Guilford Press.

McGoldrick, M., & Gerson, R. (1985). *Genograms in family assessment.* New York: Norton.

McGoldrick, M., Pearce, J., & Giordano, J. (Eds.). (1982). *Ethnicity and family therapy.* New York: Guilford Press.

Menses, G., & Durrant, M. (1987). Contextual residential care: The application of the principles of cybernetic therapy to the residential treatment of irresponsible adolescents and their families. *Journal of Strategic and Systemic Therapies, 6,* 3–15.

Miller, S., Nunnally, E., Wackman, D., & Miller, P. (1988). *Connecting with self and others.* Littleton, CO: Interpersonal Communication Programs.

Minuchin, S. (1974). *Families and family therapy.* Cambridge, MA: Harvard University Press.

Minuchin, S. (1984). *Family kaleidoscope.* Cambridge, MA: Harvard University Press.

Minuchin, S. (1987). My many voices. In J. K. Zeig (Ed.), *The evolution of psychotherapy* (pp. 5–28). New York: Brunner/Mazel.

Minuchin, S., & Fishman, H. C. (1981). *Family therapy techniques.* Cambridge, MA: Harvard University Press.

Minuchin, S., Montalvo, B., Guerney, B., Rosman, B., & Schumer, F. (1967). *Families of the slums: An exploration of their structure and treatment.* New York: Basic Books.

Napier, A., & Whitaker, C. (1978). *The family crucible: The intense experience of family therapy.* New York: Harper & Row.

Newfield, N. A., Kuehl, B. P., Joanning, H., & Quinn, W. H. (1991). We can tell you about "psychos and shrinks": An ethnography of the family therapy of adolescent drug abusers. In T. Todd & M. Selekman (Eds.), *Family therapy approaches with adolescent substance abusers* (pp. 277–316). Needham Heights, MA: Allyn & Bacon.

Nichols, M., & Schwartz, R. (1991). *Family therapy: Concepts and methods* (2nd ed.). Needham Heights, MA: Allyn & Bacon.

Nichols, W., & Everett, C. (1988). *Systemic family therapy: An integrative approach*. New York: Guilford Press.

O'Callaghan, J. B. (1988). *Family school consultation, state of the art analysis and blueprint*. Workshop presented at the 46th annual conference of the American Association for Marriage and Family Therapy, New Orleans, LA.

O'Hanlon, W. H. (1982). Two generic patterns in Ericksonian therapy. *Journal of Strategic and Systemic Therapies, 1*(4), 21–25.

O'Hanlon, W. H. (1987). *Taproots*. New York: Norton.

O'Hanlon, W. H. (1991). *Acknowledgement and possibility*. Paper presented at the Family and Children's Agency, Louisville, KY.

O'Hanlon, W. H., & Weiner-Davis, M. (1989). *In search of solutions: A new direction in psychotherapy*. New York: Norton.

Olson, D. H., Porter, J., & Ravee, Y. (1985). *FACES I*. St. Paul: Family Social Science, University of Minnesota.

Papp, P. (1980). The use of fantasy in a couples group. In M. Andolfi & I. Zwerling (Eds.), *Dimensions of family therapy* (pp. 73–90). New York: Guilford Press.

Papp, P. (1983). *The process of change*. New York: Guilford Press.

Paul, G. L. (1967). Strategy of outcome research in psychotherapy. *Journal of Consulting Psychology, 31*, 109–118.

Paul, N., & Paul, B. B. (1975). *A marital puzzle*. New York: Norton.

Penn, P. (1982). Circular questioning. *Family Process, 19*, 267–280.

Petker, S. (1982). The domino effect in a system with two or more generations of unresolved mourning. *The Family, 9*(2), 75–79.

Piercy, F., Laird, R., & Mohammed, Z. (1983). A family therapist rating scale. *Journal of Marital and Family Therapy, 9*, 49–59.

Piercy, F., & Sprenkle, D. (1986). *Family therapy source book*. New York: Guilford Press.

Pinsof, W. M., & Catherall, D. (1986). The integrative psychotherapy alliance. *Journal of Marital and Family Therapy, 12*, 137–152.

Pittman, F. (1991). The secret passions of men. *Journal of Marital and Family Therapy, 17*, 17–23.

Pittman, F., DeYoung, C., Flomenhaft, K., Kaplan, D., & Langsley, D. (1966). Crisis family therapy. In J. H. Masserman (Ed.), *Current psychiatric therapies* (Vol. 6, pp. 187–196). New York: Grune & Stratton.

Quinn, W., & Davidson, B. (1984). Prevalence of family therapy models: A research note. *Journal of Marital and Family Therapy, 10*(4), 393–398.

Rappaport, A. F. (1976). Conjugal relationship enhancement program. In D. H. L. Olson (Ed.), *Treating relationships* (pp. 41–66). Lake Mills, IA: Graphic Publishing.

Rogers, C. (1961). *On becoming a person*. Boston: Houghton Mifflin.

Ruesch, J., & Bateson, G. (1951). *Communication: The social matrix of psychiatry*. New York: Norton.

Sager, C. (1981). Couples therapy and marriage contracts. In A. S. Gurman & D. P. Kniskern (Eds.), *Handbook of family therapy* (pp. 85–132). New York: Brunner/Mazel.

Satir, V. (1972). *Peoplemaking*. Palo Alto, CA: Science & Behavior Books.

Scalise, J. (1992). Life or death: A family suicide watch. *GrassRoutes: Stories from Family and Systemic Therapists, 1*(1), 22.

Segal, L., & Bavelas, J. B. (1983). Human systems and communications theory. In B. B. Wolman & G. Strickler (Eds.), *Handbook of family and marital therapy* (pp. 11–27). New York: Plenum.

Selekman, M. D., & Todd, T. (Eds.). (1991). Major issues from family therapy research and theory: Implications for the future. In T. Todd & M. D. Selekman (Eds.), *Family therapy approaches with adolescent substance abusers* (pp. 311–325). Needham Heights, MA: Allyn & Bacon.

Selvini Palazzoli, M. (1978). *Self starvation.* New York: Jason Aronson.

Selvini Palazzoli, M. (1985). The problem of the sibling as the referring person. *Journal of Marital and Family Therapy, 11*(1), 21–34.

Selvini Palazzoli, M. (1986). Towards a general model of psychotic family games. *Journal of Marital and Family Therapy, 12,* 339–349.

Selvini Palazzoli, M., Boscolo, L., Cecchin, G., & Prata, G. (1978). *Paradox and counterparadox.* New York: Jason Aronson.

Selvini Palazzoli, M., Boscolo, L., Cecchin, G., & Prata, G. (1980a). Hypothesizing, circularity, neutrality: Three guidelines for the conduct of the session. *Family Process, 19*(1), 7–19.

Selvini Palazzoli, M., Boscolo, L., Cecchin, G., & Prata, G. (1980b). Why a long interval between sessions? The therapeutic control of the family-therapist supersystem. In M. Andolfi & I. Zwerling (Eds.), *Dimensions of family therapy* (pp. 161–169). New York: Guilford Press.

Selvini Palazzoli, M., Cirillo, S., Selvini, M., & Sorrentino, A. M. (1989). *Family games: General models of psychotic processes in the family.* New York: Norton.

Selvini Palazzoli, M., & Prata, G. (1982). Snares in family therapy. *Journal of Marital and Family Therapy, 8*(4), 443–450.

Sheinberg, M. (1992). Navigating treatment impasses at the disclosure of incest: Combining ideas from feminism and social constructionism. *Family Process, 31*(3), 201–216.

Sheinberg, M., & Penn, P. (1991). Gender dilemmas, gender questions and the gender mantra. *Journal of Marital and Family Therapy, 17*(1), 33–44.

Sluzki, C. (1992). Transformations: A blueprint for narrative changes in therapy. *Family Process, 31*(3), 217–230.

Snider, M. (1992). *Process family therapy.* Needham Heights, MA: Simon & Schuster.

Spanier, G. B. (1976). Measuring dyadic adjustment: New scales for assessing the quality of marriage and similar dyads. *Journal of Marriage and the Family, 38,* 15–28.

Stanton, M. D. (1981). Strategic approaches to family therapy. In A. S. Gurman & D. P. Kniskern (Eds.), *Handbook of family therapy* (pp. 361–402). New York: Brunner/Mazel.

Stanton, M. D. (1992). The time line and the "Why now?" question: A technique and rationale for therapy, training, organizational consultation and research. *Journal of Marital and Family Therapy, 18*(4), 331–344.

Steinglass, P., Bennett, L., Wolin, S., & Reiss, D. (1987). *The alcoholic family.* New York: Basic Books.

Stuart, R. B. (1976). An operant interpersonal program for couples. In D. H. L. Olsen (Ed.), *Treating relationships* (pp. 119–132). Lake Mills, IA: Graphic Publishing.

Stuart, R. B. (1980). *Helping couples change: A social learning approach to marital therapy.* Champaign, IL: Research Press.

Stuart, R. B., & Stuart, F. (1972). *Marital pre-counseling inventory.* Champaign, IL: Research Press.

Todd, T., & Selekman, M. D. (Eds.). (1991). *Family therapy approaches with adolescent substance abusers*. Needham Heights, MA: Allyn & Bacon.

Todd, T. C. (1986). Structural-strategic marital therapy. In N. S. Jacobson & A. S. Gurman (Eds.), *Clinical handbook of marital therapy* (pp. 71–106). New York: Guilford Press.

Tomm, K. M. (1984). One perspective on the Milan systemic approach: I. Overview of development, theory and practice. *Journal of Marital and Family Therapy, 10*, 113–125.

Tomm, K. M., & Wright, L. M. (1979). Training in family therapy: Perceptual, conceptual and executive skills. *Family Process, 18*, 227–250.

Treadway, D. (1989). *Before it's too late: Working with substance abuse in the family*. New York: Norton.

Van Deusen, J., Stanton, M. D., Scott, S., Todd, T., & Mowatt, D. (1982). Getting the addict to agree to involve his family of origin: The initial contact. In M. Stanton & T. Todd (Eds.), *The family therapy of drug abuse and addiction* (pp. 39–59). New York: Guilford Press.

Waldegrave, C. (1990). Social justice and family therapy. *Dulwich Centre Newsletter*.

Wamboldt, F., & Wolin, S. (1989). Reality and myth in family life: Changes across generations. In S. Anderson & D. Bagarozzi (Eds.), *Family myths: Psychotherapy implications* (pp. 141–166). New York: Haworth Press.

Warner, R., & Hansen, J. (1970). Verbal-reinforcement and model-reinforcement group counseling with alienated students. *Journal of Counseling Psychology, 14*, 168–172.

Warner, R., Swisher, J., & Horan, J. (1973). Drug abuse prevention: A behavioral approach. *NAASP Bulletin, 372*, 49–54.

Watzlawick, P., Beavin, J., & Jackson, D. (1967). *Pragmatics of human communication*. New York: Norton.

Watzlawick, P., Weakland, J. H., & Fisch, R. (1974). *Change: Principles of problem formation and problem resolution*. New York: Norton.

Weakland, J., Fisch, R., Watzlawick, P., & Bodin, A. (1974). Brief therapy: Focused problem resolution. *Family Process, 13*, 141–168.

Weber, T., McKeever, J., & McDaniel, S. (1985). The beginning guide to the problem-oriented first family interview. *Family Process, 24*(3), 356–364.

Weeks, G. K., & Abate, L. (1982). *Paradoxical psychotherapy: Theory and technique*. New York: Brunner/Mazel.

Weiss, R. L., & Perry, B. A. (1979). *Assessment and treatment of marital dysfunction*. Eugene, OR: Marital Studies Program.

Whitaker, C. (1976). Comment: Live supervision in psychotherapy. *Voices, 12*, 24–25.

Whitaker, C. (1986). Personal communication.

Whitaker, C. A. (1982). The ongoing training of the psychotherapist. In J. R. Neill & D. P. Kniskern (Eds.), *From psyche to system: The evolving therapy of Carl Whitaker* (pp. 121–138). New York: Guilford Press.

White, M. (1986). Negative explanation, restraint, and double description: A template for family therapy. *Family Process, 25*(2), 169–184.

White, M. (1990, October). *Couple therapy and deconstruction*. Paper presented at the meeting of the American Association for Marriage and Family Therapy, Washington, DC.

White, M., & Epston, D. (1991). *Narrative means to therapeutic ends*. New York: Norton.

Williamson, D. (1981). Personal authority via termination of the intergenerational hierarchical boundary: A "new" stage in the family lifecycle. *Journal of Marital and Family Therapy, 7*, 441–452.

Wright, L., & Leahey, M. (1984). *Nurses and families: A guide to family assessment and intervention.* Philadelphia: Davis.

Zeig, J., & Lankton, S. (1988). *Developing Ericksonian therapy: State of the art.* New York: Brunner/Mazel.

Name Index

Subject Index

TO THE OWNER OF THIS BOOK:

We hope that you have found *The Practice of Family Therapy* useful. So that this book can be improved in a future edition, would you take the time to complete this sheet and return it? Thank you.

School and address: ————————————————————————

Department: ————————————————————————

Instructor's name: ————————————————————————

1. What I like most about this book is: ——————————————————

————————————————————————————————

————————————————————————————————

2. What I like least about this book is: ——————————————————

————————————————————————————————

————————————————————————————————

3. My general reaction to this book is: ——————————————————

————————————————————————————————

4. The name of the course in which I used this book is: ——————————

————————————————————————————————

5. Were all of the chapters of the book assigned for you to read? ——————

   If not, which ones weren't? ————————————————————

6. In the space below, or on a separate sheet of paper, please write specific suggestions for improving this book and anything else you'd care to share about your experience in using the book.

————————————————————————————————

————————————————————————————————

————————————————————————————————

————————————————————————————————

————————————————————————————————

Optional:

Your name: _____ Date: _____

May Brooks/Cole quote you, either in promotion for *The Practice of Family Therapy* or in future publishing ventures?

Yes: _____ No: _____

Sincerely,

Suzanne Midori Hanna
Joseph H. Brown

Brooks/Cole is dedicated to publishing quality books for the helping professions.
If you would like to learn more about our publications, please use this mailer to
request our catalog.

Name: _____

Street Address: _____

City, State, and Zip: _____